MznLnx

Missing Links Exam Preps

Exam Prep for

Fundamentals of Investments

Jordan & Miller, 4th Edition

The MznLnx Exam Prep is your link from the texbook and lecture to your exams.
The MznLnx Exam Preps are unauthorized and comprehensive reviews of your textbooks.

All material provided by MznLnx and Rico Publications (c) 2010
Textbook publishers and textbook authors do not particpate in or contribute to these reviews.

MznLnx

Rico Publications

Exam Prep for Fundamentals of Investments
4th Edition
Jordan & Miller

Publisher: Raymond Houge
Assistant Editor: Michael Rouger
Text and Cover Designer: Lisa Buckner
Marketing Manager: Sara Swagger
Project Manager, Editorial Production: Jerry Emerson
Art Director: Vernon Lowerui

Product Manager: Dave Mason
Editorial Assitant: Rachel Guzmanji
Pedagogy: Debra Long
Cover Image: Jim Reed/Getty Images
Text and Cover Printer: City Printing, Inc.
Compositor: Media Mix, Inc.

(c) 2010 Rico Publications

ALL RIGHTS RESERVED. No part of this work covered by the copyright may be reproduced or used in any form or by an means--graphic, electronic, or mechanical, including photocopying, recording, taping, Web distribution, information storage, and retrieval systems, or in any other manner--without the written permission of the publisher.

Printed in the United States
ISBN:

For more information about our products, contact us at:
Dave.Mason@RicoPublications.com

For permission to use material from this text or product, submit a request online to:
Dave.Mason@RicoPublications.com

Contents

CHAPTER 1
A Brief History of Risk and Return — 1

CHAPTER 2
Buying and Selling Securities — 9

CHAPTER 3
Overview of Security Types — 22

CHAPTER 4
Mutual Funds — 33

CHAPTER 5
The Stock Market — 43

CHAPTER 6
Common Stock Valuation — 51

CHAPTER 7
Stock Price Behavior and Market Efficiency — 62

CHAPTER 8
Behavioral Finance and the Psychology of Investing — 70

CHAPTER 9
Interest Rates — 78

CHAPTER 10
Bond Prices and Yields — 94

CHAPTER 11
Diversification and Risky Asset Allocation — 100

CHAPTER 12
Return, Risk, and the Security Market Line — 106

CHAPTER 13
Performance Evaluation and Risk Management — 113

CHAPTER 14
Futures Contracts — 120

CHAPTER 15
Stock Options — 129

CHAPTER 16
Option Valuation — 135

CHAPTER 17
Projecting Cash Flow and Earnings — 141

CHAPTER 18
Corporate Bonds — 154

CHAPTER 19
Government Bonds — 166

CHAPTER 20
Mortgage-Backed Securities — 176

ANSWER KEY — 183

TO THE STUDENT

COMPREHENSIVE

The *MznLnx* Exam Prep series is designed to help you pass your exams. Editors at MznLnx review your textbooks and then prepare these practice exams to help you master the textbook material. Unlike study guides, workbooks, and practice tests provided by the texbook publisher and textbook authors, *MznLnx* gives you **all** of the material in each chapter in exam form, not just samples, so you can be sure to nail your exam.

MECHANICAL

The MznLnx Exam Prep series creates exams that will help you learn the subject matter as well as test you on your understanding. Each question is designed to help you master the concept. Just working through the exams, you gain an understanding of the subject--its a simple mechanical process that produces success.

INTEGRATED STUDY GUIDE AND REVIEW

MznLnx is not just a set of exams designed to test you, its also a comprehensive review of the subject content. Each exam question is also a review of the concept, making sure that you will get the answer correct without having to go to other sources of material. You learn as you go! Its the easiest way to pass an exam.

HUMOR

Studying can be tedious and dry. MznLnx's instructional design includes moderate humor within the exam questions on occassion, to break the tedium and revitalize the brain

Chapter 1. A Brief History of Risk and Return

1. The _____ is the market for securities, where companies and governments can raise longterm funds. The _____ includes the stock market and the bond market. Financial regulators, such as the U.S. Securities and Exchange Commission, oversee the _____s in their designated countries to ensure that investors are protected against fraud.
   - a. Forward market
   - b. Capital market
   - c. Delta neutral
   - d. Spot rate

2. _____ mature in one year or less. Like zero-coupon bonds, they do not pay interest prior to maturity; instead they are sold at a discount of the par value to create a positive yield to maturity. Many regard _____ as the least risky investment available to U.S. investors.
   - a. Treasury Inflation Protected Securities
   - b. 4-4-5 Calendar
   - c. Treasury securities
   - d. Treasury bills

3. In business and finance, a _____ (also referred to as equity _____) of stock means a _____ of ownership in a corporation (company.) In the plural, stocks is often used as a synonym for _____s especially in the United States, but it is less commonly used that way outside of North America.

   In the United Kingdom, South Africa, and Australia, stock can also refer to completely different financial instruments such as government bonds or, less commonly, to all kinds of marketable securities.
   - a. Margin
   - b. Share
   - c. Procter ' Gamble
   - d. Bucket shop

4. A _____ is a profit that results from investments into a capital asset, such as stocks, bonds or real estate, which exceeds the purchase price. It is the difference between a higher selling price and a lower purchase price, resulting in a financial gain for the seller. Conversely, a capital loss arises if the proceeds from the sale of a capital asset are less than the purchase price.
   - a. Payroll tax
   - b. Capital gains tax
   - c. Tax brackets
   - d. Capital gain

5. A _____ is a payment made by a corporation to its shareholder members. When a corporation earns a profit or surplus, that money can be put to two uses: it can either be re-invested in the business (called retained earnings), or it can be paid to the shareholders as a _____. Many corporations retain a portion of their earnings and pay the remainder as a _____.
   - a. Dividend yield
   - b. Dividend
   - c. Dividend puzzle
   - d. Special dividend

6. _____ is a form of corporation equity ownership represented in the securities. It is dangerous in comparison to preferred shares and some other investment options, in that in the event of bankruptcy, _____ investors receive their funds after preferred stockholders, bondholders, creditors, etc. On the other hand, common shares on average perform better than preferred shares or bonds over time.
   - a. Stop-limit order
   - b. Stock market bubble
   - c. Common stock
   - d. Stock split

7. The _____ on a company stock is the company's annual dividend payments divided by its market cap, or the dividend per share divided by the price per share. It is often expressed as a percentage.

   Dividend payments on preferred shares are stipulated by the prospectus.

Chapter 1. A Brief History of Risk and Return

    a. Special dividend
    b. Dividend imputation
    c. Dividend reinvestment plan
    d. Dividend yield

8. In finance, _____, also known as return on investment is the ratio of money gained or lost on an investment relative to the amount of money invested. The amount of money gained or lost may be referred to as interest, profit/loss, gain/loss, or net income/loss. The money invested may be referred to as the asset, capital, principal, or the cost basis of the investment.
    a. Composiition of Creditors
    b. Stock or scrip dividends
    c. Rate of return
    d. Doctrine of the Proper Law

9. In finance, the term _____ describes the amount in cash that returns to the owners of a security. Normally it does not include the price variations, at the difference of the total return. _____ applies to various stated rates of return on stocks (common and preferred, and convertible), fixed income instruments (bonds, notes, bills, strips, zero coupon), and some other investment type insurance products (e.g. annuities.)
    a. Macaulay duration
    b. Yield to maturity
    c. 4-4-5 Calendar
    d. Yield

10. In finance, a _____ is a debt security, in which the authorized issuer owes the holders a debt and, depending on the terms of the _____, is obliged to pay interest (the coupon) and/or to repay the principal at a later date, termed maturity.

Thus a _____ is a loan: the issuer is the borrower, the _____ holder is the lender, and the coupon is the interest. _____s provide the borrower with external funds to finance long-term investments, or, in the case of government _____s, to finance current expenditure.

    a. Puttable bond
    b. Convertible bond
    c. Catastrophe bonds
    d. Bond

11. _____ (also trust indenture or deed of trust) is a legal document issued to lenders and describes key terms such as the interest rate, maturity date, convertibility, pledge, promises, representations, covenants, and other terms of the bond offering. When the Offering Memorandum is prepared in advance of marketing a Bond, the indenture will typically be summarised in the 'Description of Notes' section.
    a. McFadden Act
    b. Court of Audit of Belgium
    c. Fair Labor Standards Act
    d. Bond indenture

12. A _____ is a bond issued by a corporation. The term is usually applied to longer-term debt instruments, generally with a maturity date falling at least a year after their issue date. (The term 'commercial paper' is sometimes used for instruments with a shorter maturity.)
    a. Serial bond
    b. Brady bonds
    c. Corporate bond
    d. Government bond

13. The _____ is one of several stock market indices, created by nineteenth-century Wall Street Journal editor and Dow Jones ' Company co-founder Charles Dow. Dow compiled the index to gauge the performance of the industrial sector of the American stock market. It is the second-oldest U.S. market index, after the Dow Jones Transportation Average, which Dow also created.

a. Dow Jones Industrial Average
b. 7-Eleven
c. 4-4-5 Calendar
d. 529 plan

14. A _____ is a bond issued by a national government denominated in the country's own currency. Bonds issued by national governments in foreign currencies are normally referred to as sovereign bonds. The first ever _____ was issued by the British government in 1693 to raise money to fund a war against France.
   a. Collateralized debt obligations
   b. Zero-coupon bond
   c. Municipal bond
   d. Government bond

15. In the United States, a _____ is a bond issued by a city or other local government, or their agencies. Potential issuers of these bonds include cities, counties, redevelopment agencies, school districts, publicly owned airports and seaports, and any other governmental entity (or group of governments) below the state level. They may be general obligations of the issuer or secured by specified revenues.
   a. Municipal bond
   b. Senior debt
   c. Premium bond
   d. Puttable bond

16. In economic models, the _____ time frame assumes no fixed factors of production. Firms can enter or leave the marketplace, and the cost (and availability) of land, labor, raw materials, and capital goods can be assumed to vary. In contrast, in the short-run time frame, certain factors are assumed to be fixed, because there is not sufficient time for them to change.
   a. Short-run
   b. 4-4-5 Calendar
   c. 529 plan
   d. Long-run

17. A _____ is a fungible, negotiable instrument representing financial value. They are broadly categorized into debt securities (such as banknotes, bonds and debentures), and equity securities; e.g., common stocks. The company or other entity issuing the _____ is called the issuer.
   a. Securities lending
   b. Tracking stock
   c. Book entry
   d. Security

18. A _____ is a measure of the average price of consumer goods and services purchased by households. The _____ can be used to index (i.e., adjust for the effects of inflation) wages, salaries, pensions, or regulated or contracted prices. The _____ is, along with the population census and the National Income and Product Accounts, one of the most closely watched national economic statistics.
   a. 4-4-5 Calendar
   b. Divisia index
   c. 529 plan
   d. Consumer price index

19. In economics, _____ is a rise in the general level of prices of goods and services in an economy over a period of time. The term '_____' once referred to increases in the money supply (monetary _____); however, economic debates about the relationship between money supply and price levels have led to its primary use today in describing price _____. _____ can also be described as a decline in the real value of money--a loss of purchasing power in the medium of exchange which is also the monetary unit of account.
   a. AAB
   b. A Random Walk Down Wall Street
   c. ABN Amro
   d. Inflation

20. _____ is a measurement of corporate or economic size equal to the share price times the number of shares outstanding of a public company. As owning stock represents owning the company, including all its equity, capitalization could represent the public opinion of a company's net worth and is a determining factor in stock valuation. Likewise, the capitalization of stock markets or economic regions may be compared to other economic indicators.

a. Proxy fight
b. Just-in-time
c. Market capitalization
d. Synthetic CDO

21. A _____ is a normalized average (typically a weighted average) of prices for a given class of goods or services in a given region, during a given interval of time. It is a statistic designed to help to compare how these prices, taken as a whole, differ between time periods or geographical locations.

a. Price discrimination
b. Transfer pricing
c. Price Index
d. Discounts and allowances

22. _____ in finance is a risk management technique, related to hedging, that mixes a wide variety of investments within a portfolio. Because the fluctuations of a single security have less impact on a diverse portfolio, _____ minimizes the risk from any one investment.

A simple example of _____ is the following: On a particular island the entire economy consists of two companies: one that sells umbrellas and another that sells sunscreen.

a. Diversification
b. 529 plan
c. 4-4-5 Calendar
d. 7-Eleven

23. In finance and economics _____ refers to the rate of interest before adjustment for inflation (in contrast with the real interest rate); or, for interest balls stated' without adjustment for the full effect of compounding (also referred to as the nominal annual rate.) An interest rate is called nominal if the frequency of compounding (e.g. a month) is not identical to the basic time unit (normally a year.)

The real interest rate includes compensation for the lender's lost value due to inflation, whereas the _____ excludes inflation.

a. Cash accumulation equation
b. Shanghai Interbank Offered Rate
c. SIBOR
d. Nominal interest rate

24. _____ is a fee paid on borrowed assets. It is the price paid for the use of borrowed money , or, money earned by deposited funds . Assets that are sometimes lent with _____ include money, shares, consumer goods through hire purchase, major assets such as aircraft, and even entire factories in finance lease arrangements.

a. Insolvency
b. A Random Walk Down Wall Street
c. AAB
d. Interest

25. An _____ is the price a borrower pays for the use of money they do not own, and the return a lender receives for deferring the use of funds, by lending it to the borrower. _____s are normally expressed as a percentage rate over the period of one year.

_____s targets are also a vital tool of monetary policy and are used to control variables like investment, inflation, and unemployment.

a. A Random Walk Down Wall Street
b. AAB
c. ABN Amro
d. Interest rate

26. The _____ on a portfolio of investments takes into account not only the capital appreciation on the portfolio, but also the income received on the portfolio. The income typically consists of interest, dividends, and securities lending fees. This contrasts with the price return, which takes into account only the capital gain on an investment.
   a. Total return
   b. Global tactical asset allocation
   c. Capitalization rate
   d. Profitability index

27. Depending on the nature of the investment, the type of _____ will vary.

A common concern with any investment is that you may lose the money you invest - your capital. This risk is therefore often referred to as 'capital risk.'

If the assets you invest in are held in another currency there is a risk that currency movements alone may affect the value.

   a. AAB
   b. A Random Walk Down Wall Street
   c. ABN Amro
   d. Investment risk

28.

In finance, the _____ can be the expected rate of return above the risk-free interest rate. When measuring risk, a common sense approach is to compare the risk-free return on T-bills and the very risky return on other investments. The difference between these two returns can be interpreted as a measure of the excess return on the average risky asset. This excess return is known as the _____.

   a. Risk aversion
   b. Risk premium
   c. Risk adjusted return on capital
   d. Risk modeling

29. In business and accounting, _____s are everything of value that is owned by a person or company. The balance sheet of a firm records the monetary value of the _____s owned by the firm. The two major _____ classes are tangible _____s and intangible _____s.
   a. Income
   b. Asset
   c. Accounts payable
   d. EBITDA

30. _____ is the discipline of identifying, monitoring and limiting risks. In some cases the acceptable risk may be near zero. Risks can come from accidents, natural causes and disasters as well as deliberate attacks from an adversary.
   a. Penny stock
   b. FIFO
   c. 4-4-5 Calendar
   d. Risk management

31. In finance, _____ are stocks that appreciate in value and yield a high return on equity (ROE.) Analysts compute ROE by taking the company's net income and dividing it by the company's equity. To be classified as a growth stock, analysts expect to see at least 15 percent return on equity.

Chapter 1. A Brief History of Risk and Return

a. Security Analysis
b. Growth stocks
c. 4-4-5 Calendar
d. Stock valuation

32. A _____ is a professionally managed type of collective investment scheme that pools money from many investors and invests it in stocks, bonds, short-term money market instruments, and/or other securities. The _____ will have a fund manager that trades the pooled money on a regular basis. Currently, the worldwide value of all _____s totals more than $26 trillion.

Since 1940, there have been three basic types of investment companies in the United States: open-end funds, also known in the US as _____s; unit investment trusts (UITs); and closed-end funds.

a. Net asset value
b. Mutual Fund
c. Trust company
d. Financial intermediary

33. A _____ is a tax designation for a corporation investing in real estate that reduces or eliminates corporate income taxes. In return, _____s are required to distribute 95% of their income, which may be taxable in the hands of the investors. The _____ structure was designed to provide a similar structure for investment in real estate as mutual funds provide for investment in stocks.

a. REIT
b. Real Estate Investment Trust
c. Real estate investing
d. Liquidation value

34. _____ is a term used to refer to how an investor distributes his or her investments among various classes of investment vehicles (e.g., stocks and bonds.)

A large part of financial planning is finding an _____ that is appropriate for a given person in terms of their appetite for and ability to shoulder risk. This can depend on various factors; see investor profile.

a. Investing online
b. Investment performance
c. Alternative investment
d. Asset allocation

35. A _____ is the direction in which a financial market is moving. _____s can be classified as primary trends, secondary trends (short-term), and secular trends (long-term.) This principle incorporates the idea that market cycles occur with regularity and persistence.

a. Market trend
b. 529 plan
c. 4-4-5 Calendar
d. 7-Eleven

36. The coupon or _____ of a bond is the amount of interest paid per year expressed as a percentage of the face value of the bond.

For example if you hold $10,000 nominal of a bond described as a 4.5% loan stock, you will receive $450 in interest each year (probably in two installments of $225 each.)

Not all bonds have coupons.

Chapter 1. A Brief History of Risk and Return

    a. Zero-coupon bond
    b. Revenue bonds
    c. Puttable bond
    d. Coupon rate

37.   A _____ is a unit that is equal to 1/100th of a percentage point. It is frequently used to express percentage point changes of less than 1%. It avoids the ambiguity between relative and absolute discussions about rates.
    a. 4-4-5 Calendar
    b. 529 plan
    c. Bond market
    d. Basis point

38.   In statistics, a _____ is a tabulation of the values that one or more variables take in a sample.

Univariate _____s are often presented as lists ordered by quantity showing the number of times each value appears. For example, if 100 people rate a five-point Likert scale assessing their agreement with a statement on a scale on which 1 denotes strong agreement and 5 strong disagreement, the _____ of their responses might look like:

This simple tabulation has two drawbacks.

    a. Covariance
    b. Variance
    c. Random variables
    d. Frequency distribution

39.   In probability and statistics, the _____ of a collection of numbers is a measure of the dispersion of the numbers from their expected (mean) value. It can apply to a probability distribution, a random variable, a population or a data set. The _____ is usually denoted with the letter σ (lowercase sigma.)
    a. Standard deviation
    b. Mean
    c. Sample size
    d. Kurtosis

40.   In probability theory and statistics, the _____ of a random variable, probability distribution averaging the squared distance of its possible values from the expected value (mean.) Whereas the mean is a way to describe the location of a distribution, the _____ is a way to capture its scale or degree of being spread out. The unit of _____ is the square of the unit of the original variable.
    a. Variance
    b. Semivariance
    c. Harmonic mean
    d. Monte Carlo methods

41.   The _____ is an important family of continuous probability distributions, applicable in many fields. Each member of the family may be defined by two parameters, location and scale: the mean and variance respectively. The standard _____ is the _____ with a mean of zero and a variance of one
    a. Normal distribution
    b. Random variables
    c. Probability distribution
    d. Correlation

42.   _____ is a heterodox theory on stock price movements that is used as the basis for technical analysis. The theory was derived from 255 Wall Street Journal editorials written by Charles H. Dow (1851-1902), journalist, founder and first editor of the Wall Street Journal and co-founder of Dow Jones and Company. Following Dow's death, William P. Hamilton, Robert Rhea and E. George Schaefer organized and collectively represented '_____,' based on Dow's editorials.
    a. Point and figure
    b. Money flow
    c. Technical analysis
    d. Dow theory

43. A _____ is a situation that involves losing one quality or aspect of something in return for gaining another quality or aspect. It implies a decision to be made with full comprehension of both the upside and downside of a particular choice.

In economics the term is expressed as opportunity cost, referring the most preferred alternative given up.

   a. Trade-off
   b. Total revenue
   c. Break-even point
   d. Capital outflow

44. In finance, the value of an option consists of two components, its intrinsic value and its _____. Time value is simply the difference between option value and intrinsic value. _____ is also known as theta, extrinsic value, or instrumental value.
   a. Debt buyer
   b. Global Squeeze
   c. Conservatism
   d. Time value

45. Simply put, _____ is the value of money figuring in a given amount of interest for a given amount of time. For example 100 dollars of todays money held for a year at 5 percent interest is worth 105 dollars, therefore 100 dollars paid now or 105 dollars paid exactly one year from now is the same amount of payment of money with that given intersest at that given amount of time. This notion dates at least to Martín de Azpilcueta of the School of Salamanca.

All of the standard calculations for _____ derive from the most basic algebraic expression for the present value of a future sum, 'discounted' to the present by an amount equal to the _____. For example, a sum of FV to be received in one year is discounted (at the rate of interest r) to give a sum of PV at present: PV = FV -- r·PV = FV/(1+r).

   a. Coefficient of variation
   b. Current account
   c. Zero-coupon bond
   d. Time value of money

Chapter 2. Buying and Selling Securities

1. A '_____' is a 'Charge' that is paid to obtain the right to delay a payment. Essentially, the payer purchases the right to make a given payment in the future instead of in the Present. The '_____', or 'Charge' that must be paid to delay the payment, is simply the difference between what the payment amount would be if it were paid in the present and what the payment amount would be paid if it were paid in the future.

   a. Value at risk
   b. Risk aversion
   c. Risk modeling
   d. Discount

2. _____, in bookkeeping, refers to assets, liabilities, income, and expenses recorded on individual pages of the so called book of final entry or ledger. Changes in _____ value are made by chronologically posting debit (DR) and credit (CR) entries to its page. Examples of _____s are cash, _____s receivable, mortgages, loans, land and buildings, common stock, sales, services provided, wages, and payroll overhead.

   a. Alpha
   b. Option
   c. Accretion
   d. Account

3. Behavioral economics and _____ are closely related fields that have evolved to be a separate branch of economic and financial analysis which applies scientific research on human and social, cognitive and emotional factors to better understand economic decisions by, say, consumers, borrowers, investors, and how they affect market prices, returns and the allocation of resources.

The field is primarily concerned with the bounds of rationality (selfishness, self-control) of economic agents. Behavioral models typically integrate insights from psychology with neo-classical economic theory.

   a. Behavioral finance
   b. Recession
   c. Market structure
   d. Medium of exchange

4. _____ is a form of corporation equity ownership represented in the securities. It is dangerous in comparison to preferred shares and some other investment options, in that in the event of bankruptcy, _____ investors receive their funds after preferred stockholders, bondholders, creditors, etc. On the other hand, common shares on average perform better than preferred shares or bonds over time.

   a. Stock split
   b. Stop-limit order
   c. Stock market bubble
   d. Common stock

5. The institution most often referenced by the word '_____' is a public or publicly traded _____, the shares of which are traded on a public stock exchange (e.g., the New York Stock Exchange or Nasdaq in the United States) where shares of stock of _____s are bought and sold by and to the general public. Most of the largest businesses in the world are publicly traded _____s. However, the majority of _____s are said to be closely held, privately held or close _____s, meaning that no ready market exists for the trading of shares.

   a. Depository Trust Company
   b. Federal Home Loan Mortgage Corporation
   c. Protect
   d. Corporation

6. Explicit _____ is a measure implemented in many countries to protect bank depositors, in full or in part, from losses caused by a bank's inability to pay its debts when due. _____ systems are one component of a financial system safety net that promotes financial stability.

   a. Reserve requirement
   b. Banking panic
   c. Time deposit
   d. Deposit Insurance

Chapter 2. Buying and Selling Securities

7. The _____ is a United States government corporation created by the Glass-Steagall Act of 1933. It provides deposit insurance, which guarantees the safety of checking and savings deposits in member banks, currently up to $250,000 per depositor per bank. Insured deposits are backed by the full faith and credit of the United States.
   a. FASB
   b. Ford Foundation
   c. NYSE Group
   d. Federal Deposit Insurance Corporation

8. The _____ is a federally mandated non-profit corporation in the United States that protects securities investors from harm if a broker-dealer company fails. Investors are not insured for any potential loss while invested in the market.

Congress created _____ in 1970 through the _____ (15 U.S.C.

   a. Rule 144A
   b. SIPC
   c. Prudent man rule
   d. Williams Act

9. A _____ is a fungible, negotiable instrument representing financial value. They are broadly categorized into debt securities (such as banknotes, bonds and debentures), and equity securities; e.g., common stocks. The company or other entity issuing the _____ is called the issuer.
   a. Book entry
   b. Tracking stock
   c. Securities lending
   d. Security

10. _____ is an estimate of the fair value of corporations and their stocks, by using fundamental economic criteria. This theoretical valuation has to be perfected with market criteria, as the final purpose is to determine potential market prices.
    a. 4-4-5 Calendar
    b. Stock valuation
    c. Growth stocks
    d. Security Analysis

11. In finance, _____ is the process of estimating the potential market value of a financial asset or liability. they can be done on assets (for example, investments in marketable securities such as stocks, options, business enterprises, or intangible assets such as patents and trademarks) or on liabilities (e.g., Bonds issued by a company.) _____s are required in many contexts including investment analysis, capital budgeting, merger and acquisition transactions, financial reporting, taxable events to determine the proper tax liability, and in litigation.
    a. Margin
    b. Valuation
    c. Share
    d. Procter ' Gamble

12. In economics and finance, _____ is the practice of taking advantage of a price differential between two or more markets: striking a combination of matching deals that capitalize upon the imbalance, the profit being the difference between the market prices. When used by academics, an _____ is a transaction that involves no negative cash flow at any probabilistic or temporal state and a positive cash flow in at least one state; in simple terms, a risk-free profit.
    a. Efficient-market hypothesis
    b. Initial margin
    c. Issuer
    d. Arbitrage

13. _____ , in finance, is a general theory of asset pricing, that has become influential in the pricing of stocks.

Chapter 2. Buying and Selling Securities

_____ holds that the expected return of a financial asset can be modeled as a linear function of various macro-economic factors or theoretical market indices, where sensitivity to changes in each factor is represented by a factor-specific beta coefficient. The model-derived rate of return will then be used to price the asset correctly - the asset price should equal the expected end of period price discounted at the rate implied by model.

a. A Random Walk Down Wall Street
b. Arbitrage pricing theory
c. AAB
d. ABN Amro

14. In finance, a _____ is collateral that the holder of a position in securities, options, or futures contracts has to deposit to cover the credit risk of his counterparty (most often his broker.) This risk can arise if the holder has done any of the following:

- borrowed cash from the counterparty to buy securities or options,
- sold securities or options short, or
- entered into a futures contract.

The collateral can be in the form of cash or securities, and it is deposited in a _____ account. On U.S. futures exchanges, '_____' was formally called performance bond.

_____ buying is buying securities with cash borrowed from a broker, using other securities as collateral.

a. Share
b. Margin
c. Credit
d. Procter ' Gamble

15. The collateral can be in the form of cash or securities, and it is deposited in a _____. On U.S. futures exchanges, 'margin' was formally called performance bond.

Margin buying is buying securities with cash borrowed from a broker, using other securities as collateral.

a. Risk-neutral measure
b. Margin account
c. Dollar roll
d. Forward contract

16. _____ mature in one year or less. Like zero-coupon bonds, they do not pay interest prior to maturity; instead they are sold at a discount of the par value to create a positive yield to maturity. Many regard _____ as the least risky investment available to U.S. investors.

a. Treasury Inflation Protected Securities
b. Treasury securities
c. 4-4-5 Calendar
d. Treasury bills

17. In finance, the yield curve is the relation between the interest rate (or cost of borrowing) and the time to maturity of the debt for a given borrower in a given currency. For example, the current U.S. dollar interest rates paid on U.S. Treasury securities for various maturities are closely watched by many traders, and are commonly plotted on a graph such as the one on the right which is informally called 'the yield curve.' More formal mathematical descriptions of this relation are often called the _____.

The yield of a debt instrument is the annualized percentage increase in the value of the investment.

a. 7-Eleven
b. 529 plan
c. Term structure of interest rates
d. 4-4-5 Calendar

18. In financial accounting, a _____ or statement of financial position is a summary of a person's or organization's balances. Assets, liabilities and ownership equity are listed as of a specific date, such as the end of its financial year. A _____ is often described as a snapshot of a company's financial condition.
   a. Statement on Auditing Standards No. 70: Service Organizations
   b. Balance sheet
   c. Financial statements
   d. Statement of retained earnings

19. _____ is a fee paid on borrowed assets. It is the price paid for the use of borrowed money, or, money earned by deposited funds . Assets that are sometimes lent with _____ include money, shares, consumer goods through hire purchase, major assets such as aircraft, and even entire factories in finance lease arrangements.
   a. Insolvency
   b. A Random Walk Down Wall Street
   c. AAB
   d. Interest

20. An _____ is the price a borrower pays for the use of money they do not own, and the return a lender receives for deferring the use of funds, by lending it to the borrower. _____s are normally expressed as a percentage rate over the period of one year.

   _____s targets are also a vital tool of monetary policy and are used to control variables like investment, inflation, and unemployment.

   a. AAB
   b. A Random Walk Down Wall Street
   c. ABN Amro
   d. Interest rate

21. In finance, _____ refers to Monday, October 19, 1987, when stock markets around the world crashed, shedding a huge value in a very short time. The crash began in Hong Kong, spread west through international time zones to Europe, hitting the United States after other markets had already declined by a significant margin. The Dow Jones Industrial Average (DJIA) dropped by 508 points to 1738.74 (22.61%).
   a. 529 plan
   b. 4-4-5 Calendar
   c. 7-Eleven
   d. Black Monday

22. A _____ is a bond issued by a national government denominated in the country's own currency. Bonds issued by national governments in foreign currencies are normally referred to as sovereign bonds. The first ever _____ was issued by the British government in 1693 to raise money to fund a war against France.
   a. Zero-coupon bond
   b. Municipal bond
   c. Collateralized debt obligations
   d. Government bond

23. The _____ requirement is the amount required to be collateralized in order to open a position. Thereafter, the amount required to be kept in collateral until the position is closed is the maintenance requirement. The maintenance requirement is the minimum amount to be collateralized in order to keep an open position.
   a. Efficient-market hypothesis
   b. Arbitrage
   c. Issuer
   d. Initial margin

Chapter 2. Buying and Selling Securities

24. The variation margin or _____ is not collateral, but a daily offsetting of profits and losses. Futures are marked-to-market every day, so the current price is compared to the previous day's price. The profit or loss on the day of a position is then paid to or debited from the holder by the futures exchange.
    a. Delivery month
    b. Total return swap
    c. SPI 200 futures contract
    d. Maintenance margin

25. The _____ is the amount required to be collateralized in order to open a position. Thereafter, the amount required to be kept in collateral until the position is closed is the maintenance requirement. The maintenance requirement is the minimum amount to be collateralized in order to keep an open position.
    a. ABN Amro
    b. A Random Walk Down Wall Street
    c. AAB
    d. Initial margin requirement

26. In the United States, a _____ is a bond issued by a city or other local government, or their agencies. Potential issuers of these bonds include cities, counties, redevelopment agencies, school districts, publicly owned airports and seaports, and any other governmental entity (or group of governments) below the state level. They may be general obligations of the issuer or secured by specified revenues.
    a. Puttable bond
    b. Premium bond
    c. Municipal bond
    d. Senior debt

27. The U.S. Securities and Exchange Commission's (SEC's) Regulation Fair Disclosure, also commonly referred to as _____ was an SEC ruling implemented in October 2000 (.) It mandated that all publicly traded companies must disclose material information to all investors at the same time.

The regulation sought to stamp out selective disclosure, in which some investors (often large institutional investors) received market moving information before others (often smaller, individual investors.)

    a. Regulation Fair Disclosure
    b. Revenue recognition
    c. Commodity Pool Operator
    d. Regulation FD

28. In financial accounting, the term _____ is most commonly used to describe any part of shareholders' equity, except for basic share capital. Sometimes, the term is used instead of the term provision; such a use, however, is inconsistent with the terminology suggested by International Accounting Standards Board. For more information about provisions, see provision (accounting.)
    a. FIFO and LIFO accounting
    b. Closing entries
    c. Treasury stock
    d. Reserve

29. A _____, reserve bank, or monetary authority is the entity responsible for the monetary policy of a country or of a group of member states. It is a bank that can lend money to other banks in times of need. Its primary responsibility is to maintain the stability of the national currency and money supply, but more active duties include controlling subsidized-loan interest rates, and acting as a lender of last resort to the banking sector during times of financial crisis (private banks often being integral to the national financial system.)
    a. 4-4-5 Calendar
    b. Central bank
    c. 529 plan
    d. 7-Eleven

Chapter 2. Buying and Selling Securities

30. The _____ of 1934 is a law governing the secondary trading of securities (stocks, bonds, and debentures) in the United States of America. The Act, 48 Stat. 881 (enacted June 6, 1934), codified at 15 U.S.C. § 78a et seq., was a sweeping piece of legislation. The Act and related statutes form the basis of regulation of the financial markets and their participants in the United States.

    a. 4-4-5 Calendar
    b. 529 plan
    c. 7-Eleven
    d. Securities Exchange Act

31. In finance, a _____ is a debt security, in which the authorized issuer owes the holders a debt and, depending on the terms of the _____, is obliged to pay interest (the coupon) and/or to repay the principal at a later date, termed maturity.

Thus a _____ is a loan: the issuer is the borrower, the _____ holder is the lender, and the coupon is the interest. _____s provide the borrower with external funds to finance long-term investments, or, in the case of government _____s, to finance current expenditure.

    a. Puttable bond
    b. Bond
    c. Catastrophe bonds
    d. Convertible bond

32. The _____, sometimes called the maintenance margin requirement, is the ratio set for:

- (Stock Equity - Leveraged Dollars) to Stock Equity

- Stock Equity being the stock price * no. of stocks bought and Leveraged Dollars being the amount borrowed in the margin account.

- E.g. An investor bought 1000 shares of ABC company each priced at $50. If the initial margin requirement were 60%:

- Stock Equity: $50 * 1000 = $50,000

- Leveraged Dollars or amount borrowed: ($50 * 1000)* (1-60%) = $20,000

So the maintenance margin requirement uses the above variables to form a ratio that investors have to abide by in order to keep the account active.

The point is, let's say the maintenance margin requirement is reduced from 60% to 25% - At what price would the investor be getting a margin call? Let P be the price, so 1000P in our case is the Stock Equity.

- (Stock Equity - Leveraged Dollars) divided by Stock Equity = 25%

- (1000P - $20,000)/1000P = 0.25

- (1000P - $20,000) = 250P

- P = $26.67

Chapter 2. Buying and Selling Securities

So if the stock price drops from $50 to $26.67, investors will be called to add additional funds to the account to make up for the loss in stock equity.

Margin requirements are reduced for positions that offset each other.

a. 4-4-5 Calendar
b. 529 plan
c. 7-Eleven
d. Minimum margin requirement

33. The _____ generally prohibits short selling of securities except on an uptick. The rule was defined by U.S. Securities and Exchange Commission (SEC) which summarized it: 'Rule 10a-1(a)(1) provided that, subject to certain exceptions, a listed security may be sold short (A) at a price above the price at which the immediately preceding sale was effected (plus tick), or (B) at the last sale price if it is higher than the last different price (zero-plus tick.) Short sales were not permitted on minus ticks or zero-minus ticks, subject to narrow exceptions.'

The rule went into effect in 1938 and was removed when Rule 201 Regulation SHO became effective in 2007.

a. AAB
b. A Random Walk Down Wall Street
c. Uptick rule
d. ABN Amro

34. In finance, _____ (or gearing) is borrowing money to supplement existing funds for investment in such a way that the potential positive or negative outcome is magnified and/or enhanced. It generally refers to using borrowed funds, or debt, so as to attempt to increase the returns to equity. Deleveraging is the action of reducing borrowings.

a. Limited partnership
b. Financial endowment
c. Pension fund
d. Leverage

35. A _____ is the price of a single share of a no. of saleable stocks of the company. Once the stock is purchased, the owner becomes a shareholder of the company that issued the share.

a. Stock split
b. Trading curb
c. Whisper numbers
d. Share price

36. The _____, effective annual interest rate, Annual Equivalent Rate (AER) or simply effective rate is the interest rate on a loan or financial product restated from the nominal interest rate as an interest rate with annual compound interest. It is used to compare the annual interest between loans with different compounding terms (daily, monthly, annually, or other.)

The _____ differs in two important respects from the annual percentage rate (APR):

1. the _____ generally does not incorporate one-time charges such as front-end fees;
2. the _____ is (generally) not defined by legal or regulatory authorities (as APR is in many jurisdictions.)

By contrast, the 'effective APR' is used as a legal term, where front-fees and other costs can be included, as defined by local law.

Chapter 2. Buying and Selling Securities

Annual Percentage Yield or effective annual yield is the analogous concept used for savings or investment products, such as a certificate of deposit.

   a. Effective interest rate
   b. ABN Amro
   c. A Random Walk Down Wall Street
   d. AAB

37. The _____ is the weighted-average most likely outcome in gambling, probability theory, economics or finance.

In gambling and probability theory, there is usually a discrete set of possible outcomes. In this case, _____ is a measure of the relative balance of win or loss weighted by their chances of occurring.

   a. ABN Amro
   b. A Random Walk Down Wall Street
   c. AAB
   d. Expected return

38. Generally, in English and American law, a contract of mortgage or pledge as collateral for a debt in which the subject matter is not delivered into the possession of the pledgee or pawnee. The arrangement is common with modern mortgages - the borrower retains legal ownership of the property but provides the lender with a lien over the property until the debt is paid off.

_____ and re-_____, respectively, are commonly used to describe the means by which securities brokers and dealers first extend credit on margin to their customers using pledged securities as collateral, and then pledge the client-owned securities held in the client's margin account as collateral for the brokerage's bank loan.

   a. 529 plan
   b. 7-Eleven
   c. 4-4-5 Calendar
   d. Hypothecation

39. In business and accounting, _____s are everything of value that is owned by a person or company. The balance sheet of a firm records the monetary value of the _____s owned by the firm. The two major _____ classes are tangible _____s and intangible _____s.

   a. Asset
   b. Income
   c. Accounts payable
   d. EBITDA

40. The term _____ is often used to refer to the investment management of collective investments, (not necessarily) whilst the more generic fund management may refer to all forms of institutional investment as well as investment management for private investors. Investment managers who specialize in advisory or discretionary management on behalf of (normally wealthy) private investors may often refer to their services as wealth management or portfolio management often within the context of so-called 'private banking'.

The provision of 'investment management services' includes elements of financial analysis, asset selection, stock selection, plan implementation and ongoing monitoring of investments.

   a. ABN Amro
   b. AAB
   c. A Random Walk Down Wall Street
   d. Asset management

Chapter 2. Buying and Selling Securities

41. In finance, a _____ in a security, such as a stock or a bond means the holder of the position owns the security and will profit if the price of the security goes up.

Similarly, a _____ in a futures contract or similar derivative, means the holder of the position will profit if the price of the underlying security goes up. Going long is the more conventional practice of investing and is contrasted with going short

- Short (finance)

a. Delta hedging
b. Forward market
c. Long position
d. Central Securities Depository

42. A _____ is a professionally managed type of collective investment scheme that pools money from many investors and invests it in stocks, bonds, short-term money market instruments, and/or other securities. The _____ will have a fund manager that trades the pooled money on a regular basis. Currently, the worldwide value of all _____s totals more than $26 trillion.

Since 1940, there have been three basic types of investment companies in the United States: open-end funds, also known in the US as _____s; unit investment trusts (UITs); and closed-end funds.

a. Financial intermediary
b. Net asset value
c. Trust company
d. Mutual fund

43. Days to Cover (DTC) is a numerical term that describes the relationship between the amount of shares in a given equity that have been short sold and the number of days of typical trading that it would require to 'cover' all _____ outstanding. For example, if there are ten million shares of XYZ Inc. that are currently short sold and the average daily volume of XYZ shares traded each day is one million, it would require ten days of trading for all _____ to be covered (10 million / 1 million.)

a. Stock or scrip dividends
b. Cash budget
c. Guaranteed investment contracts
d. Short positions

44. In finance, _____ or 'shorting' is the practice of selling a financial instrument that the seller does not own at the time of the sale. _____ is done with intent of later purchasing the financial instrument at a lower price. Short-sellers attempt to profit from an expected decline in the price of a financial instrument.

a. Short selling
b. 4-4-5 Calendar
c. 529 plan
d. Short ratio

45. A _____ is one in which a brokerage manages an investor's portfolio for a flat quarterly or annual fee. This fee covers all administrative, commission, and management expenses. Sometimes this also includes funds of funds. This type of account is also known as an investment platform.

a. Payback period
b. Net worth
c. Wrap account
d. Floating charge

46. An _____ is a document a company presents at an annual general meeting for approval by its shareholders, or a charitable organization presents its trustees. The report is made up of reports, which may include the following:

- Chairman's report
- CEO's report
- Auditor's report on corporate governance
- Mission statement
- Corporate governance statement of compliance
- Statement of directors' responsibilities
- Invitation to the company's AGM

as well as financial statements including:

- Auditor's report on the financial statements
- Balance sheet
- Statement of retained earnings
- Income statement
- Cash flow statement
- Notes to the financial statements
- Accounting policies

Other information deemed relevant to stakeholders may be included, such as a report on operations for manufacturing firms. In the case of larger companies, it is usually a sleek, colorful, high gloss publication.

The details provided in the report are of use to investors to understand the company's financial position and future direction.

a. Outstanding balance
b. Accrued liabilities
c. Amortization schedule
d. Annual report

47. The _____ is usually the number of shares outstanding of a publicly traded company that is sold short, divided by the average daily trading volume (daily transaction).

It is one measure of the market's outlook on a given stock; a higher short interest ratio indicates more pessimism, because a higher proportion of a company's total float has already been sold short.

The short interest and _____ can be deceiving, however, when a company has many convertible securities outstanding and is perceived to be at risk, because convertible and options arbitrageurs will often sell the stock short to manage risk with their long positions in these other instruments.

a. 529 plan
b. Short ratio
c. Short selling
d. 4-4-5 Calendar

Chapter 2. Buying and Selling Securities

48. In finance, the term _____ describes the amount in cash that returns to the owners of a security. Normally it does not include the price variations, at the difference of the total return. _____ applies to various stated rates of return on stocks (common and preferred, and convertible), fixed income instruments (bonds, notes, bills, strips, zero coupon), and some other investment type insurance products (e.g. annuities.)
   a. Yield to maturity
   c. Macaulay duration
   b. 4-4-5 Calendar
   d. Yield

49. _____ in finance is a risk management technique, related to hedging, that mixes a wide variety of investments within a portfolio. Because the fluctuations of a single security have less impact on a diverse portfolio, _____ minimizes the risk from any one investment.

A simple example of _____ is the following: On a particular island the entire economy consists of two companies: one that sells umbrellas and another that sells sunscreen.

   a. Diversification
   c. 529 plan
   b. 4-4-5 Calendar
   d. 7-Eleven

50. _____ is a March 2000 book written by Yale University professor Robert Shiller, named after Alan Greenspan's '_____' quote. Published at the height of the dot-com boom, it put forth several arguments demonstrating how the stock markets were overvalued at the time. Shiller was soon proven right when the Nasdaq peaked on the very month of the book's publication, and the stock markets collapsed right after.
   a. A Random Walk Down Wall Street
   c. AAB
   b. ABN Amro
   d. Irrational Exuberance

51. A _____ is a pool of assets forming an independent legal entity that are bought with the contributions to a pension plan for the exclusive purpose of financing pension plan benefits.

_____s are important shareholders of listed and private companies. They are especially important to the stock market where large institutional investors like the Ontario Teachers' Pension Plan dominate.

   a. Leverage
   c. Pension fund
   b. Leveraged buyout
   d. Limited liability company

52. A _____ is a fixed point of time in the future at which point certain processes will be evaluated or assumed to end. It is necessary in an accounting, finance or risk management regime to assign such a fixed horizon time so that alternatives can be evaluated for performance over the same period of time.
   a. 529 plan
   c. 7-Eleven
   b. 4-4-5 Calendar
   d. Time horizon

53. An _____ is an investment vehicle traded on stock exchanges, much like stocks. An ETF holds assets such as stocks or bonds and trades at approximately the same price as the net asset value of its underlying assets over the course of the trading day. Most ETFs track an index, such as the Dow Jones Industrial Average or the S'P 500.
   a. Exchange-traded fund
   c. ABN Amro
   b. AAB
   d. A Random Walk Down Wall Street

Chapter 2. Buying and Selling Securities

54. An _____ is a retirement plan account that provides some tax advantages for retirement savings in the United States.

   a. AAB
   b. A Random Walk Down Wall Street
   c. ABN Amro
   d. Individual Retirement Arrangement

55. A _____ is a periodic payment that is paid by investors in a pooled investment fund to the fund's investment adviser for investment and portfolio management services.

In a mutual fund, the _____ will include any fees payable to the fund's investment adviser or its affiliates, and administrative fees payable to the investment adviser that are not included in the 'Other Expenses' category.)

In a private equity fund, the _____ is an annual payment made by the limited partners in the fund to the fund's manager (e.g., the private equity firm) to pay for the private equity firm's investment operations..

   a. 4-4-5 Calendar
   b. 7-Eleven
   c. Management fee
   d. 529 plan

56. An _____ or index tracker is a collective investment scheme (usually a mutual fund or exchange-traded fund) that aims to replicate the movements of an index of a specific financial market regardless of market conditions.

Tracking can be achieved by trying to hold all of the securities in the index, in the same proportions as the index. Other methods include statistically sampling the market and holding 'representative' securities.

   a. Investment company
   b. AAB
   c. Index fund
   d. A Random Walk Down Wall Street

57. An _____ is a contract written by a seller that conveys to the buyer the right -- but not the obligation -- to buy (in the case of a call _____) or to sell (in the case of a put _____) a particular asset, such as a piece of property such as, among others, a futures contract. In return for granting the _____, the seller collects a payment (the premium) from the buyer.

For example, buying a call _____ provides the right to buy a specified quantity of a security at a set strike price at some time on or before expiration, while buying a put _____ provides the right to sell.

   a. AT'T Mobility LLC
   b. Amortization
   c. Annuity
   d. Option

58. _____ is a term used to refer to how an investor distributes his or her investments among various classes of investment vehicles (e.g., stocks and bonds.)

A large part of financial planning is finding an _____ that is appropriate for a given person in terms of their appetite for and ability to shoulder risk. This can depend on various factors; see investor profile.

Chapter 2. Buying and Selling Securities

a. Asset allocation
b. Investment performance
c. Investing online
d. Alternative investment

59. _____ is the strategy of making buy or sell decisions of financial assets (often stocks) by attempting to predict future market price movements. The prediction may be based on an outlook of market or economic conditions resulting from technical or fundamental analysis. This is an investment strategy based on the outlook for an aggregate market, rather than for a particular financial asset.
   a. Late trading
   b. Divestment
   c. Portable alpha
   d. Market timing

60. A _____ is a collective investment scheme that invests in bonds and other debt securities. _____s yield monthly dividends that include interest payments on the fund's underlying securities plus any capital appreciation in the prices of the portfolio's bonds. _____s tend to pay higher dividends than CDs and money market accounts, and they generally pay out dividends more frequently and regularly than individual bonds.
   a. Gilts
   b. Premium bond
   c. Private activity bond
   d. Bond fund

61. _____, authored by professors Benjamin Graham and David Dodd of Columbia Business School, laid the intellectual foundation for what would later be called value investing. The work was first published in 1934, following unprecedented losses on Wall Street. In summing up lessons learned, Graham and Dodd chided Wall Street for its myopic focus on a company's reported earnings per share, and were particularly harsh on the favored 'earnings trends.' They encouraged investors to take an entirely different approach by gauging the rough value of the operating business that lay behind the security.
   a. Growth stocks
   b. Stock valuation
   c. 4-4-5 Calendar
   d. Security analysis

Chapter 3. Overview of Security Types

1. A _____ is a fungible, negotiable instrument representing financial value. They are broadly categorized into debt securities (such as banknotes, bonds and debentures), and equity securities; e.g., common stocks. The company or other entity issuing the _____ is called the issuer.

   a. Security
   c. Securities lending
   b. Tracking stock
   d. Book entry

2. In business and accounting, _____s are everything of value that is owned by a person or company. The balance sheet of a firm records the monetary value of the _____s owned by the firm. The two major _____ classes are tangible _____s and intangible _____s.

   a. Accounts payable
   c. Asset
   b. EBITDA
   d. Income

3. In finance, a _____ is a debt security, in which the authorized issuer owes the holders a debt and, depending on the terms of the _____, is obliged to pay interest (the coupon) and/or to repay the principal at a later date, termed maturity.

   Thus a _____ is a loan: the issuer is the borrower, the _____ holder is the lender, and the coupon is the interest. _____s provide the borrower with external funds to finance long-term investments, or, in the case of government _____s, to finance current expenditure.

   a. Convertible bond
   c. Puttable bond
   b. Bond
   d. Catastrophe bonds

4. A _____ s a time deposit, a financial product commonly offered to consumers by banks, thrift institutions, and credit unions.

   They are similar to savings accounts in that they are insured and thus virtually risk-free; they are 'money in the bank'. They are different from savings accounts in that they have a specific, fixed term (often three months, six months, or one to five years), and, usually, a fixed interest rate.

   a. Time deposit
   c. Variable rate mortgage
   b. Reserve requirement
   d. Certificate of deposit

5. The coupon or _____ of a bond is the amount of interest paid per year expressed as a percentage of the face value of the bond.

   For example if you hold $10,000 nominal of a bond described as a 4.5% loan stock, you will receive $450 in interest each year (probably in two installments of $225 each.)

   Not all bonds have coupons.

   a. Puttable bond
   c. Coupon rate
   b. Revenue bonds
   d. Zero-coupon bond

Chapter 3. Overview of Security Types

6. In finance, _____ occurs when a debtor has not met its legal obligations according to the debt contract, e.g. it has not made a scheduled payment, or has violated a loan covenant (condition) of the debt contract. _____ may occur if the debtor is either unwilling or unable to pay their debt. This can occur with all debt obligations including bonds, mortgages, loans, and promissory notes.

   a. Default
   b. Credit crunch
   c. Debt validation
   d. Vendor finance

7. _____ is the risk of loss due to a debtor's non-payment of a loan or other line of credit (either the principal or interest (coupon) or both)

Most lenders employ their own models (credit scorecards) to rank potential and existing customers according to risk, and then apply appropriate strategies. With products such as unsecured personal loans or mortgages, lenders charge a higher price for higher risk customers and vice versa. With revolving products such as credit cards and overdrafts, risk is controlled through careful setting of credit limits.

   a. Liquidity risk
   b. Market risk
   c. Transaction risk
   d. Credit risk

8. A '_____' is a 'Charge' that is paid to obtain the right to delay a payment. Essentially, the payer purchases the right to make a given payment in the future instead of in the Present. The '_____', or 'Charge' that must be paid to delay the payment, is simply the difference between what the payment amount would be if it were paid in the present and what the payment amount would be paid if it were paid in the future.

   a. Value at risk
   b. Risk modeling
   c. Discount
   d. Risk aversion

9. _____ in finance is a risk management technique, related to hedging, that mixes a wide variety of investments within a portfolio. Because the fluctuations of a single security have less impact on a diverse portfolio, _____ minimizes the risk from any one investment.

A simple example of _____ is the following: On a particular island the entire economy consists of two companies: one that sells umbrellas and another that sells sunscreen.

   a. 7-Eleven
   b. 4-4-5 Calendar
   c. Diversification
   d. 529 plan

10. _____ refers to any type of investment that yields a regular (or fixed) return.

For example, if you lend money to a borrower and the borrower has to pay interest once a month, you have been issued a fixed-income security. When a company does this, it is often called a bond or corporate bank debt (although preferred stock is also sometimes considered to be _____).

   a. 529 plan
   b. Bond market
   c. 4-4-5 Calendar
   d. Fixed income

11. In finance, the _____ is the global financial market for short-term borrowing and lending. It provides short-term liquidity funding for the global financial system. The _____ is where short-term obligations such as Treasury bills, commercial paper and bankers' acceptances are bought and sold.
   a. Debt-for-equity swap
   b. Consumer debt
   c. Cramdown
   d. Money market

12. _____ mature in one year or less. Like zero-coupon bonds, they do not pay interest prior to maturity; instead they are sold at a discount of the par value to create a positive yield to maturity. Many regard _____ as the least risky investment available to U.S. investors.
   a. Treasury bills
   b. Treasury securities
   c. Treasury Inflation Protected Securities
   d. 4-4-5 Calendar

13. _____ are government bonds issued by the United States Department of the Treasury through the Bureau of the Public Debt. They are the debt financing instruments of the U.S. Federal government, and they are often referred to simply as Treasuries or Treasurys. There are four types of marketable _____: Treasury bills, Treasury notes, Treasury bonds, and Treasury Inflation Protected Securities (TIPS.)
   a. Treasury securities
   b. Treasury Inflation-Protected Securities
   c. 4-4-5 Calendar
   d. Treasury Inflation Protected Securities

14. A _____ is a unit that is equal to 1/100th of a percentage point. It is frequently used to express percentage point changes of less than 1%. It avoids the ambiguity between relative and absolute discussions about rates.
   a. 4-4-5 Calendar
   b. 529 plan
   c. Bond market
   d. Basis point

15. _____ (also trust indenture or deed of trust) is a legal document issued to lenders and describes key terms such as the interest rate, maturity date, convertibility, pledge, promises, representations, covenants, and other terms of the bond offering. When the Offering Memorandum is prepared in advance of marketing a Bond, the indenture will typically be summarised in the 'Description of Notes' section.
   a. McFadden Act
   b. Court of Audit of Belgium
   c. Fair Labor Standards Act
   d. Bond indenture

16. A _____ is a bond issued by a corporation. The term is usually applied to longer-term debt instruments, generally with a maturity date falling at least a year after their issue date. (The term 'commercial paper' is sometimes used for instruments with a shorter maturity.)
   a. Serial bond
   b. Government bond
   c. Brady bonds
   d. Corporate bond

17. The _____, interest yield, income yield, flat yield or running yield is a financial term used in reference to bonds and other fixed-interest securities such as gilts. It is the ratio of the annual interest payment and the bond's current price.

The _____ only therefore refers to the yield of the bond at the current moment. It does not reflect the total return over the life of the bond. In particular, it takes no account of reinvestment risk (the uncertainty about the rate at which future cashflows can be reinvested) or the fact that bonds usually mature at par value, which can be an important component of a bond's return.

a. Perpetuity
b. Modified Internal Rate of Return
c. Stochastic volatility
d. Current yield

18. In finance, the term _____ describes the amount in cash that returns to the owners of a security. Normally it does not include the price variations, at the difference of the total return. _____ applies to various stated rates of return on stocks (common and preferred, and convertible), fixed income instruments (bonds, notes, bills, strips, zero coupon), and some other investment type insurance products (e.g. annuities.)

a. Yield to maturity
b. Macaulay duration
c. Yield
d. 4-4-5 Calendar

19. The _____ or redemption yield is the yield promised to the bondholder on the assumption that the bond or other fixed-interest security such as gilts will be held to maturity, that all coupon and principal payments will be made and coupon payments are reinvested at the bond's promised yield at the same rate as invested. It is a measure of the return of the bond. This technique in theory allows investors to calculate the fair value of different financial instruments.

a. Macaulay duration
b. 4-4-5 Calendar
c. Yield
d. Yield to maturity

20. In finance, _____ is the interest that has accumulated since the principal investment, or since the previous interest payment if there has been one already. For a financial instrument such as a bond, interest is calculated and paid in set intervals.

The primary formula for calculating the interest accrued in a given period is:

$$I_A = T \times P \times R$$

where I_A is the _____, T is the fraction of the year, P is the principal, and R is the annualized interest rate.

a. AAB
b. A Random Walk Down Wall Street
c. ABN Amro
d. Accrued interest

21. _____ is a fee paid on borrowed assets. It is the price paid for the use of borrowed money, or, money earned by deposited funds. Assets that are sometimes lent with _____ include money, shares, consumer goods through hire purchase, major assets such as aircraft, and even entire factories in finance lease arrangements.

a. Insolvency
b. Interest
c. AAB
d. A Random Walk Down Wall Street

22. _____ is a life of security. It may also refer to the final payment date of a loan or other financial instrument, at which point all remaining interest and principal is due to be paid.

1, 3, 6 months _____ band can be calculated by using 30-day per month periods.

a. Replacement cost
b. False billing
c. Primary market
d. Maturity

Chapter 3. Overview of Security Types

23. _____ is a form of corporation equity ownership represented in the securities. It is dangerous in comparison to preferred shares and some other investment options, in that in the event of bankruptcy, _____ investors receive their funds after preferred stockholders, bondholders, creditors, etc. On the other hand, common shares on average perform better than preferred shares or bonds over time.
    a. Common stock
    b. Stock split
    c. Stock market bubble
    d. Stop-limit order

24. A _____ is a payment made by a corporation to its shareholder members. When a corporation earns a profit or surplus, that money can be put to two uses: it can either be re-invested in the business (called retained earnings), or it can be paid to the shareholders as a _____. Many corporations retain a portion of their earnings and pay the remainder as a _____.
    a. Dividend yield
    b. Dividend
    c. Dividend puzzle
    d. Special dividend

25. _____ is typically a higher ranking stock than voting shares, and its terms are negotiated between the corporation and the investor.

    _____ usually carry no voting rights, but may carry superior priority over common stock in the payment of dividends and upon liquidation. _____ may carry a dividend that is paid out prior to any dividends to common stock holders.

    a. Second lien loan
    b. Preferred stock
    c. Follow-on offering
    d. Trade-off theory

26. _____ is a term used to refer to how an investor distributes his or her investments among various classes of investment vehicles (e.g., stocks and bonds.)

    A large part of financial planning is finding an _____ that is appropriate for a given person in terms of their appetite for and ability to shoulder risk. This can depend on various factors; see investor profile.

    a. Investment performance
    b. Asset allocation
    c. Investing online
    d. Alternative investment

27. _____ are those dividends paid out in form of additional stock shares of the issuing corporation or other corporation They are usually issued in proportion to shares owned (for example for every 100 shares of stock owned, 5% stock dividend will yield 5 extra shares). If this payment involves the issue of new shares, this is very similar to a stock split in that it increases the total number of shares while lowering the price of each share and does not change the market capitalization or the total value of the shares held
    a. The Hong Kong Securities Institute
    b. Time-based currency
    c. Database auditing
    d. Stock or scrip dividends

28. In business and finance, a _____ (also referred to as equity _____) of stock means a _____ of ownership in a corporation (company.) In the plural, stocks is often used as a synonym for _____s especially in the United States, but it is less commonly used that way outside of North America.

Chapter 3. Overview of Security Types 27

In the United Kingdom, South Africa, and Australia, stock can also refer to completely different financial instruments such as government bonds or, less commonly, to all kinds of marketable securities.

a. Share
b. Margin
c. Procter ' Gamble
d. Bucket shop

29. In finance, a _____ is a type of bond that can be converted into shares of stock in the issuing company, usually at some pre-announced ratio. It is a hybrid security with debt- and equity-like features. Although it typically has a low coupon rate, the holder is compensated with the ability to convert the bond to common stock, usually at a substantial discount to the stock's market value.

a. Gilts
b. Bond fund
c. Corporate bond
d. Convertible bond

30. A _____ is a bond issued by a national government denominated in the country's own currency. Bonds issued by national governments in foreign currencies are normally referred to as sovereign bonds. The first ever _____ was issued by the British government in 1693 to raise money to fund a war against France.

a. Zero-coupon bond
b. Government bond
c. Municipal bond
d. Collateralized debt obligations

31. In the United States, a _____ is a bond issued by a city or other local government, or their agencies. Potential issuers of these bonds include cities, counties, redevelopment agencies, school districts, publicly owned airports and seaports, and any other governmental entity (or group of governments) below the state level. They may be general obligations of the issuer or secured by specified revenues.

a. Senior debt
b. Puttable bond
c. Municipal bond
d. Premium bond

32. The _____ is an American stock exchange. It is the largest electronic screen-based equity securities trading market in the United States. With approximately 3,200 companies, it has more trading volume per day than any other stock exchange in the world.

a. 4-4-5 Calendar
b. NASDAQ
c. 7-Eleven
d. 529 plan

33. The institution most often referenced by the word '_____' is a public or publicly traded _____, the shares of which are traded on a public stock exchange (e.g., the New York Stock Exchange or Nasdaq in the United States) where shares of stock of _____s are bought and sold by and to the general public. Most of the largest businesses in the world are publicly traded _____s. However, the majority of _____s are said to be closely held, privately held or close _____s, meaning that no ready market exists for the trading of shares.

a. Federal Home Loan Mortgage Corporation
b. Depository Trust Company
c. Protect
d. Corporation

34. The _____, in terms of finance and investing, describes how the expected return of a stock or portfolio is correlated to the return of the financial market as a whole.

An asset with a beta of 0 means that its price is not at all correlated with the market; that asset is independent. A positive beta means that the asset generally follows the market.

a. LIBOR market model
b. Perpetuity
c. Beta coefficient
d. Current yield

35. A _____ is a collective investment scheme that invests in bonds and other debt securities. _____s yield monthly dividends that include interest payments on the fund's underlying securities plus any capital appreciation in the prices of the portfolio's bonds. _____s tend to pay higher dividends than CDs and money market accounts, and they generally pay out dividends more frequently and regularly than individual bonds.

a. Private activity bond
b. Gilts
c. Premium bond
d. Bond fund

36. _____ is the provision of resources (such as granting a loan) by one party to another party where that second party does not reimburse the first party immediately, thereby generating a debt, and instead arranges either to repay or return those resources (or material(s) of equal value) at a later date. The first party is called a creditor, also known as a lender, while the second party is called a debtor, also known as a borrower.

Movements of financial capital are normally dependent on either _____ or equity transfers.

a. Warrant
b. Clearing house
c. Credit
d. Comparable

37. A _____ assesses the credit worthiness of an individual, corporation, or even a country. _____s are calculated from financial history and current assets and liabilities. Typically, a _____ tells a lender or investor the probability of the subject being able to pay back a loan.

a. Credit cycle
b. Debenture
c. Credit report monitoring
d. Credit rating

38. Modern portfolio theory (MPT) proposes how rational investors will use diversification to optimize their portfolios, and how a risky asset should be priced. The basic concepts of the theory are Markowitz diversification, the _____, capital asset pricing model, the alpha and beta coefficients, the Capital Market Line and the Securities Market Line.

MPT models an asset's return as a random variable, and models a portfolio as a weighted combination of assets so that the return of a portfolio is the weighted combination of the assets' returns.

a. AAB
b. A Random Walk Down Wall Street
c. ABN Amro
d. Efficient frontier

39. A _____ is a pool of assets forming an independent legal entity that are bought with the contributions to a pension plan for the exclusive purpose of financing pension plan benefits.

_____s are important shareholders of listed and private companies. They are especially important to the stock market where large institutional investors like the Ontario Teachers' Pension Plan dominate.

a. Leverage
b. Leveraged buyout
c. Pension fund
d. Limited liability company

Chapter 3. Overview of Security Types

40. _____ is the action of bringing a portfolio of investments that has deviated away from one's target asset allocation back into line. Under-weighted securities can be purchased with newly saved money; alternatively, over-weighted securities can be sold to purchase under-weighted securities.

The investments in a portfolio will perform according to the market.

a. Divestment
b. Security market line
c. Market timing
d. Rebalancing

41. An _____ is an investment product other than traditional investments such as stocks, bonds or cash.

This broad definition makes it impossible to list all alternative strategies, but the most important areas are real estate, private equity, venture capital,commodities, and hedged or absolute return strategies. Wine, art and antiques, indeed any business of value, might also be considered as an _____.

a. Asset allocation
b. Alternative investment
c. Investing online
d. Investment decisions

42. _____ are the inflation-indexed bonds issued by the U.S. Treasury. The principal is adjusted to the Consumer Price Index, the commonly used measure of inflation. The coupon rate is constant, but generates a different amount of interest when multiplied by the inflation-adjusted principal, thus protecting the holder against inflation. _____ are currently offered in 5-year, 10-year and 20-year maturities.

a. Treasury Inflation-Protected Securities
b. Treasury securities
c. 4-4-5 Calendar
d. Treasury Inflation Protected Securities

43. A _____ is a financial contract whose value is derived from the value of something else (known as the underlying.) The underlying on which a _____ is based can be an asset, weather conditions bonds or other forms of credit.

a. 7-Eleven
b. 4-4-5 Calendar
c. 529 plan
d. Derivative

44. In finance, a _____ is a standardized contract, to buy or sell a specified commodity of standardized quality at a certain date in the future, at a market determined price (the futures price.)

The price is determined by the instantaneous equilibrium between the forces of supply and demand among competing buy and sell orders on the exchange at the time of the purchase or sale of the contract.

In many cases, the items may be such non-traditional 'commodities' as foreign currencies, commercial or government paper [e.g., bonds], or 'baskets' of corporate equity ['stock indices'] or other financial instruments.

a. Financial future
b. Futures contract
c. Heston model
d. Repurchase agreement

45. A _____ is an exchange of promises between two or more parties to do an act which is enforceable in a court of law. It is where an unqualified offer meets a qualified acceptance and the parties reach Consensus ad Idem. The parties must have the necessary capacity to _____ and the _____ must not be either trifling, indeterminate, impossible or illegal.
   a. 7-Eleven
   b. 529 plan
   c. 4-4-5 Calendar
   d. Contract

46. A _____ is something for which there is demand, but which is supplied without qualitative differentiation across a market. It is a product that is the same no matter who produces it, such as petroleum, notebook paper, or milk. In other words, copper is copper.
   a. 7-Eleven
   b. 529 plan
   c. Commodity
   d. 4-4-5 Calendar

47. A _____ is a futures contract on a short term interest rate (STIR.) Contracts vary, but are often defined on an interest rate index such as 3-month sterling or US dollar LIBOR.

They are traded across a wide range of currencies, including the G12 country currencies and many others.

   a. Dual currency deposit
   b. Notional amount
   c. Real estate derivatives
   d. Financial future

48. The _____ is an American financial and commodity derivative exchange based in Chicago. The _____ was founded in 1898 as the Chicago Butter and Egg Board. Originally, the exchange was a non-profit organization.
   a. Chicago Mercantile Exchange
   b. Public Company Accounting Oversight Board
   c. Financial Crimes Enforcement Network
   d. Gamelan Council

49. A _____ is a financial contract between two parties, the buyer and the seller of this type of option. Often it is simply labeled a 'call'. The buyer of the option has the right, but not the obligation to buy an agreed quantity of a particular commodity or financial instrument (the underlying instrument) from the seller of the option at a certain time (the expiration date) for a certain price (the strike price.)
   a. Call option
   b. Bear call spread
   c. Bull spread
   d. Bear spread

50. In banking and finance, _____ denotes all activities from the time a commitment is made for a transaction until it is settled. _____ is necessary because the speed of trades is much faster than the cycle time for completing the underlying transaction.

In its widest sense _____ involves the management of post-trading, pre-settlement credit exposures, to ensure that trades are settled in accordance with market rules, even if a buyer or seller should become insolvent prior to settlement.

   a. Procter ' Gamble
   b. Clearing
   c. Clearing house
   d. Share

51. In options, the _____ is a key variable in a derivatives contract between two parties. Where the contract requires delivery of the underlying instrument, the trade will be at the _____, regardless of the spot price (market price) of the underlying instrument at that time.

Definition - The fixed price at which the owner of an option can purchase, in the case of a call in the case of a put, the underlying security or commodity.

a. Swaption
c. Naked put
b. Moneyness
d. Strike price

52. An _____ is a contract written by a seller that conveys to the buyer the right -- but not the obligation -- to buy (in the case of a call _____) or to sell (in the case of a put _____) a particular asset, such as a piece of property such as, among others, a futures contract. In return for granting the _____, the seller collects a payment (the premium) from the buyer.

For example, buying a call _____ provides the right to buy a specified quantity of a security at a set strike price at some time on or before expiration, while buying a put _____ provides the right to sell.

a. Annuity
c. AT'T Mobility LLC
b. Option
d. Amortization

53. An _____ is defined as 'a promise which meets the requirements for the formation of a contract and limits the promisor's power to revoke an offer.' Restatement (Second) of Contracts § 25 (1981.)

Quite simply, an _____ is a type of contract that protects an offeree from an offeror's ability to revoke the contract.

Consideration for the _____ is still required as it is still a form of contract.

a. Option contract
c. A Random Walk Down Wall Street
b. ABN Amro
d. AAB

54. The _____ is the price the buyer of the options contract pays for the right to buy or sell a security at a specified price in the future.
a. ABN Amro
c. AAB
b. A Random Walk Down Wall Street
d. Option premium

55. A _____ is a financial contract between two parties, the seller (writer) and the buyer of the option. The put allows its buyer the right but not the obligation to sell a commodity or financial instrument (the underlying instrument) to the writer (seller) of the option at a certain time for a certain price (the strike price.) The writer (seller) has the obligation to purchase the underlying asset at that strike price, if the buyer exercises the option.
a. Debit spread
c. Bear call spread
b. Bear spread
d. Put option

56. In finance, _____ is the process of estimating the potential market value of a financial asset or liability. they can be done on assets (for example, investments in marketable securities such as stocks, options, business enterprises, or intangible assets such as patents and trademarks) or on liabilities (e.g., Bonds issued by a company.) _____s are required in many contexts including investment analysis, capital budgeting, merger and acquisition transactions, financial reporting, taxable events to determine the proper tax liability, and in litigation.

    a. Share
    b. Procter ' Gamble
    c. Margin
    d. Valuation

57. _____ is the difference between price and the costs of bringing to market whatever it is that is accounted as an enterprise (whether by harvest, extraction, manufacture, or purchase) in terms of the component costs of delivered goods and/or services and any operating or other expenses.

A key difficulty in measuring profit is in defining costs. Pure economic monetary profits can be zero or negative even in competitive equilibrium when accounted monetized costs exceed monetized price.

    a. Economic profit
    b. A Random Walk Down Wall Street
    c. AAB
    d. Accounting profit

Chapter 4. Mutual Funds

1. A _____, is a collective investment scheme with a limited number of shares.

New shares are rarely issued after the fund is launched; shares are not normally redeemable for cash or securities until the fund liquidates. Typically an investor can acquire shares in a _____ by buying shares on a secondary market from a broker, market maker, or other investor as opposed to an open-end fund where all transactions eventually involve the fund company creating new shares on the fly (in exchange for either cash or securities) or redeeming shares (for cash or securities.)

   a. Money market funds   b. Stock fund
   c. Mutual fund fees and expenses   d. Closed-end fund

2. An _____ is a company whose main business is holding securities of other companies purely for investment purposes. The _____ invests money on behalf of its shareholders who in turn share in the profits and losses.
   a. AAB   b. Unit investment trust
   c. A Random Walk Down Wall Street   d. Investment company

3. A _____ is a professionally managed type of collective investment scheme that pools money from many investors and invests it in stocks, bonds, short-term money market instruments, and/or other securities. The _____ will have a fund manager that trades the pooled money on a regular basis. Currently, the worldwide value of all _____s totals more than $26 trillion.

Since 1940, there have been three basic types of investment companies in the United States: open-end funds, also known in the US as _____s; unit investment trusts (UITs); and closed-end funds.

   a. Trust company   b. Net asset value
   c. Mutual fund   d. Financial intermediary

4. The _____ is an American stock exchange. It is the largest electronic screen-based equity securities trading market in the United States. With approximately 3,200 companies, it has more trading volume per day than any other stock exchange in the world.
   a. 4-4-5 Calendar   b. 529 plan
   c. 7-Eleven   d. NASDAQ

5. An _____ is a document a company presents at an annual general meeting for approval by its shareholders, or a charitable organization presents its trustees. The report is made up of reports, which may include the following:

- Chairman's report
- CEO's report
- Auditor's report on corporate governance
- Mission statement
- Corporate governance statement of compliance
- Statement of directors' responsibilities
- Invitation to the company's AGM

as well as financial statements including:

- Auditor's report on the financial statements
- Balance sheet
- Statement of retained earnings
- Income statement
- Cash flow statement
- Notes to the financial statements
- Accounting policies

Other information deemed relevant to stakeholders may be included, such as a report on operations for manufacturing firms. In the case of larger companies, it is usually a sleek, colorful, high gloss publication.

The details provided in the report are of use to investors to understand the company's financial position and future direction.

    a. Outstanding balance   b. Amortization schedule
    c. Accrued liabilities   d. Annual report

6. _____ is a term used to describe the value of an entity's assets less the value of its liabilities. The term is commonly used in relation to collective investment schemes. It may also be used as a synonym for the book value of a firm.

    a. Financial intermediary   b. Passive management
    c. Retail broker   d. Net asset value

7. In business and accounting, _____s are everything of value that is owned by a person or company. The balance sheet of a firm records the monetary value of the _____s owned by the firm. The two major _____ classes are tangible _____s and intangible _____s.

    a. Income   b. Accounts payable
    c. EBITDA   d. Asset

8. An _____ is a contract written by a seller that conveys to the buyer the right -- but not the obligation -- to buy (in the case of a call _____) or to sell (in the case of a put _____) a particular asset, such as a piece of property such as, among others, a futures contract. In return for granting the _____, the seller collects a payment (the premium) from the buyer.

For example, buying a call _____ provides the right to buy a specified quantity of a security at a set strike price at some time on or before expiration, while buying a put _____ provides the right to sell.

    a. Annuity   b. Amortization
    c. AT'T Mobility LLC   d. Option

9. An _____ is an investment vehicle traded on stock exchanges, much like stocks. An ETF holds assets such as stocks or bonds and trades at approximately the same price as the net asset value of its underlying assets over the course of the trading day. Most ETFs track an index, such as the Dow Jones Industrial Average or the S'P 500.

Chapter 4. Mutual Funds

a. A Random Walk Down Wall Street
b. ABN Amro
c. AAB
d. Exchange-traded fund

10. In business, _____ is income that a company receives from its normal business activities, usually from the sale of goods and services to customers. Some companies also receive _____ from interest, dividends or royalties paid to them by other companies. _____ may refer to business income in general, or it may refer to the amount, in a monetary unit, received during a period of time, as in 'Last year, Company X had _____ of $32 million.'

In many countries, including the UK, _____ is referred to as turnover.

a. Matching principle
b. Bottom line
c. Furniture, Fixtures and Equipment
d. Revenue

11. In economics, business, and accounting, a _____ is the value of money that has been used up to produce something, and hence is not available for use anymore. In business, the _____ may be one of acquisition, in which case the amount of money expended to acquire it is counted as _____. In this case, money is the input that is gone in order to acquire the thing.

a. Sliding scale fees
b. Fixed costs
c. Cost
d. Marginal cost

12. An _____ or index tracker is a collective investment scheme (usually a mutual fund or exchange-traded fund) that aims to replicate the movements of an index of a specific financial market regardless of market conditions.

Tracking can be achieved by trying to hold all of the securities in the index, in the same proportions as the index. Other methods include statistically sampling the market and holding 'representative' securities.

a. A Random Walk Down Wall Street
b. Investment company
c. Index fund
d. AAB

13. _____ also known as Deferred Sales Charge, is a fee paid when shares are sold. This fee typically goes to the brokers that sell the fund's shares. The amount of this type of load will depend on how long the investor holds his or her shares and typically decreases to zero if the investor holds his or her shares long enough.

a. Closed-end fund
b. Money market funds
c. Mutual fund fees and expenses
d. Back-end load

14. The U.S. Securities and Exchange Commission's (SEC's) Regulation Fair Disclosure, also commonly referred to as _____ was an SEC ruling implemented in October 2000 (.) It mandated that all publicly traded companies must disclose material information to all investors at the same time.

The regulation sought to stamp out selective disclosure, in which some investors (often large institutional investors) received market moving information before others (often smaller, individual investors.)

a. Regulation Fair Disclosure
b. Commodity Pool Operator
c. Revenue recognition
d. Regulation FD

15. _____, in accrual accounting, is any account where the asset or liability is not realized until a future date, e.g. annuities, charges, taxes, income, etc. The _____ item may be carried, dependent on type of deferral, as either an asset or liability. See also: accrual

_____ is also used in the university admissions process. It is the action by which a school rejects a student for early admission but still opts to review that student in the general admissions pool.

a. Current asset
c. Deferred
b. Net profit
d. Revenue

16. A _____ is a periodic payment that is paid by investors in a pooled investment fund to the fund's investment adviser for investment and portfolio management services.

In a mutual fund, the _____ will include any fees payable to the fund's investment adviser or its affiliates, and administrative fees payable to the investment adviser that are not included in the 'Other Expenses' category.)

In a private equity fund, the _____ is an annual payment made by the limited partners in the fund to the fund's manager (e.g., the private equity firm) to pay for the private equity firm's investment operations..

a. 4-4-5 Calendar
c. 7-Eleven
b. 529 plan
d. Management fee

17. A _____ or equity fund is a fund that invests in Equities more commonly known as stocks. Such funds are typically held either in stock or cash, as opposed to Bonds, notes, or other securities. This may be a mutual fund or exchange-traded fund.

a. Closed-end fund
c. Money market funds
b. Stock Fund
d. Mutual fund fees and expenses

18. In finance, the _____ is the global financial market for short-term borrowing and lending. It provides short-term liquidity funding for the global financial system. The _____ is where short-term obligations such as Treasury bills, commercial paper and bankers' acceptances are bought and sold.

a. Consumer debt
c. Cramdown
b. Debt-for-equity swap
d. Money market

19. In economics, the concept of the _____ refers to the decision-making time frame of a firm in which at least one factor of production is fixed. Costs which are fixed in the _____ have no impact on a firms decisions. For example a firm can raise output by increasing the amount of labour through overtime.

a. 529 plan
c. Long-run
b. Short-run
d. 4-4-5 Calendar

20. In the United States, a _____ is a bond issued by a city or other local government, or their agencies. Potential issuers of these bonds include cities, counties, redevelopment agencies, school districts, publicly owned airports and seaports, and any other governmental entity (or group of governments) below the state level. They may be general obligations of the issuer or secured by specified revenues.

Chapter 4. Mutual Funds

a. Premium bond
c. Puttable bond
b. Senior debt
d. Municipal bond

21. In finance, a _____ is a debt security, in which the authorized issuer owes the holders a debt and, depending on the terms of the _____, is obliged to pay interest (the coupon) and/or to repay the principal at a later date, termed maturity.

Thus a _____ is a loan: the issuer is the borrower, the _____ holder is the lender, and the coupon is the interest. _____s provide the borrower with external funds to finance long-term investments, or, in the case of government _____s, to finance current expenditure.

a. Catastrophe bonds
c. Puttable bond
b. Convertible bond
d. Bond

22. Money funds (or _____, money market mutual funds) are mutual funds that invest in short-term debt instruments.

_____, also known as principal stability funds, seek to limit exposure to losses due to credit, market and liquidity risks. _____, in the United States, are regulated by the Securities and Exchange Commission's (SEC) Investment Company Act of 1940.

a. Closed-end fund
c. Mutual fund fees and expenses
b. Stock fund
d. Money market funds

23. A _____ is a fungible, negotiable instrument representing financial value. They are broadly categorized into debt securities (such as banknotes, bonds and debentures), and equity securities; e.g., common stocks. The company or other entity issuing the _____ is called the issuer.

a. Book entry
c. Tracking stock
b. Securities lending
d. Security

24. The institution most often referenced by the word '_____' is a public or publicly traded _____, the shares of which are traded on a public stock exchange (e.g., the New York Stock Exchange or Nasdaq in the United States) where shares of stock of _____s are bought and sold by and to the general public. Most of the largest businesses in the world are publicly traded _____s. However, the majority of _____s are said to be closely held, privately held or close _____s, meaning that no ready market exists for the trading of shares.

a. Federal Home Loan Mortgage Corporation
c. Depository Trust Company
b. Corporation
d. Protect

25. Explicit _____ is a measure implemented in many countries to protect bank depositors, in full or in part, from losses caused by a bank's inability to pay its debts when due. _____ systems are one component of a financial system safety net that promotes financial stability.

a. Time deposit
c. Deposit Insurance
b. Banking panic
d. Reserve requirement

26. The _____ is a United States government corporation created by the Glass-Steagall Act of 1933. It provides deposit insurance, which guarantees the safety of checking and savings deposits in member banks, currently up to $250,000 per depositor per bank. Insured deposits are backed by the full faith and credit of the United States.

a. NYSE Group
b. FASB
c. Ford Foundation
d. Federal Deposit Insurance Corporation

27. In economic models, the _____ time frame assumes no fixed factors of production. Firms can enter or leave the marketplace, and the cost (and availability) of land, labor, raw materials, and capital goods can be assumed to vary. In contrast, in the short-run time frame, certain factors are assumed to be fixed, because there is not sufficient time for them to change.
   a. 529 plan
   b. Short-run
   c. 4-4-5 Calendar
   d. Long-run

28. _____, in bookkeeping, refers to assets, liabilities, income, and expenses recorded on individual pages of the so called book of final entry or ledger. Changes in _____ value are made by chronologically posting debit (DR) and credit (CR) entries to its page. Examples of _____s are cash, _____s receivable, mortgages, loans, land and buildings, common stock, sales, services provided, wages, and payroll overhead.
   a. Accretion
   b. Option
   c. Account
   d. Alpha

29. A _____ is a current account at a banking institution that allows money to be deposited and withdrawn by the account holder, with the transactions and resulting balance being recorded on the bank's books. Some banks charge a fee for this service, while others may pay the customer interest on the funds deposited.

Although restrictions placed on access depend upon the terms and conditions of the account and the provider, the account holder retains rights to have their funds repaid on demand.

   a. Deposit account
   b. Contractum trinius
   c. Bilateral netting
   d. 4-4-5 Calendar

30. A _____ is a pool of assets forming an independent legal entity that are bought with the contributions to a pension plan for the exclusive purpose of financing pension plan benefits.

_____s are important shareholders of listed and private companies. They are especially important to the stock market where large institutional investors like the Ontario Teachers' Pension Plan dominate.

   a. Leveraged buyout
   b. Limited liability company
   c. Leverage
   d. Pension fund

31. A _____ is a collective investment scheme that invests in bonds and other debt securities. _____s yield monthly dividends that include interest payments on the fund's underlying securities plus any capital appreciation in the prices of the portfolio's bonds. _____s tend to pay higher dividends than CDs and money market accounts, and they generally pay out dividends more frequently and regularly than individual bonds.
   a. Private activity bond
   b. Premium bond
   c. Gilts
   d. Bond fund

32. _____ in finance is a risk management technique, related to hedging, that mixes a wide variety of investments within a portfolio. Because the fluctuations of a single security have less impact on a diverse portfolio, _____ minimizes the risk from any one investment.

Chapter 4. Mutual Funds

A simple example of _____ is the following: On a particular island the entire economy consists of two companies: one that sells umbrellas and another that sells sunscreen.

a. 4-4-5 Calendar
c. 529 plan
b. 7-Eleven
d. Diversification

33. The _____ is a U.S. government-owned corporation within the Department of Housing and Urban Development

Ginnie Mae provides guarantees on mortgage-backed securities backed by federally insured or guaranteed loans, mainly loans issued by the Federal Housing Administration, Department of Veterans Affairs, Rural Housing Service, and Office of Public and Indian Housing. Ginnie Mae securities are the only MBS that are guaranteed by the United States government.

a. GNMA
c. Certified Emission Reductions
b. Case-Shiller Home Price Indices
d. Cash budget

34. The _____ is a U.S. government-owned corporation within the Department of Housing and Urban Development

Ginnie Mae provides guarantees on mortgage-backed securities backed by federally insured or guaranteed loans, mainly loans issued by the Federal Housing Administration, Department of Veterans Affairs, Rural Housing Service, and Office of Public and Indian Housing. Ginnie Mae securities are the only MBS that are guaranteed by the United States government.

a. Jumbo mortgage
c. Graduated payment mortgage
b. 4-4-5 Calendar
d. Government National Mortgage Association

35. _____ is a measurement of corporate or economic size equal to the share price times the number of shares outstanding of a public company. As owning stock represents owning the company, including all its equity, capitalization could represent the public opinion of a company's net worth and is a determining factor in stock valuation. Likewise, the capitalization of stock markets or economic regions may be compared to other economic indicators.

a. Synthetic CDO
c. Proxy fight
b. Market capitalization
d. Just-in-time

36. A _____, securities exchange or (in Europe) bourse is a corporation or mutual organization which provides 'trading' facilities for stock brokers and traders, to trade stocks and other securities. _____s also provide facilities for the issue and redemption of securities as well as other financial instruments and capital events including the payment of income and dividends. The securities traded on a _____ include: shares issued by companies, unit trusts and other pooled investment products and bonds.

a. 529 plan
c. 7-Eleven
b. Stock exchange
d. 4-4-5 Calendar

37. _____ is a term used in accounting relating to the increase in value of an asset. In this sense it is the reverse of depreciation, which measures the fall in value of assets over their normal life-time.

_____ is a rise of a currency in a floating exchange rate.

a. A Random Walk Down Wall Street
c. Other Comprehensive Basis of Accounting
b. Operating cash flow
d. Appreciation

38. In finance, _____ are stocks that appreciate in value and yield a high return on equity (ROE.) Analysts compute ROE by taking the company's net income and dividing it by the company's equity. To be classified as a growth stock, analysts expect to see at least 15 percent return on equity.

a. Stock valuation
c. 4-4-5 Calendar
b. Growth stocks
d. Security Analysis

39. _____, refers to consumption opportunity gained by an entity within a specified time frame, which is generally expressed in monetary terms. However, for households and individuals, '_____ is the sum of all the wages, salaries, profits, interests payments, rents and other forms of earnings received... in a given period of time.' For firms, _____ generally refers to net-profit: what remains of revenue after expenses have been subtracted.

a. OIBDA
c. Accrual
b. Annual report
d. Income

40. In business and finance, a _____ (also referred to as equity _____) of stock means a _____ of ownership in a corporation (company.) In the plural, stocks is often used as a synonym for _____s especially in the United States, but it is less commonly used that way outside of North America.

In the United Kingdom, South Africa, and Australia, stock can also refer to completely different financial instruments such as government bonds or, less commonly, to all kinds of marketable securities.

a. Margin
c. Procter ' Gamble
b. Bucket shop
d. Share

41. The term _____ is used to describe a nation's social, or business activity in the process of rapid industrialization. _____ are generally less-wealthy than the developed world, and are wealthier (or the wealthiest of) the developing world. According to The Economist many people find the term dated, but a new term has yet to gain much traction.

a. A Random Walk Down Wall Street
c. Emerging markets
b. ABN Amro
d. AAB

42. _____ is a term used to refer to how an investor distributes his or her investments among various classes of investment vehicles (e.g., stocks and bonds.)

A large part of financial planning is finding an _____ that is appropriate for a given person in terms of their appetite for and ability to shoulder risk. This can depend on various factors; see investor profile.

a. Asset allocation
c. Investing online
b. Investment performance
d. Alternative investment

43. In finance, a _____ is a type of bond that can be converted into shares of stock in the issuing company, usually at some pre-announced ratio. It is a hybrid security with debt- and equity-like features. Although it typically has a low coupon rate, the holder is compensated with the ability to convert the bond to common stock, usually at a substantial discount to the stock's market value.

Chapter 4. Mutual Funds

a. Gilts
b. Corporate bond
c. Bond fund
d. Convertible bond

44. In finance, a _____ (non-investment grade bond, speculative grade bond or junk bond) is a bond that is rated below investment grade at the time of purchase. These bonds have a higher risk of default or other adverse credit events, but typically pay higher yields than better quality bonds in order to make them attractive to investors.
a. Private equity
b. Sharpe ratio
c. Volatility
d. High yield bond

45. _____ is the weighted average maturity of a bond where the weights are the relative discounted cash flows in each period.

It will be seen that this is the same formula for the duration as given above.

Macaulay showed that an unweighted average maturity is not useful in predicting interest rate risk.

a. Yield
b. Yield to maturity
c. 4-4-5 Calendar
d. Macaulay duration

46. In finance, the _____ of a financial asset measures the sensitivity of the asset's price to interest rate movements, expressed as a number of years. The reason for expressing this sensitivity in years is that the time that will elapse until a cash flow is received allows more interest to accumulate. Therefore the price of an asset with long term cashflows has more interest rate sensitivity than an asset with cashflows in the near future.
a. Macaulay duration
b. Yield to maturity
c. Duration
d. 4-4-5 Calendar

47. In finance, the term _____ describes the amount in cash that returns to the owners of a security. Normally it does not include the price variations, at the difference of the total return. _____ applies to various stated rates of return on stocks (common and preferred, and convertible), fixed income instruments (bonds, notes, bills, strips, zero coupon), and some other investment type insurance products (e.g. annuities.)
a. Yield to maturity
b. Macaulay duration
c. 4-4-5 Calendar
d. Yield

48. Behavioral economics and _____ are closely related fields that have evolved to be a separate branch of economic and financial analysis which applies scientific research on human and social, cognitive and emotional factors to better understand economic decisions by, say, consumers, borrowers, investors, and how they affect market prices, returns and the allocation of resources.

The field is primarily concerned with the bounds of rationality (selfishness, self-control) of economic agents. Behavioral models typically integrate insights from psychology with neo-classical economic theory.

a. Recession
b. Medium of exchange
c. Market structure
d. Behavioral finance

49. _____ is a risk-adjusted measure of the so-called active return on an investment. It is the return in excess of the compensation for the risk borne, and thus commonly used to assess active managers' performances. Often, the return of a benchmark is subtracted in order to consider relative performance, which yields Jensen's _____.
   a. Alpha
   b. Option
   c. Annuity
   d. Amortization

50. _____ Â® funds are shares of a family of exchange-traded funds (ETFs) traded in the United States and managed by State Street Global Advisors (SSgA.) Informally, they are also known as Spyders or Spiders. _____ Â® is a trademark of the McGraw-Hill Companies, Inc.
   a. Federal Agricultural Mortgage Corporation
   b. Microfinance
   c. SPDR
   d. Federal Deposit Insurance Corporation

51. In finance, a _____ is a position established in one market in an attempt to offset exposure to the price risk of an equal but opposite obligation or position in another market -- usually, but not always, in the context of one's commercial activity. Hedging is a strategy designed to minimize exposure to such business risks as a sharp contraction in demand for one's inventory, while still allowing the business to profit from producing and maintaining that inventory. A typical hedger might be a farmer with 2000 acres of unharvested wheat in the ground, who would rather tend his crop without the distraction of uncertain prices.
   a. 7-Eleven
   b. 4-4-5 Calendar
   c. 529 plan
   d. Hedge

52. A _____ is a private investment fund open to a limited range of investors that is permitted by regulators to undertake a wider range of activities than other investment funds and also pays a performance fee to its investment manager. Each fund will have its own strategy which determines the type of investments and the methods of investment it undertakes. _____s as a class invest in a broad range of investments extending over shares, debt, commodities and beyond.
   a. 529 plan
   b. Hedge fund
   c. 7-Eleven
   d. 4-4-5 Calendar

53. A '_____' (FoF) is an investment fund that uses an investment strategy of holding a portfolio of other investment funds rather than investing directly in shares, bonds or other securities. This type of investing is often referred to as multi-manager investment.

There are different types of '_____', each investing in a different type of collective investment scheme (typically one type per FoF), eg.

   a. Leverage
   b. Pension fund
   c. Fund of funds
   d. Limited liability company

Chapter 5. The Stock Market

1. In finance, _____ refers to Monday, October 19, 1987, when stock markets around the world crashed, shedding a huge value in a very short time. The crash began in Hong Kong, spread west through international time zones to Europe, hitting the United States after other markets had already declined by a significant margin. The Dow Jones Industrial Average (DJIA) dropped by 508 points to 1738.74 (22.61%).
   a. Black Monday
   c. 4-4-5 Calendar
   b. 529 plan
   d. 7-Eleven

2. _____ is a form of corporation equity ownership represented in the securities. It is dangerous in comparison to preferred shares and some other investment options, in that in the event of bankruptcy, _____ investors receive their funds after preferred stockholders, bondholders, creditors, etc. On the other hand, common shares on average perform better than preferred shares or bonds over time.
   a. Stock market bubble
   c. Stop-limit order
   b. Stock split
   d. Common stock

3. _____, is when a company issues common stock or shares to the public for the first time. They are often issued by smaller, younger companies seeking capital to expand, but can also be done by large privately-owned companies looking to become publicly traded.

   In an _____ the issuer may obtain the assistance of an underwriting firm, which helps it determine what type of security to issue (common or preferred), best offering price and time to bring it to market.

   a. Asian Financial Crisis
   c. Insolvency
   b. Interest
   d. Initial public offering

4. The _____ is an American stock exchange. It is the largest electronic screen-based equity securities trading market in the United States. With approximately 3,200 companies, it has more trading volume per day than any other stock exchange in the world.
   a. 7-Eleven
   c. 529 plan
   b. 4-4-5 Calendar
   d. NASDAQ

5. The _____ is that part of the capital markets that deals with the issuance of new securities. Companies, governments or public sector institutions can obtain funding through the sale of a new stock or bond issue. This is typically done through a syndicate of securities dealers.
   a. Primary market
   c. Peer group analysis
   b. Volatility clustering
   d. Sector rotation

6. The U.S. _____ is an independent agency of the United States government which holds primary responsibility for enforcing the federal securities laws and regulating the securities industry, the nation's stock and options exchanges, and other electronic securities markets. The SEC was created by section 4 of the SEC of 1934 (now codified as 15 U.S.C. § 78d and commonly referred to as the 1934 Act.)
   a. 4-4-5 Calendar
   c. Securities and Exchange Commission
   b. 7-Eleven
   d. 529 plan

7. The _____ is the financial market where previously issued securities and financial instruments such as stock, bonds, options, and futures are bought and sold. The term '_____' is also used refer to the market for any used goods or assets, or an alternative use for an existing product or asset where the customer base is the second market

With primary issuances of securities or financial instruments, or the primary market, investors purchase these securities directly from issuers such as corporations issuing shares in an IPO or private placement, or directly from the federal government in the case of treasuries.

a. Financial market
b. Delta neutral
c. Performance attribution
d. Secondary market

8. A _____ is a fungible, negotiable instrument representing financial value. They are broadly categorized into debt securities (such as banknotes, bonds and debentures), and equity securities; e.g., common stocks. The company or other entity issuing the _____ is called the issuer.
a. Tracking stock
b. Book entry
c. Securities lending
d. Security

9. In business and accounting, _____s are everything of value that is owned by a person or company. The balance sheet of a firm records the monetary value of the _____s owned by the firm. The two major _____ classes are tangible _____s and intangible _____s.
a. Income
b. EBITDA
c. Asset
d. Accounts payable

10. _____ is a term used to refer to how an investor distributes his or her investments among various classes of investment vehicles (e.g., stocks and bonds.)

A large part of financial planning is finding an _____ that is appropriate for a given person in terms of their appetite for and ability to shoulder risk. This can depend on various factors; see investor profile.

a. Alternative investment
b. Investing online
c. Investment performance
d. Asset allocation

11. In business and finance, a _____ (also referred to as equity _____) of stock means a _____ of ownership in a corporation (company.) In the plural, stocks is often used as a synonym for _____s especially in the United States, but it is less commonly used that way outside of North America.

In the United Kingdom, South Africa, and Australia, stock can also refer to completely different financial instruments such as government bonds or, less commonly, to all kinds of marketable securities.

a. Bucket shop
b. Share
c. Margin
d. Procter ' Gamble

12. _____ offer, asking price is a price a seller of a good is willing to accept for that particular good.

In bid and ask, the term _____ is used in contrast to the term bid price. The difference between the _____ and the bid price is called the spread.

Chapter 5. The Stock Market

a. Interest rate parity
c. AAB
b. Ask price
d. A Random Walk Down Wall Street

13. A _____ is the highest price that a buyer (i.e., bidder) is willing to pay for a good. It is usually referred to simply as the 'bid.'

In bid and ask, the _____ stands in contrast to the ask price or 'offer', and the difference between the two is called the bid/ask spread.

An unsolicited bid or offer is when a person or company receives a bid even though they are not looking to sell.

a. Settlement date
c. Mid price
b. Political risk
d. Bid price

14. A _____ is a payment made by a corporation to its shareholder members. When a corporation earns a profit or surplus, that money can be put to two uses: it can either be re-invested in the business (called retained earnings), or it can be paid to the shareholders as a _____. Many corporations retain a portion of their earnings and pay the remainder as a _____.

a. Dividend yield
c. Dividend puzzle
b. Special dividend
d. Dividend

15. The _____ is a stock exchange based in New York City, New York. It is the largest stock exchange in the world by dollar value of its listed companies securities. As of October 2008, the combined capitalization of all domestic _____ listed companies was $10.1 trillion.

a. 4-4-5 Calendar
c. 7-Eleven
b. 529 plan
d. New York Stock Exchange

16. A _____, securities exchange or (in Europe) bourse is a corporation or mutual organization which provides 'trading' facilities for stock brokers and traders, to trade stocks and other securities. _____s also provide facilities for the issue and redemption of securities as well as other financial instruments and capital events including the payment of income and dividends. The securities traded on a _____ include: shares issued by companies, unit trusts and other pooled investment products and bonds.

a. Stock Exchange
c. 4-4-5 Calendar
b. 7-Eleven
d. 529 plan

17. A _____ is a private or public market for the trading of company stock and derivatives of company stock at an agreed price; these are securities listed on a stock exchange as well as those only traded privately.

The size of the world _____ is estimated at about $36.6 trillion US at the beginning of October 2008. The world derivatives market has been estimated at about $480 trillion face or nominal value, 12 times the size of the entire world economy.

a. Anton Gelonkin
c. Andrew Tobias
b. Adolph Coors
d. Stock market

18. A _____ is a point at which a stock market will stop trading for a period of time in response to substantial drops in value.

On the New York Stock Exchange, one type of _____ is referred to as a 'circuit breaker.' These limits were put in place after Black Monday in order to reduce market volatility and massive panic sell-offs, giving traders time to reconsider their transactions.

At the start of each quarter, the NYSE sets three circuit breaker levels at levels of 10%, 20%, and 30% of the average closing price of the Dow Jones Industrial Average for the month preceding the start of the quarter, rounded to the nearest 50-point interval.

    a. Trading curb
    b. Stock market index
    c. Stock repurchase
    d. Common stock

19. A '_____' is a 'Charge' that is paid to obtain the right to delay a payment. Essentially, the payer purchases the right to make a given payment in the future instead of in the Present. The '_____', or 'Charge' that must be paid to delay the payment, is simply the difference between what the payment amount would be if it were paid in the present and what the payment amount would be paid if it were paid in the future.

    a. Risk aversion
    b. Risk modeling
    c. Discount
    d. Value at risk

20. An _____ is a contract written by a seller that conveys to the buyer the right -- but not the obligation -- to buy (in the case of a call _____) or to sell (in the case of a put _____) a particular asset, such as a piece of property such as, among others, a futures contract. In return for granting the _____, the seller collects a payment (the premium) from the buyer.

For example, buying a call _____ provides the right to buy a specified quantity of a security at a set strike price at some time on or before expiration, while buying a put _____ provides the right to sell.

    a. Amortization
    b. Annuity
    c. Option
    d. AT'T Mobility LLC

21. A _____ is a member of an exchange who is an employee of a member firm and executes orders, as agent, on the floor of the exchange for clients. The _____ receives an order via teletype machine from his firm's trading department and then proceeds to the appropriate trading post on the exchange floor. There he joins other brokers and the specialist in the security being bought or sold and executes the trade at the best competitive price available.

    a. Floor broker
    b. Business valuation standards
    c. Case-Shiller Home Price Indices
    d. Multivariate normal distribution

22. A _____ is a firm that quotes both a buy and a sell price in a financial instrument or commodity, hoping to make a profit on the bid/offer spread, or turn.

In foreign exchange trading, where most deals are conducted over-the-counter and are, therefore, completely virtual, the _____ sells to and buys from its clients. Hence, the client's loss and the spread is the _____ firm's profit, which gets thus compensated for the effort of providing liquidity in a competitive market.

Chapter 5. The Stock Market

a. Market maker
c. 4-4-5 Calendar
b. 7-Eleven
d. 529 plan

23. In economics and finance, _____ is the practice of taking advantage of a price differential between two or more markets: striking a combination of matching deals that capitalize upon the imbalance, the profit being the difference between the market prices. When used by academics, an _____ is a transaction that involves no negative cash flow at any probabilistic or temporal state and a positive cash flow in at least one state; in simple terms, a risk-free profit.
    a. Arbitrage
    c. Initial margin
    b. Efficient-market hypothesis
    d. Issuer

24. A _____ is a buy or sell order to be executed by the broker immediately at current market prices. As long as there are willing sellers and buyers, _____s are filled.

A _____ is the simplest of the order types.

    a. Block premium
    c. Stockholder
    b. Market order
    d. Trading curb

25. A _____ is an order to buy a security at no more (or sell at no less) than a specific price. This gives the customer some control over the price at which the trade is executed, but may prevent the order from being executed ('filled'.)

A buy _____ can only be executed by the broker at the limit price or lower.

    a. Commercial mortgage-backed securities
    c. Block premium
    b. Limit order
    d. Common stock

26. A _____ is an order to buy (or sell) a security once the price of the security has climbed above (or dropped below) a specified stop price. When the specified stop price is reached, the _____ is entered as a market order (no limit.)

With a _____, the customer does not have to actively monitor how a stock is performing.

    a. Share price
    c. Wash sale
    b. Stop order
    d. Stock split

27. In finance, _____ or 'shorting' is the practice of selling a financial instrument that the seller does not own at the time of the sale. _____ is done with intent of later purchasing the financial instrument at a lower price. Short-sellers attempt to profit from an expected decline in the price of a financial instrument.
    a. 529 plan
    c. Short selling
    b. Short ratio
    d. 4-4-5 Calendar

28. A _____ combines the features of a stop order and a limit order. Once the stop price is reached, the _____ becomes a limit order to buy (or to sell) at no more (or less) than a specified price. As with all limit orders, a _____ doesn't get filled if the security's price never reaches the specified limit price.
    a. Wash sale
    c. Stop price
    b. Box spread
    d. Stop-limit order

Chapter 5. The Stock Market

29. The _____ generally prohibits short selling of securities except on an uptick. The rule was defined by U.S. Securities and Exchange Commission (SEC) which summarized it: 'Rule 10a-1(a)(1) provided that, subject to certain exceptions, a listed security may be sold short (A) at a price above the price at which the immediately preceding sale was effected (plus tick), or (B) at the last sale price if it is higher than the last different price (zero-plus tick.) Short sales were not permitted on minus ticks or zero-minus ticks, subject to narrow exceptions.'

The rule went into effect in 1938 and was removed when Rule 201 Regulation SHO became effective in 2007.

a. ABN Amro
b. Uptick rule
c. A Random Walk Down Wall Street
d. AAB

30. The _____ is the market for securities, where companies and governments can raise longterm funds. The _____ includes the stock market and the bond market. Financial regulators, such as the U.S. Securities and Exchange Commission, oversee the _____s in their designated countries to ensure that investors are protected against fraud.

a. Delta neutral
b. Spot rate
c. Forward market
d. Capital Market

31. An _____ is the term used in financial circles for a type of computer system that facilitates trading of financial products outside of stock exchanges. The primary products that are traded on an _____ are stocks and currencies. They came into existence in 1998 when the SEC authorized their creation.

a. Insider trading
b. Electronic communication network
c. Intellidex
d. Open outcry

32. The institution most often referenced by the word '_____' is a public or publicly traded _____, the shares of which are traded on a public stock exchange (e.g., the New York Stock Exchange or Nasdaq in the United States) where shares of stock of _____s are bought and sold by and to the general public. Most of the largest businesses in the world are publicly traded _____s. However, the majority of _____s are said to be closely held, privately held or close _____s, meaning that no ready market exists for the trading of shares.

a. Protect
b. Federal Home Loan Mortgage Corporation
c. Depository Trust Company
d. Corporation

33. _____ trading refers to direct institution-to-institution trading without using the service of broker-dealers. It is impossible to estimate the volume of _____ activity because trades are not subject to reporting requirements. Studies have suggested that several millions shares are traded per day.

a. 529 plan
b. Fourth market
c. 7-Eleven
d. 4-4-5 Calendar

34. In finance, _____ trading is the trading of exchange listed securities in the over-the-counter (OTC) market. Bernard Madoff was engaged in _____ trading.

a. 4-4-5 Calendar
b. 529 plan
c. 7-Eleven
d. Third market

35. An _____ is a call option on the common stock of a company, issued as a form of non-cash compensation. Restrictions on the option (such as vesting and limited transferability) attempt to align the holder's interest with those of the business' shareholders. If the company's stock rises, holders of options experience a direct financial benefit.

Chapter 5. The Stock Market

a. Employee stock option
b. Underwriting contract
c. Operating ratio
d. Internal financing

36. The _____ is one of several stock market indices, created by nineteenth-century Wall Street Journal editor and Dow Jones ' Company co-founder Charles Dow. Dow compiled the index to gauge the performance of the industrial sector of the American stock market. It is the second-oldest U.S. market index, after the Dow Jones Transportation Average, which Dow also created.

a. 7-Eleven
b. Dow Jones Industrial Average
c. 4-4-5 Calendar
d. 529 plan

37. _____ is an American publishing and financial information firm.

The company was founded in 1882 by three reporters: Charles Dow, Edward Jones, and Charles Bergstresser. Like The New York Times and the Washington Post, the company was in recent years publicly traded but privately controlled.

a. The Dun ' Bradstreet Corporation
b. Holding company
c. Federal National Mortgage Association
d. Dow Jones ' Company

38. _____ was formed in 1997 as an entity within Dow Jones ' Co. It produces, maintains, licenses and markets indexes as benchmarks and as the basis of investible products such as exchange traded funds (ETFs), mutual funds and structured products. The company currently has employees in 18 cities worldwide, including Princeton, NJ, New York, Boston, Chicago, Los Angeles, London, Frankfurt, Zurich, Paris, Madrid, Stockholm, Singapore, Hong Kong, Beijing, Mexico City, Sao Paolo, Santiago and Dubai (its latest office.)

a. Payback period
b. Dow Jones indexes
c. Tick size
d. Pattern day trader

39. _____ is a heterodox theory on stock price movements that is used as the basis for technical analysis. The theory was derived from 255 Wall Street Journal editorials written by Charles H. Dow (1851-1902), journalist, founder and first editor of the Wall Street Journal and co-founder of Dow Jones and Company. Following Dow's death, William P. Hamilton, Robert Rhea and E. George Schaefer organized and collectively represented '_____,' based on Dow's editorials.

a. Dow theory
b. Point and figure
c. Technical analysis
d. Money flow

40. In finance, the term _____ describes the amount in cash that returns to the owners of a security. Normally it does not include the price variations, at the difference of the total return. _____ applies to various stated rates of return on stocks (common and preferred, and convertible), fixed income instruments (bonds, notes, bills, strips, zero coupon), and some other investment type insurance products (e.g. annuities.)

a. Macaulay duration
b. Yield to maturity
c. 4-4-5 Calendar
d. Yield

41. _____ Â® funds are shares of a family of exchange-traded funds (ETFs) traded in the United States and managed by State Street Global Advisors (SSgA.) Informally, they are also known as Spyders or Spiders. _____ Â® is a trademark of the McGraw-Hill Companies, Inc.

a. Microfinance
b. Federal Agricultural Mortgage Corporation
c. Federal Deposit Insurance Corporation
d. SPDR

42. A _____ is a method of measuring a section of the stock market. Many indices are cited by news or financial services firms and are used to benchmark the performance of portfolios such as mutual funds.

a. Program trading
b. Trading curb
c. Stop order
d. Stock market index

43. A _____ index is a stock market index where each constituent makes up a fraction of the index that is proportional to its price. For a stock market index this implies that stocks are included in proportions based on their quoted prices. A stock trading at $100 will thus be making up 10 times more of the total index compared to a stock trading at $10.

a. Golden parachute
b. Trade finance
c. Product life cycle
d. Price-weighted

44. A _____ or stock divide increases or decreases the number of shares in a public company. The price is adjusted such that the before and after market capitalization of the company remains the same and dilution does not occur. Options and warrants are included.

a. Stop price
b. Stop order
c. Contract for difference
d. Stock split

45. _____ means regulating, adapting or settling in a variety of contexts:

In commercial law, _____ means the settlement of a loss incurred on insured goods. The calculation of the amounts of compensation to be paid by or to the several interests is a complicated matter. It involves much detail and arithmetic, and requires a full and accurate knowledge of the principles of the subject.

a. Adjustment
b. Intelligent investor
c. Equity method
d. Asset recovery

Chapter 6. Common Stock Valuation

1. _____ is a form of corporation equity ownership represented in the securities. It is dangerous in comparison to preferred shares and some other investment options, in that in the event of bankruptcy, _____ investors receive their funds after preferred stockholders, bondholders, creditors, etc. On the other hand, common shares on average perform better than preferred shares or bonds over time.
   - a. Stock split
   - b. Common stock
   - c. Stock market bubble
   - d. Stop-limit order

2. _____ of a business involves analyzing its financial statements and health, its management and competitive advantages, and its competitors and markets. The term is used to distinguish such analysis from other types of investment analysis, such as quantitative analysis and technical analysis.

   _____ is performed on historical and present data, but with the goal of making financial forecasts.
   - a. Stock valuation
   - b. Growth stocks
   - c. Fundamental analysis
   - d. 4-4-5 Calendar

3. A _____ is a fungible, negotiable instrument representing financial value. They are broadly categorized into debt securities (such as banknotes, bonds and debentures), and equity securities; e.g., common stocks. The company or other entity issuing the _____ is called the issuer.
   - a. Securities lending
   - b. Book entry
   - c. Security
   - d. Tracking stock

4. _____, authored by professors Benjamin Graham and David Dodd of Columbia Business School, laid the intellectual foundation for what would later be called value investing. The work was first published in 1934, following unprecedented losses on Wall Street. In summing up lessons learned, Graham and Dodd chided Wall Street for its myopic focus on a company's reported earnings per share, and were particularly harsh on the favored 'earnings trends.' They encouraged investors to take an entirely different approach by gauging the rough value of the operating business that lay behind the security.
   - a. Growth stocks
   - b. 4-4-5 Calendar
   - c. Stock valuation
   - d. Security analysis

5. A '_____' is a 'Charge' that is paid to obtain the right to delay a payment. Essentially, the payer purchases the right to make a given payment in the future instead of in the Present. The '_____', or 'Charge' that must be paid to delay the payment, is simply the difference between what the payment amount would be if it were paid in the present and what the payment amount would be paid if it were paid in the future.
   - a. Value at risk
   - b. Risk modeling
   - c. Risk aversion
   - d. Discount

6. A _____ is a payment made by a corporation to its shareholder members. When a corporation earns a profit or surplus, that money can be put to two uses: it can either be re-invested in the business (called retained earnings), or it can be paid to the shareholders as a _____. Many corporations retain a portion of their earnings and pay the remainder as a _____.
   - a. Special dividend
   - b. Dividend puzzle
   - c. Dividend yield
   - d. Dividend

Chapter 6. Common Stock Valuation

7. _____ is an estimate of the fair value of corporations and their stocks, by using fundamental economic criteria. This theoretical valuation has to be perfected with market criteria, as the final purpose is to determine potential market prices.
   a. Growth stocks
   b. Security Analysis
   c. Stock valuation
   d. 4-4-5 Calendar

8. In finance, _____ is the process of estimating the potential market value of a financial asset or liability. they can be done on assets (for example, investments in marketable securities such as stocks, options, business enterprises, or intangible assets such as patents and trademarks) or on liabilities (e.g., Bonds issued by a company.) _____s are required in many contexts including investment analysis, capital budgeting, merger and acquisition transactions, financial reporting, taxable events to determine the proper tax liability, and in litigation.
   a. Procter ' Gamble
   b. Share
   c. Margin
   d. Valuation

9. A _____ is a financial contract between two parties, the buyer and the seller of this type of option. Often it is simply labeled a 'call'. The buyer of the option has the right, but not the obligation to buy an agreed quantity of a particular commodity or financial instrument (the underlying instrument) from the seller of the option at a certain time (the expiration date) for a certain price (the strike price.)
   a. Bear spread
   b. Bear call spread
   c. Bull spread
   d. Call option

10. An _____ is a contract written by a seller that conveys to the buyer the right -- but not the obligation -- to buy (in the case of a call _____) or to sell (in the case of a put _____) a particular asset, such as a piece of property such as, among others, a futures contract. In return for granting the _____, the seller collects a payment (the premium) from the buyer.

For example, buying a call _____ provides the right to buy a specified quantity of a security at a set strike price at some time on or before expiration, while buying a put _____ provides the right to sell.

   a. AT'T Mobility LLC
   b. Annuity
   c. Amortization
   d. Option

11. _____ is the fraction of net income a firm pays to its stockholders in dividends:

The part of the earnings not paid to investors is left for investment to provide for future earnings growth. Investors seeking high current income and limited capital growth prefer companies with high _____. However investors seeking capital growth may prefer lower payout ratio because capital gains are taxed at a lower rate.

   a. Dividend imputation
   b. Dividend payout ratio
   c. Dividend yield
   d. Dividend puzzle

Chapter 6. Common Stock Valuation

12. In accounting, _____ refers to the portion of net income which is retained by the corporation rather than distributed to its owners as dividends. Similarly, if the corporation makes a loss, then that loss is retained and called variously retained losses, accumulated losses or accumulated deficit. _____ and losses are cumulative from year to year with losses offsetting earnings.
    a. Retained earnings
    b. Generally Accepted Accounting Principles
    c. Matching principle
    d. Historical cost

13. _____ indicates the percentage of a company's earnings that are not paid out in dividends but credited to retained earnings. It is the opposite of the dividend payout ratio, so that also called the retention rate.

    _____ = 1 - Dividend Payout Ratio

    a. Fair market value
    b. Retention ratio
    c. Bankassurer
    d. Dow Jones Indexes

14. _____ measures the rate of return on the ownership interest (shareholders' equity) of the common stock owners. _____ is viewed as one of the most important financial ratios. It measures a firm's efficiency at generating profits from every dollar of shareholders' equity (also known as net assets or assets minus liabilities.)
    a. Return on equity
    b. Diluted Earnings Per Share
    c. Return of capital
    d. Return on sales

15. _____ is the maximum rate at which a company can grow revenue without having to invest new equity capital. If a company earns a 15% return on equity (ROE), it can grow 15% simply by reinvesting all the earnings in new opportunities and maintaining a stable debt to equity ratio. In order to grow faster, the company would have to invest more equity capital or increase its financial leverage.
    a. Current ratio
    b. Price/cash flow ratio
    c. Return on capital employed
    d. Sustainable growth rate

16. A _____ rocket is a rocket that uses two or more stages, each of which contains its own engines and propellant. A tandem or serial stage is mounted on top of another stage; a parallel stage is attached alongside another stage. The result is effectively two or more rockets stacked on top of or attached next to each other.
    a. 529 plan
    b. 4-4-5 Calendar
    c. 7-Eleven
    d. Multistage

17. The _____, in terms of finance and investing, describes how the expected return of a stock or portfolio is correlated to the return of the financial market as a whole.

    An asset with a beta of 0 means that its price is not at all correlated with the market; that asset is independent. A positive beta means that the asset generally follows the market.

    a. LIBOR market model
    b. Current yield
    c. Beta coefficient
    d. Perpetuity

54 *Chapter 6. Common Stock Valuation*

18. In finance, the _____ is used to determine a theoretically appropriate required rate of return of an asset, if that asset is to be added to an already well-diversified portfolio, given that asset's non-diversifiable risk. The model takes into account the asset's sensitivity to non-diversifiable risk (also known as systemic risk or market risk), often represented by the quantity beta (β) in the financial industry, as well as the expected return of the market and the expected return of a theoretical risk-free asset.

The model was introduced by Jack Treynor (1961, 1962), William Sharpe (1964), John Lintner (1965a,b) and Jan Mossin (1966) independently, building on the earlier work of Harry Markowitz on diversification and modern portfolio theory.

- a. Random walk hypothesis
- b. Cox-Ingersoll-Ross model
- c. Hull-White model
- d. Capital asset pricing model

19. The term _____ has three unrelated technical definitions, and is also used in a variety of non-technical ways.

- In financial economics, it refers to any asset used to make money, as opposed to assets used for personal enjoyment or consumption. This is an important distinction because two people can disagree sharply about the value of personal assets, one person might think a sports car is more valuable than a pickup truck, another person might have the opposite taste. But if an asset is held for the purpose of making money, taste has nothing to do with it, only differences of opinion about how much money the asset will produce. With the further assumption that people agree on the probability distribution of future cash flows, it is possible to have an objective _____ pricing model. Even without the assumption of agreement, it is possible to set rational limits on _____ value.
- In governmental accounting, it is defined as any asset used in operations with an initial useful life extending beyond one reporting period. Generally, government managers have a 'stewardship' duty to maintain _____s under their control. See International Public Sector Accounting Standards for details.
- In US tax accounting, it is defined as any property other than a list of exceptions. The main exceptions are anything held for sale, and any real estate or depreciable property used in business. Almost everything you own and use for personal purposes, pleasure or investment is a _____. If something is a _____ for tax purposes, gains or losses on sale or disposition are capital gains or capital losses. For individuals, however, capital losses on property held for personal use are generally not deductible. See the IRS publication Tax Facts about Capital Gains and Losses for details.

A well-known financial accounting textbook advises that the term be avoided except in tax accounting because it is used in so many different senses, not all of them well-defined. For example it is often used as a synonym for fixed assets or for investments in securities.

A common non-technical usage occurs when people ask that employees or the environment or something else be treated as a _____.

- a. Political risk
- b. Solvency
- c. Settlement date
- d. Capital asset

20. The _____ is an interest rate a central bank charges depository institutions that borrow reserves from it.

Chapter 6. Common Stock Valuation

The term _____ has two meanings:

- the same as interest rate; the term 'discount' does not refer to the meaning of the word, but to the purpose of using the quantity, such as computations of present value, e.g. net present value / discounted cash flow

- the annual effective _____, which is the annual interest divided by the capital including that interest; this rate is lower than the interest rate; it corresponds to using the value after a year as the nominal value, and seeing the initial value as the nominal value minus a discount; it is used for Treasury Bills and similar financial instruments

The annual effective _____ is the annual interest divided by the capital including that interest, which is the interest rate divided by 100% plus the interest rate. It is the annual discount factor to be applied to the future cash flow, to find the discount, subtracted from a future value to find the value one year earlier.

For example, suppose there is a government bond that sells for $95 and pays $100 in a year's time.

a. Discount rate
b. Fisher equation
c. Black-Scholes
d. Stochastic volatility

21. Depending on the nature of the investment, the type of _____ will vary.

A common concern with any investment is that you may lose the money you invest - your capital. This risk is therefore often referred to as 'capital risk.'

If the assets you invest in are held in another currency there is a risk that currency movements alone may affect the value.

a. Investment risk
b. ABN Amro
c. A Random Walk Down Wall Street
d. AAB

22.

In finance, the _____ can be the expected rate of return above the risk-free interest rate. When measuring risk, a common sense approach is to compare the risk-free return on T-bills and the very risky return on other investments. The difference between these two returns can be interpreted as a measure of the excess return on the average risky asset. This excess return is known as the _____.

a. Risk premium
b. Risk adjusted return on capital
c. Risk aversion
d. Risk modeling

Chapter 6. Common Stock Valuation

23. In finance, the yield curve is the relation between the interest rate (or cost of borrowing) and the time to maturity of the debt for a given borrower in a given currency. For example, the current U.S. dollar interest rates paid on U.S. Treasury securities for various maturities are closely watched by many traders, and are commonly plotted on a graph such as the one on the right which is informally called 'the yield curve.' More formal mathematical descriptions of this relation are often called the _____.

The yield of a debt instrument is the annualized percentage increase in the value of the investment.

 a. 7-Eleven
 b. 4-4-5 Calendar
 c. 529 plan
 d. Term structure of interest rates

24. In finance, the value of an option consists of two components, its intrinsic value and its _____. Time value is simply the difference between option value and intrinsic value. _____ is also known as theta, extrinsic value, or instrumental value.
 a. Conservatism
 b. Global Squeeze
 c. Time value
 d. Debt buyer

25. Simply put, _____ is the value of money figuring in a given amount of interest for a given amount of time. For example 100 dollars of todays money held for a year at 5 percent interest is worth 105 dollars, therefore 100 dollars paid now or 105 dollars paid exactly one year from now is the same amount of payment of money with that given intersest at that given amount of time. This notion dates at least to Martín de Azpilcueta of the School of Salamanca.

All of the standard calculations for _____ derive from the most basic algebraic expression for the present value of a future sum, 'discounted' to the present by an amount equal to the _____. For example, a sum of FV to be received in one year is discounted (at the rate of interest r) to give a sum of PV at present: PV = FV -- r·PV = FV/(1+r).

 a. Time value of money
 b. Current account
 c. Coefficient of variation
 d. Zero-coupon bond

26. In business and accounting, _____s are everything of value that is owned by a person or company. The balance sheet of a firm records the monetary value of the _____s owned by the firm. The two major _____ classes are tangible _____s and intangible _____s.
 a. Accounts payable
 b. EBITDA
 c. Income
 d. Asset

27. _____ is a fee paid on borrowed assets. It is the price paid for the use of borrowed money , or, money earned by deposited funds . Assets that are sometimes lent with _____ include money, shares, consumer goods through hire purchase, major assets such as aircraft, and even entire factories in finance lease arrangements.
 a. AAB
 b. Insolvency
 c. A Random Walk Down Wall Street
 d. Interest

28. An _____ is the price a borrower pays for the use of money they do not own, and the return a lender receives for deferring the use of funds, by lending it to the borrower. _____s are normally expressed as a percentage rate over the period of one year.

Chapter 6. Common Stock Valuation

_____s targets are also a vital tool of monetary policy and are used to control variables like investment, inflation, and unemployment.

- a. Interest rate
- b. ABN Amro
- c. AAB
- d. A Random Walk Down Wall Street

29. _____ is the discipline of identifying, monitoring and limiting risks. In some cases the acceptable risk may be near zero. Risks can come from accidents, natural causes and disasters as well as deliberate attacks from an adversary.
- a. 4-4-5 Calendar
- b. Risk management
- c. Penny stock
- d. FIFO

30. A _____ is a situation that involves losing one quality or aspect of something in return for gaining another quality or aspect. It implies a decision to be made with full comprehension of both the upside and downside of a particular choice.

In economics the term is expressed as opportunity cost, referring the most preferred alternative given up.

- a. Capital outflow
- b. Trade-off
- c. Total revenue
- d. Break-even point

31. In corporate finance, _____ is an estimate of true economic profit after making corrective adjustments to GAAP accounting, including deducting the opportunity cost of equity capital. GAAP is estimated to ignore US$300 billion in shareholder opportunity costs. _____ can be measured as Net Operating Profit After Taxes(or NOPAT) less the money cost of capital.
- a. Economic value added
- b. ABN Amro
- c. A Random Walk Down Wall Street
- d. AAB

32. _____ is a rent received on a regular basis, with little effort required to maintain it. It is advocated by some authors, especially by Robert Kiyosaki.

Some examples of _____ are:

- Repeated regular income, earned by a sales person, generated from the payment of a product or service that must be renewed on a regular basis, in order to continue receiving its benefits - also called residual income.
- Rental from property;
- Royalties from publishing a book or from licensing a patent or other form of intellectual property;
- Earnings from internet advertisement on your websites;
- Earnings from a business that does not require direct involvement from the owner or merchant;
- Dividend and interest income from owning securities, such as stocks and bonds, are usually referred to as portfolio income, which can be considered a form of _____;
- Pensions.

_____ is usually taxable. The American Internal Revenue Service defines _____ as 'any activity...

a. 4-4-5 Calendar
b. Passive income
c. Horizontal merger
d. Fixed exchange rate system

33. _____, refers to consumption opportunity gained by an entity within a specified time frame, which is generally expressed in monetary terms. However, for households and individuals, '_____ is the sum of all the wages, salaries, profits, interests payments, rents and other forms of earnings received... in a given period of time.' For firms, _____ generally refers to net-profit: what remains of revenue after expenses have been subtracted.

a. OIBDA
b. Accrual
c. Income
d. Annual report

34. _____ refers to the additional value of a commodity over the cost of commodities used to produce it from the previous stage of production. An example is the price of gasoline at the pump over the price of the oil in it. In national accounts used in macroeconomics, it refers to the contribution of the factors of production, i.e., land, labor, and capital goods, to raising the value of a product and corresponds to the incomes received by the owners of these factors.

a. Demand shock
b. Supply shock
c. Deregulation
d. Value added

35. In the United States, the Financial Industry Regulatory Authority (FINRA) is a self-regulatory organization (SRO) under the Securities Exchange Act of 1934, successor to the _____, Inc.

FINRA is responsible for regulatory oversight of all securities firms that do business with the public; professional training, testing and licensing of registered persons; arbitration and mediation; market regulation by contract for The NASDAQ Stock Market, Inc., the American Stock Exchange LLC, and the International Securities Exchange, LLC; and industry utilities, such as Trade Reporting Facilities and other over-the-counter operations.

a. 529 plan
b. 7-Eleven
c. 4-4-5 Calendar
d. National Association of Securities Dealers

36. _____ is the quotient of earnings per share divided by the share price. It is the reciprocal of the P/E ratio--the E/P or the EPS.

The _____ is quoted as a percentage, allowing an easy comparison to going bond rates.

a. Average accounting return
b. Earnings yield
c. Assets turnover
d. Asset turnover

37. The _____ of a stock is a measure of the price paid for a share relative to the annual income or profit earned by the firm per share. It is a financial ratio used for valuation: a higher _____ means that investors are paying more for each unit of income, so the stock is more expensive compared to one with lower _____.

The _____ has units of years, which can be interpreted as 'number of years of earnings to pay back purchase price'.

a. Sustainable growth rate
b. Return of capital
c. Quick ratio
d. P/E ratio

Chapter 6. Common Stock Valuation

38. In finance, the term _____ describes the amount in cash that returns to the owners of a security. Normally it does not include the price variations, at the difference of the total return. _____ applies to various stated rates of return on stocks (common and preferred, and convertible), fixed income instruments (bonds, notes, bills, strips, zero coupon), and some other investment type insurance products (e.g. annuities.)
   a. Yield to maturity
   b. Macaulay duration
   c. 4-4-5 Calendar
   d. Yield

39. _____ is the balance of the amounts of cash being received and paid by a business during a defined period of time, sometimes tied to a specific project. Measurement of _____ can be used

   - to evaluate the state or performance of a business or project.
   - to determine problems with liquidity. Being profitable does not necessarily mean being liquid. A company can fail because of a shortage of cash, even while profitable.
   - to generate project rate of returns. The time of _____s into and out of projects are used as inputs to financial models such as internal rate of return, and net present value.
   - to examine income or growth of a business when it is believed that accrual accounting concepts do not represent economic realities. Alternately, _____ can be used to 'validate' the net income generated by accrual accounting.

   _____ as a generic term may be used differently depending on context, and certain _____ definitions may be adapted by analysts and users for their own uses. Common terms include operating _____ and free _____.

   _____s can be classified into:

   1. Operational _____s: Cash received or expended as a result of the company's core business activities.
   2. Investment _____s: Cash received or expended through capital expenditure, investments or acquisitions.
   3. Financing _____s: Cash received or expended as a result of financial activities, such as interests and dividends.

   All three together - the net _____ - are necessary to reconcile the beginning cash balance to the ending cash balance. Loan draw downs or equity injections, that is just shifting of capital but no expenditure as such, are not considered in the net _____.

   a. Cash flow
   b. Corporate finance
   c. Shareholder value
   d. Real option

40. The institution most often referenced by the word '_____' is a public or publicly traded _____, the shares of which are traded on a public stock exchange (e.g., the New York Stock Exchange or Nasdaq in the United States) where shares of stock of _____s are bought and sold by and to the general public. Most of the largest businesses in the world are publicly traded _____s. However, the majority of _____s are said to be closely held, privately held or close _____s, meaning that no ready market exists for the trading of shares.
   a. Federal Home Loan Mortgage Corporation
   b. Corporation
   c. Depository Trust Company
   d. Protect

Chapter 6. Common Stock Valuation

41. _____ is a term used in accounting, economics and finance to spread the cost of an asset over the span of several years.

In simple words we can say that _____ is the reduction in the value of an asset due to usage, passage of time, wear and tear, technological outdating or obsolescence, depletion or other such factors.

In accounting, _____ is a term used to describe any method of attributing the historical or purchase cost of an asset across its useful life, roughly corresponding to normal wear and tear.

   a. Bottom line
   b. Depreciation
   c. Deferred financing costs
   d. Matching principle

42. In finance, _____ are stocks that appreciate in value and yield a high return on equity (ROE.) Analysts compute ROE by taking the company's net income and dividing it by the company's equity. To be classified as a growth stock, analysts expect to see at least 15 percent return on equity.

   a. Growth stocks
   b. Stock valuation
   c. 4-4-5 Calendar
   d. Security Analysis

43. _____ is equal to the income that a firm has after subtracting costs and expenses from the total revenue. _____ can be distributed among holders of common stock as a dividend or held by the firm as retained earnings. _____ is an accounting term; in some countries (such as the UK) profit is the usual term.

   a. Furniture, Fixtures and Equipment
   b. Write-off
   c. Historical cost
   d. Net income

44. An _____ is a call option on the common stock of a company, issued as a form of non-cash compensation. Restrictions on the option (such as vesting and limited transferability) attempt to align the holder's interest with those of the business' shareholders. If the company's stock rises, holders of options experience a direct financial benefit.

   a. Operating ratio
   b. Employee stock option
   c. Underwriting contract
   d. Internal financing

45. In business and finance, a _____ (also referred to as equity _____) of stock means a _____ of ownership in a corporation (company.) In the plural, stocks is often used as a synonym for _____s especially in the United States, but it is less commonly used that way outside of North America.

In the United Kingdom, South Africa, and Australia, stock can also refer to completely different financial instruments such as government bonds or, less commonly, to all kinds of marketable securities.

   a. Bucket shop
   b. Procter ' Gamble
   c. Margin
   d. Share

46. A _____ is a bond issued by a national government denominated in the country's own currency. Bonds issued by national governments in foreign currencies are normally referred to as sovereign bonds. The first ever _____ was issued by the British government in 1693 to raise money to fund a war against France.

   a. Zero-coupon bond
   b. Municipal bond
   c. Government bond
   d. Collateralized debt obligations

Chapter 6. Common Stock Valuation

47. In finance, a _____ is a debt security, in which the authorized issuer owes the holders a debt and, depending on the terms of the _____, is obliged to pay interest (the coupon) and/or to repay the principal at a later date, termed maturity.

Thus a _____ is a loan: the issuer is the borrower, the _____ holder is the lender, and the coupon is the interest. _____s provide the borrower with external funds to finance long-term investments, or, in the case of government _____s, to finance current expenditure.

a. Puttable bond
c. Bond

b. Convertible bond
d. Catastrophe bonds

48. The _____ is a financial ratio used to compare a company's book value to its current market price. Book value is an accounting term denoting the portion of the company held by the shareholders; in other words, the company's total tangible assets less its total liabilities. The calculation can be performed in two ways, but the result should be the same each way. In the first way, the company's market capitalization can be divided by the company's total book value from its balance sheet. The second way, using per-share values, is to divide the company's current share price by the book value per share (i.e. its book value divided by the number of outstanding shares).

a. Stock repurchase
c. Whisper numbers

b. Stop order
d. Price-to-book ratio

Chapter 7. Stock Price Behavior and Market Efficiency

1. In economics and finance, _____ is the practice of taking advantage of a price differential between two or more markets: striking a combination of matching deals that capitalize upon the imbalance, the profit being the difference between the market prices. When used by academics, an _____ is a transaction that involves no negative cash flow at any probabilistic or temporal state and a positive cash flow in at least one state; in simple terms, a risk-free profit.
   a. Initial margin
   b. Issuer
   c. Efficient-market hypothesis
   d. Arbitrage

2. Behavioral economics and _____ are closely related fields that have evolved to be a separate branch of economic and financial analysis which applies scientific research on human and social, cognitive and emotional factors to better understand economic decisions by, say, consumers, borrowers, investors, and how they affect market prices, returns and the allocation of resources.

   The field is primarily concerned with the bounds of rationality (selfishness, self-control) of economic agents. Behavioral models typically integrate insights from psychology with neo-classical economic theory.

   a. Medium of exchange
   b. Behavioral finance
   c. Recession
   d. Market structure

3. _____ is a risk-adjusted measure of the so-called active return on an investment. It is the return in excess of the compensation for the risk borne, and thus commonly used to assess active managers' performances. Often, the return of a benchmark is subtracted in order to consider relative performance, which yields Jensen's _____.
   a. Alpha
   b. Option
   c. Amortization
   d. Annuity

4. In economics, _____ describes the state of a market with respect to competition.

   - Perfect competition, in which the market consists of a very large number of firms producing a homogeneous product.
   - Monopolistic competition where there are a large number of independent firms which have a very small proportion of the market share.
   - Oligopoly, in which a market is dominated by a small number of firms which own more than 40% of the market share.
   - Oligopsony, a market dominated by many sellers and a few buyers.
   - Monopoly, where there is only one provider of a product or service.
   - Natural monopoly, a monopoly in which economies of scale cause efficiency to increase continuously with the size of the firm. A firm is a natural monopoly if it is able to serve the entire market demand at a lower cost than any combination of two or more smaller, more specialized firms.
   - Monopsony, when there is only one buyer in a market.

   The imperfectly competitive structure is quite identical to the realistic market conditions where some monopolistic competitors, monopolists, oligopolists, and duopolists exist and dominate the market conditions. The elements of _____ include the number and size distribution of firms, entry conditions, and the extent of differentiation.

   These somewhat abstract concerns tend to determine some but not all details of a specific concrete market system where buyers and sellers actually meet and commit to trade.

   a. Market structure
   b. Fixed exchange rate
   c. Human capital
   d. Gross domestic product

Chapter 7. Stock Price Behavior and Market Efficiency

5. _____, in bookkeeping, refers to assets, liabilities, income, and expenses recorded on individual pages of the so called book of final entry or ledger. Changes in _____ value are made by chronologically posting debit (DR) and credit (CR) entries to its page. Examples of _____s are cash, _____s receivable, mortgages, loans, land and buildings, common stock, sales, services provided, wages, and payroll overhead.
   a. Account
   b. Accretion
   c. Alpha
   d. Option

6. A _____ is a fungible, negotiable instrument representing financial value. They are broadly categorized into debt securities (such as banknotes, bonds and debentures), and equity securities; e.g., common stocks. The company or other entity issuing the _____ is called the issuer.
   a. Securities lending
   b. Tracking stock
   c. Book entry
   d. Security

7. The _____ is the tendency of the stock market to rise between December 31 and the end of the first week in January. There are many theories for why this happens, the main one being that it occurs because many investors choose to sell some of their stock right before the end of the year in order to claim a capital loss for tax purposes. Once the tax calendar rolls over to a new year on January 1st these same investors quickly reinvest their money in the market, causing stock prices to rise.
   a. Sector rotation
   b. Death spiral financing
   c. Revaluation
   d. January effect

8. _____ is a form of corporation equity ownership represented in the securities. It is dangerous in comparison to preferred shares and some other investment options, in that in the event of bankruptcy, _____ investors receive their funds after preferred stockholders, bondholders, creditors, etc. On the other hand, common shares on average perform better than preferred shares or bonds over time.
   a. Common stock
   b. Stock market bubble
   c. Stop-limit order
   d. Stock split

9. The institution most often referenced by the word '_____' is a public or publicly traded _____, the shares of which are traded on a public stock exchange (e.g., the New York Stock Exchange or Nasdaq in the United States) where shares of stock of _____s are bought and sold by and to the general public. Most of the largest businesses in the world are publicly traded _____s. However, the majority of _____s are said to be closely held, privately held or close _____s, meaning that no ready market exists for the trading of shares.
   a. Depository Trust Company
   b. Corporation
   c. Federal Home Loan Mortgage Corporation
   d. Protect

10. An _____ is a contract written by a seller that conveys to the buyer the right -- but not the obligation -- to buy (in the case of a call _____) or to sell (in the case of a put _____) a particular asset, such as a piece of property such as, among others, a futures contract. In return for granting the _____, the seller collects a payment (the premium) from the buyer.

For example, buying a call _____ provides the right to buy a specified quantity of a security at a set strike price at some time on or before expiration, while buying a put _____ provides the right to sell.

Chapter 7. Stock Price Behavior and Market Efficiency

a. Amortization
c. AT'T Mobility LLC
b. Annuity
d. Option

11. A _____, is a mathematical formalization of a trajectory that consists of taking successive random steps. The results of _____ analysis have been applied to computer science, physics, ecology, economics and a number of other fields as a fundamental model for random processes in time. For example, the path traced by a molecule as it travels in a liquid or a gas, the search path of a foraging animal, the price of a fluctuating stock and the financial status of a gambler can all be modeled as _____s.
  a. 7-Eleven
  b. 4-4-5 Calendar
  c. 529 plan
  d. Random walk

12. A _____ is the price of a single share of a no. of saleable stocks of the company. Once the stock is purchased, the owner becomes a shareholder of the company that issued the share.
  a. Share price
  b. Whisper numbers
  c. Stock split
  d. Trading curb

13. _____ is an estimate of the fair value of corporations and their stocks, by using fundamental economic criteria. This theoretical valuation has to be perfected with market criteria, as the final purpose is to determine potential market prices.
  a. 4-4-5 Calendar
  b. Security Analysis
  c. Stock valuation
  d. Growth stocks

14. In finance, _____ is the process of estimating the potential market value of a financial asset or liability. they can be done on assets (for example, investments in marketable securities such as stocks, options, business enterprises, or intangible assets such as patents and trademarks) or on liabilities (e.g., Bonds issued by a company.) _____s are required in many contexts including investment analysis, capital budgeting, merger and acquisition transactions, financial reporting, taxable events to determine the proper tax liability, and in litigation.
  a. Share
  b. Margin
  c. Procter ' Gamble
  d. Valuation

15. In finance, an _____ is the difference between the expected return of a security and the actual return. _____s are sometimes triggered by 'events.' Events can include mergers, dividend announcements, company earning announcements, interest rate increases, lawsuits, etc. all which can contribute to an _____.
  a. ABN Amro
  b. AAB
  c. A Random Walk Down Wall Street
  d. Abnormal return

16. An _____ is a statistical method to assess the impact of an event on the value of a firm. For example, the announcement of a merger between two firms can be analyzed to see whether investors believe the merger will create or destroy value. Event studies have been used in a large variety of studies, including [mergers and acquisitions], earnings announcements, debt or equity issues, corporate reorganisations, investment decisions and corporate social responsibility (MacKinlay 1997; McWilliams ' Siegel, 1997.)
  a. A Random Walk Down Wall Street
  b. AAB
  c. ABN Amro
  d. Event study

17. _____ is the trading of a corporation's stock or other securities (e.g. bonds or stock options) by individuals with potential access to non-public information about the company. In most countries, trading by corporate insiders such as officers, key employees, directors, and large shareholders may be legal, if this trading is done in a way that does not take advantage of non-public information. However, the term is frequently used to refer to a practice in which an insider or a related party trades based on material non-public information obtained during the performance of the insider's duties at the corporation, or otherwise in breach of a fiduciary duty or other relationship of trust and confidence or where the non-public information was misappropriated from the company.

   a. Equity investment   b. Intellidex
   c. Open outcry   d. Insider trading

18. _____ in finance is a risk management technique, related to hedging, that mixes a wide variety of investments within a portfolio. Because the fluctuations of a single security have less impact on a diverse portfolio, _____ minimizes the risk from any one investment.

A simple example of _____ is the following: On a particular island the entire economy consists of two companies: one that sells umbrellas and another that sells sunscreen.

   a. 7-Eleven   b. 529 plan
   c. 4-4-5 Calendar   d. Diversification

19. An _____ is a sum paid by A to B by way of compensation for a particular loss suffered by B. The indemnifying party (A) may or may not be responsible for the loss suffered by the indemnified party (B.) Forms of _____ include cash payments, repairs, replacement, and reinstatement.

In common parlance, _____ is often used as a synonym for compensation or reparation.

   a. A Random Walk Down Wall Street   b. AAB
   c. Indemnity   d. ABN Amro

20. In business and finance, a _____ (also referred to as equity _____) of stock means a _____ of ownership in a corporation (company.) In the plural, stocks is often used as a synonym for _____s especially in the United States, but it is less commonly used that way outside of North America.

In the United Kingdom, South Africa, and Australia, stock can also refer to completely different financial instruments such as government bonds or, less commonly, to all kinds of marketable securities.

   a. Procter ' Gamble   b. Margin
   c. Bucket shop   d. Share

21. An _____ or index tracker is a collective investment scheme (usually a mutual fund or exchange-traded fund) that aims to replicate the movements of an index of a specific financial market regardless of market conditions.

Tracking can be achieved by trying to hold all of the securities in the index, in the same proportions as the index. Other methods include statistically sampling the market and holding 'representative' securities.

a. Investment company
c. A Random Walk Down Wall Street
b. AAB
d. Index Fund

22. A _____ is a professionally managed type of collective investment scheme that pools money from many investors and invests it in stocks, bonds, short-term money market instruments, and/or other securities. The _____ will have a fund manager that trades the pooled money on a regular basis. Currently, the worldwide value of all _____s totals more than $26 trillion.

Since 1940, there have been three basic types of investment companies in the United States: open-end funds, also known in the US as _____s; unit investment trusts (UITs); and closed-end funds.

a. Mutual fund
c. Trust company
b. Net asset value
d. Financial intermediary

23. An _____ is a document a company presents at an annual general meeting for approval by its shareholders, or a charitable organization presents its trustees. The report is made up of reports, which may include the following:

- Chairman's report
- CEO's report
- Auditor's report on corporate governance
- Mission statement
- Corporate governance statement of compliance
- Statement of directors' responsibilities
- Invitation to the company's AGM

as well as financial statements including:

- Auditor's report on the financial statements
- Balance sheet
- Statement of retained earnings
- Income statement
- Cash flow statement
- Notes to the financial statements
- Accounting policies

Other information deemed relevant to stakeholders may be included, such as a report on operations for manufacturing firms. In the case of larger companies, it is usually a sleek, colorful, high gloss publication.

The details provided in the report are of use to investors to understand the company's financial position and future direction.

a. Amortization schedule
c. Outstanding balance
b. Accrued liabilities
d. Annual report

Chapter 7. Stock Price Behavior and Market Efficiency

24. An _____ is a call option on the common stock of a company, issued as a form of non-cash compensation. Restrictions on the option (such as vesting and limited transferability) attempt to align the holder's interest with those of the business' shareholders. If the company's stock rises, holders of options experience a direct financial benefit.

   a. Underwriting contract
   b. Internal financing
   c. Operating ratio
   d. Employee stock option

25. A _____ is any actual or hypothesized stock market trend based on the calendar, such as rises and falls associated with particular days of the week or months of the year.

Examples include:

- Halloween indicator (or the 'Sell in May' principle)
- January effect
- Mark Twain effect
- Monday effect
- Weekend effect
- Turn-of-the-Month effect
- Holiday effect

   a. 7-Eleven
   b. Calendar effect
   c. 4-4-5 Calendar
   d. 529 plan

26. The _____ of a stock is a measure of the price paid for a share relative to the annual income or profit earned by the firm per share. It is a financial ratio used for valuation: a higher _____ means that investors are paying more for each unit of income, so the stock is more expensive compared to one with lower _____.

The _____ has units of years, which can be interpreted as 'number of years of earnings to pay back purchase price'.

   a. Sustainable growth rate
   b. Quick ratio
   c. Return of capital
   d. P/E ratio

27. A _____ is a private or public market for the trading of company stock and derivatives of company stock at an agreed price; these are securities listed on a stock exchange as well as those only traded privately.

The size of the world _____ is estimated at about $36.6 trillion US at the beginning of October 2008. The world derivatives market has been estimated at about $480 trillion face or nominal value, 12 times the size of the entire world economy.

   a. Adolph Coors
   b. Andrew Tobias
   c. Anton Gelonkin
   d. Stock market

28. The _____ was the most devastating stock market crash in the history of the United States, taking into consideration the full extent and duration of its fallout.

Chapter 7. Stock Price Behavior and Market Efficiency

Three phrases--Black Thursday, Black Monday, and Black Tuesday--are commonly used to describe this collapse of stock values. All three are appropriate, for the crash was not a one-day affair. The initial crash occurred on Thursday, October 24, 1929, but the catastrophic downturn of Monday, October 28 and Tuesday, October 29 precipitated widespread alarm and the onset of an unprecedented and long-lasting economic depression for the United States and the world. This stock market collapse continued for a month.

a. Securitization
b. Wall Street Crash of 1929
c. Board of Audit
d. Legal and regulatory risk

29. In finance, _____ refers to Monday, October 19, 1987, when stock markets around the world crashed, shedding a huge value in a very short time. The crash began in Hong Kong, spread west through international time zones to Europe, hitting the United States after other markets had already declined by a significant margin. The Dow Jones Industrial Average (DJIA) dropped by 508 points to 1738.74 (22.61%).

a. 4-4-5 Calendar
b. 529 plan
c. 7-Eleven
d. Black Monday

30. _____ is casually defined as the use of computers in stock markets to engage in arbitrage and portfolio insurance strategies. However, the New York Stock Exchange (NYSE) defines the term as 'a wide range of portfolio trading strategies involving the purchase or sale of 15 or more stocks having a total market value of $1 million or more' without any direct reference to the use of computers. The word 'program' can be interpreted in its earlier, more general meaning of a defined and pre-arranged sequence of steps, rather than specifically a computer program.

a. Wash sale
b. Stop order
c. Program trading
d. Share price

31. The _____ is a stock exchange based in New York City, New York. It is the largest stock exchange in the world by dollar value of its listed companies securities. As of October 2008, the combined capitalization of all domestic _____ listed companies was $10.1 trillion.

a. 7-Eleven
b. 529 plan
c. 4-4-5 Calendar
d. New York Stock Exchange

32. _____ is a stock market index for the Tokyo Stock Exchange (TSE.) It has been calculated daily by the Nihon Keizai Shimbun (Nikkei) newspaper since 1950. It is a price-weighted average (the unit is Yen), and the components are reviewed once a year.

a. 4-4-5 Calendar
b. 7-Eleven
c. 529 plan
d. Nikkei 225

33. A _____, securities exchange or (in Europe) bourse is a corporation or mutual organization which provides 'trading' facilities for stock brokers and traders, to trade stocks and other securities. _____s also provide facilities for the issue and redemption of securities as well as other financial instruments and capital events including the payment of income and dividends. The securities traded on a _____ include: shares issued by companies, unit trusts and other pooled investment products and bonds.

a. 4-4-5 Calendar
b. 7-Eleven
c. Stock Exchange
d. 529 plan

Chapter 7. Stock Price Behavior and Market Efficiency

34. A _____ is a point at which a stock market will stop trading for a period of time in response to substantial drops in value.

On the New York Stock Exchange, one type of _____ is referred to as a 'circuit breaker.' These limits were put in place after Black Monday in order to reduce market volatility and massive panic sell-offs, giving traders time to reconsider their transactions.

At the start of each quarter, the NYSE sets three circuit breaker levels at levels of 10%, 20%, and 30% of the average closing price of the Dow Jones Industrial Average for the month preceding the start of the quarter, rounded to the nearest 50-point interval.

- a. Common stock
- b. Stock market index
- c. Stock repurchase
- d. Trading curb

Chapter 8. Behavioral Finance and the Psychology of Investing

1. Behavioral economics and _____ are closely related fields that have evolved to be a separate branch of economic and financial analysis which applies scientific research on human and social, cognitive and emotional factors to better understand economic decisions by, say, consumers, borrowers, investors, and how they affect market prices, returns and the allocation of resources.

The field is primarily concerned with the bounds of rationality (selfishness, self-control) of economic agents. Behavioral models typically integrate insights from psychology with neo-classical economic theory.

a. Recession
b. Medium of exchange
c. Behavioral finance
d. Market structure

2. _____ is a theory that describes decisions between alternatives that involve risk, i.e. alternatives with uncertain outcomes, where the probabilities are known. The model is descriptive: it tries to model real-life choices, rather than optimal decisions.

_____ was developed by Daniel Kahneman, professor at Princeton University's Department of Psychology, and Amos Tversky in 1979 as a psychologically realistic alternative to expected utility theory.

a. Herd behavior
b. Dumb agent theory
c. The equity premium puzzle
d. Prospect theory

3. In prospect theory, _____ refers to the tendency for people to strongly prefer avoiding losses than acquiring gains. Some studies suggest that losses are twice as powerful, psychologically, as gains. _____ was first convincingly demonstrated by Amos Tversky and Daniel Kahneman.

a. Perth Leadership Outcome Model
b. Loss aversion
c. Herd behavior
d. Quantitative behavioral finance

4. A concept first named by Richard Thaler (1980), _____ attempts to describe the process whereby people code, categorize and evaluate economic outcomes. _____ theorists argue that people group their assets into a number of non-fungible mental accounts.

One detailed application of _____, the behavioral life cycle hypothesis (Shefrin ' Thaler, 1988), posits that people mentally frame assets as belonging to either current income, current wealth or future income and this has implications for their behavior as the accounts are largely non-fungible and marginal propensity to consume out of each account is different.

a. Disposition effect
b. Quantitative behavioral finance
c. Psychological level
d. Mental accounting

5. In economics and business, specifically cost accounting, the _____ is the point at which cost or expenses and revenue are equal: there is no net loss or gain, and one has 'broken even'. A profit or a loss has not been made, although opportunity costs have been paid, and capital has received the risk-adjusted, expected return.

For example, if the business sells less than 200 tables each month, it will make a loss, if it sells more, it will be a profit.

Chapter 8. Behavioral Finance and the Psychology of Investing

a. Market microstructure
b. Defined contribution plan
c. Fixed asset turnover
d. Break-even point

6. The _____ is an anomaly discovered in behavioral finance. It relates to the tendency of investors to sell shares whose price has increased, while keeping assets that have dropped in value . Investors are unwilling to recognize losses (which they would be forced to do if they sold assets which had fallen in value), but are more willing to recognize gains.
   a. Psychological level
   b. Disposition effect
   c. Prospect theory
   d. Herd behavior

7. The _____ is a hypothesis that people value a good or service more once their property right to it has been established. In other words, people place a higher value on objects they own than objects that they do not. In one experiment, people demanded a higher price for a coffee mug that had been given to them but put a lower price on one they did not yet own.
   a. A Random Walk Down Wall Street
   b. AAB
   c. ABN Amro
   d. Endowment effect

8. _____ refers to the tendency of people to think of currency in nominal, rather than real, terms. In other words, the numerical/face value (nominal value) of money is mistaken for its purchasing power (real value.) This is a fallacy as modern fiat currencies have no inherent value and their real value is derived from their ability to be exchanged for goods and used for payment of taxes.
   a. 4-4-5 Calendar
   b. Fungibility
   c. 529 plan
   d. Money illusion

9. In economics, business, and accounting, a _____ is the value of money that has been used up to produce something, and hence is not available for use anymore. In business, the _____ may be one of acquisition, in which case the amount of money expended to acquire it is counted as _____. In this case, money is the input that is gone in order to acquire the thing.
   a. Sliding scale fees
   b. Cost
   c. Marginal cost
   d. Fixed costs

10. Modern portfolio theory (MPT) proposes how rational investors will use diversification to optimize their portfolios, and how a risky asset should be priced. The basic concepts of the theory are Markowitz diversification, the _____, capital asset pricing model, the alpha and beta coefficients, the Capital Market Line and the Securities Market Line.

MPT models an asset's return as a random variable, and models a portfolio as a weighted combination of assets so that the return of a portfolio is the weighted combination of the assets' returns.

   a. Efficient frontier
   b. A Random Walk Down Wall Street
   c. ABN Amro
   d. AAB

11. The _____ is a heuristic wherein people assume commonality between objects of similar appearance, or between an object and a group it appears to fit into. While often very useful in everyday life, it can also result in neglect of relevant base rates and other errors. The representative heuristic was first proposed by Amos Tversky and Daniel Kahneman.

a. 7-Eleven
b. Representativeness heuristic
c. 4-4-5 Calendar
d. 529 plan

12. The _____ refers to the tendency to erroneously perceive small samples from random distributions as having significant 'streaks' or 'clusters', caused by a human tendency to underpredict the amount of variability likely to appear in a small sample of random or semi-random data due to chance.

Thomas Gilovich found that most people thought that the sequence

'OXXXOXXXOXXOOOXOOXXOO'

looked non-random, when, in fact, it has several characteristics maximally probable for a 'random' stream, such as having an equal number of each result and the number of adjacent results with the same outcome is equal for both possible outcomes. In sequences like this, people seem to expect to see a greater number of alternations than one would predict statistically.

a. 4-4-5 Calendar
b. Hindsight bias
c. Hyperbolic discounting
d. Clustering illusion

13. In business and accounting, _____s are everything of value that is owned by a person or company. The balance sheet of a firm records the monetary value of the _____s owned by the firm. The two major _____ classes are tangible _____s and intangible _____s.
   a. EBITDA
   b. Accounts payable
   c. Income
   d. Asset

14. The term _____ is often used to refer to the investment management of collective investments, (not necessarily) whilst the more generic fund management may refer to all forms of institutional investment as well as investment management for private investors. Investment managers who specialize in advisory or discretionary management on behalf of (normally wealthy) private investors may often refer to their services as wealth management or portfolio management often within the context of so-called 'private banking'.

The provision of 'investment management services' includes elements of financial analysis, asset selection, stock selection, plan implementation and ongoing monitoring of investments.

a. ABN Amro
b. Asset Management
c. AAB
d. A Random Walk Down Wall Street

15. _____ is a term used in accounting relating to the increase in value of an asset. In this sense it is the reverse of depreciation, which measures the fall in value of assets over their normal life-time.

_____ is a rise of a currency in a floating exchange rate.

a. Other Comprehensive Basis of Accounting
b. Appreciation
c. A Random Walk Down Wall Street
d. Operating cash flow

Chapter 8. Behavioral Finance and the Psychology of Investing

16. In finance, a _____ is one who attempts to profit by investing in a manner that differs from the conventional wisdom, when the consensus opinion appears to be wrong.

A _____ believes that certain crowd behavior among investors can lead to exploitable mispricings in securities markets. For example, widespread pessimism about a stock can drive a price so low that it overstates the company's risks, and understates its prospects for returning to profitability.

 a. Secured debt
 b. Day trading
 c. Contrarian
 d. Direct access trading

17. In economics and finance, _____ is the practice of taking advantage of a price differential between two or more markets: striking a combination of matching deals that capitalize upon the imbalance, the profit being the difference between the market prices. When used by academics, an _____ is a transaction that involves no negative cash flow at any probabilistic or temporal state and a positive cash flow in at least one state; in simple terms, a risk-free profit.

 a. Initial margin
 b. Efficient-market hypothesis
 c. Arbitrage
 d. Issuer

18. _____ in finance is a risk management technique, related to hedging, that mixes a wide variety of investments within a portfolio. Because the fluctuations of a single security have less impact on a diverse portfolio, _____ minimizes the risk from any one investment.

A simple example of _____ is the following: On a particular island the entire economy consists of two companies: one that sells umbrellas and another that sells sunscreen.

 a. 4-4-5 Calendar
 b. Diversification
 c. 7-Eleven
 d. 529 plan

19. _____ is a theory which assumes that restrictions placed upon funds, that would ordinarily be used by rational traders to arbitrage away pricing inefficiencies, leave prices in a non-equilibrium state for protracted periods of time.

The efficient market hypothesis assumes that whenever mispricing of a publicly-traded stock occurs as a result of an over-reaction to news, or some similar event, an opportunity for low-risk profit is created for rational traders. The low-risk profit opportunity exists through the tool of arbitrage, which, briefly, is buying and selling differently priced items of the same value, and pocketing the difference.

 a. Limits to arbitrage
 b. Market anomaly
 c. Forward market
 d. Delta hedging

20. A _____ is described in the literature of financial research as a stock trader whose decisions to buy, sell, or hold are not based upon fundamental analysis.

In finance, noise obtained a formal definition in a 1986 paper by Fischer Black 'Noise in the sense of a large number of small events is often a cause factor much more powerful than a small number of large events can be.'

a. Portfolio insurance
c. Venture capital
b. Price-to-book ratio
d. Noise trader

21. A _____ is the direction in which a financial market is moving. _____s can be classified as primary trends, secondary trends (short-term), and secular trends (long-term.) This principle incorporates the idea that market cycles occur with regularity and persistence.
   a. 529 plan
   b. 4-4-5 Calendar
   c. 7-Eleven
   d. Market trend

22. _____ mature in one year or less. Like zero-coupon bonds, they do not pay interest prior to maturity; instead they are sold at a discount of the par value to create a positive yield to maturity. Many regard _____ as the least risky investment available to U.S. investors.
   a. Treasury Inflation Protected Securities
   b. Treasury bills
   c. 4-4-5 Calendar
   d. Treasury securities

23. The _____ is one of several stock market indices, created by nineteenth-century Wall Street Journal editor and Dow Jones ' Company co-founder Charles Dow. Dow compiled the index to gauge the performance of the industrial sector of the American stock market. It is the second-oldest U.S. market index, after the Dow Jones Transportation Average, which Dow also created.
   a. 529 plan
   b. 4-4-5 Calendar
   c. 7-Eleven
   d. Dow Jones Industrial Average

24. _____ is a heterodox theory on stock price movements that is used as the basis for technical analysis. The theory was derived from 255 Wall Street Journal editorials written by Charles H. Dow (1851-1902), journalist, founder and first editor of the Wall Street Journal and co-founder of Dow Jones and Company. Following Dow's death, William P. Hamilton, Robert Rhea and E. George Schaefer organized and collectively represented '_____,' based on Dow's editorials.
   a. Money flow
   b. Point and figure
   c. Technical analysis
   d. Dow theory

25. The _____ is a form of technical analysis that attempts to forecast trends in the financial markets and other collective activities. It is named after Ralph Nelson Elliott (1871-1948), an accountant who developed the concept in the 1930s: he proposed that market prices unfold in specific patterns, which practitioners today call Elliott waves. Elliott published his views of market behavior in the book The Wave Principle (1938), in a series of articles in Financial World magazine in 1939, and most fully in his final major work, Nature's Laws - The Secret of the Universe (1946.)
   a. A Random Walk Down Wall Street
   b. Elliott wave principle
   c. ABN Amro
   d. AAB

26. _____ is a concept in technical analysis that the movement of the price of a security will tend to stop and reverse at certain predetermined price levels.

A support level is a price level where the price tends to find support as it is going down. This means the price is more likely to 'bounce' off this level rather than break through it.

A resistance level is the opposite of a support level. It is where the price tends to find resistance as it is going up. This means the price is more likely to 'bounce' off this level rather than break through it.

Chapter 8. Behavioral Finance and the Psychology of Investing

a. Technical analysis
b. Point and figure
c. Dow theory
d. Support and resistance

27. In finance, the term _____ describes the amount in cash that returns to the owners of a security. Normally it does not include the price variations, at the difference of the total return. _____ applies to various stated rates of return on stocks (common and preferred, and convertible), fixed income instruments (bonds, notes, bills, strips, zero coupon), and some other investment type insurance products (e.g. annuities.)
   a. Yield to maturity
   b. Macaulay duration
   c. 4-4-5 Calendar
   d. Yield

28. In finance, a _____ is a trade that is usually at least 10,000 shares of a stock or $200,000 of bonds. It can also refer specifically to large trades that occur between institutional parties at a fixed price. For instance, an insurance company may hold a large stake in a company that they would like to liquidate completely.
   a. 4-4-5 Calendar
   b. 7-Eleven
   c. Block trade
   d. 529 plan

29. The _____ is a financial technical analysis momentum oscillator measuring the velocity and magnitude of directional price movement by comparing upward and downward close-to-close movements.

The _____ was developed by J. Welles Wilder and published in Commodities magazine (now called Futures magazine) in June 1978, and in his New Concepts in Technical Trading Systems the same year.

   a. Relative strength Index
   b. Global depository receipt
   c. Database auditing
   d. Stock or scrip dividends

30. An _____ is a type of chart typically used to illustrate movements in the price of a financial instrument over time. Each vertical line on the chart shows the price range (the highest and lowest prices) over one unit of time, e.g. one day or one hour. Tick marks project from each side of the line indicating the opening price (e.g. for a daily bar chart this would be the starting price for that day) on the left, and the closing price for that time period on the right.
   a. AAB
   b. ABN Amro
   c. A Random Walk Down Wall Street
   d. Open-high-low-close chart

31. A _____ is a pair of parallel trend lines that form a chart pattern for a stock or commodity. Channels may be horizontal, ascending or descending. When prices pass through and stay through a trendline representing support or resistance the trend is said to be broken and there is a 'breakout'.
   a. Mitigating Control
   b. Managerial Accounting Vs Financial Accounting
   c. Lookback options
   d. Price channel

32. In statistics, a _____, is a type of finite impulse response filter used to analyze a set of data points by creating a series of averages of different subsets of the full data set. A _____ is not a single number, but it is a set of numbers, each of which is the average of the corresponding subset of a larger set of data points. A _____ may also use unequal weights for each data value in the subset to emphasize particular values in the subset.
   a. Moving average
   b. Gordon growth model
   c. Voluntary Emissions Reductions
   d. Loans and interest, in Judaism

Chapter 8. Behavioral Finance and the Psychology of Investing

33. _____ are a technical analysis tool invented by John Bollinger in the 1980s. Having evolved from the concept of trading bands, _____ can be used to measure the highness or lowness of the price relative to previous trades.

_____ consist of:

- a middle band being an N-period simple moving average
- an upper band at K times an N-period standard deviation above the middle band
- a lower band at K times an N-period standard deviation below the middle band

Typical values for N and K are 20 and 2, respectively. The default choice for the average is a simple moving average, but other types of averages can be employed as needed.

a. Money flow
c. Point and figure
b. Dow theory
d. Bollinger bands

34. _____ in technical analysis is typical price multiplied by volume, a kind of approximation to the dollar value of a day's trading.

_____ index (Money flowI) is an oscillator calculated over an N-day period, ranging from 0 to 100, showing _____ on up days as a percentage of the total of up and down days.

The calculations are as follows. The typical price for each day is the average of high, low and close,

$$\boxed{}>$$

_____ is the product of typical price and the volume on that day.

$$\boxed{}>$$

a. Technical analysis
c. Support and resistance
b. Dow theory
d. Money flow

35. In statistics, _____ has two related meanings:

- the arithmetic _____
- the expected value of a random variable, which is also called the population _____.

It is sometimes stated that the '_____' is average. This is incorrect if '_____' is taken in the specific sense of 'arithmetic _____' as there are different types of averages: the _____, median, and mode. Other simple statistical analyses use measures of spread, such as range, interquartile range, or standard deviation. For a real-valued random variable X, the _____ is the expectation of X. Note that not every probability distribution has a defined _____; see the Cauchy distribution for an example.

a. Sample size
b. Harmonic mean
c. Mean
d. Probability distribution

36. In finance, _____ or 'shorting' is the practice of selling a financial instrument that the seller does not own at the time of the sale. _____ is done with intent of later purchasing the financial instrument at a lower price. Short-sellers attempt to profit from an expected decline in the price of a financial instrument.

a. 529 plan
b. Short ratio
c. 4-4-5 Calendar
d. Short selling

Chapter 9. Interest Rates

1. In the United States, _____ are overnight borrowings by banks to maintain their bank reserves at the Federal Reserve. Banks keep reserves at Federal Reserve Banks to meet their reserve requirements and to clear financial transactions. Transactions in the _____ market enable depository institutions with reserve balances in excess of reserve requirements to lend reserves to institutions with reserve deficiencies.

   a. Federal funds rate
   b. 4-4-5 Calendar
   c. Regulation T
   d. Federal funds

2. _____ mature in one year or less. Like zero-coupon bonds, they do not pay interest prior to maturity; instead they are sold at a discount of the par value to create a positive yield to maturity. Many regard _____ as the least risky investment available to U.S. investors.

   a. Treasury Inflation Protected Securities
   b. 4-4-5 Calendar
   c. Treasury securities
   d. Treasury bills

3. _____ are government bonds issued by the United States Department of the Treasury through the Bureau of the Public Debt. They are the debt financing instruments of the U.S. Federal government, and they are often referred to simply as Treasuries or Treasurys. There are four types of marketable _____: Treasury bills, Treasury notes, Treasury bonds, and Treasury Inflation Protected Securities (TIPS.)

   a. Treasury Inflation Protected Securities
   b. Treasury Inflation-Protected Securities
   c. 4-4-5 Calendar
   d. Treasury securities

4. In finance, _____ is the interest that has accumulated since the principal investment, or since the previous interest payment if there has been one already. For a financial instrument such as a bond, interest is calculated and paid in set intervals.

The primary formula for calculating the interest accrued in a given period is:

$$I_A = T \times P \times R$$

where I_A is the _____, T is the fraction of the year, P is the principal, and R is the annualized interest rate.

   a. Accrued interest
   b. AAB
   c. A Random Walk Down Wall Street
   d. ABN Amro

5. In finance, a _____ is a debt security, in which the authorized issuer owes the holders a debt and, depending on the terms of the _____, is obliged to pay interest (the coupon) and/or to repay the principal at a later date, termed maturity.

Thus a _____ is a loan: the issuer is the borrower, the _____ holder is the lender, and the coupon is the interest. _____s provide the borrower with external funds to finance long-term investments, or, in the case of government _____s, to finance current expenditure.

   a. Puttable bond
   b. Catastrophe bonds
   c. Convertible bond
   d. Bond

Chapter 9. Interest Rates

6. _____ is a fee paid on borrowed assets. It is the price paid for the use of borrowed money, or, money earned by deposited funds. Assets that are sometimes lent with _____ include money, shares, consumer goods through hire purchase, major assets such as aircraft, and even entire factories in finance lease arrangements.
   a. AAB
   b. A Random Walk Down Wall Street
   c. Insolvency
   d. Interest

7. An _____ is the price a borrower pays for the use of money they do not own, and the return a lender receives for deferring the use of funds, by lending it to the borrower. _____s are normally expressed as a percentage rate over the period of one year.

   _____s targets are also a vital tool of monetary policy and are used to control variables like investment, inflation, and unemployment.

   a. Interest rate
   b. ABN Amro
   c. A Random Walk Down Wall Street
   d. AAB

8. In finance, the term _____ describes the amount in cash that returns to the owners of a security. Normally it does not include the price variations, at the difference of the total return. _____ applies to various stated rates of return on stocks (common and preferred, and convertible), fixed income instruments (bonds, notes, bills, strips, zero coupon), and some other investment type insurance products (e.g. annuities.)
   a. Yield
   b. Macaulay duration
   c. 4-4-5 Calendar
   d. Yield to maturity

9. _____ is the concept of adding accumulated interest back to the principal, so that interest is earned on interest from that moment on. The act of declaring interest to be principal is called compounding (i.e., interest is compounded.) A loan, for example, may have its interest compounded every month: in this case, a loan with $100 principal and 1% interest per month would have a balance of $101 at the end of the first month.
   a. Risk management
   b. Penny stock
   c. 4-4-5 Calendar
   d. Compound interest

10. A '_____' is a 'Charge' that is paid to obtain the right to delay a payment. Essentially, the payer purchases the right to make a given payment in the future instead of in the Present. The '_____', or 'Charge' that must be paid to delay the payment, is simply the difference between what the payment amount would be if it were paid in the present and what the payment amount would be paid if it were paid in the future.
    a. Risk aversion
    b. Value at risk
    c. Risk modeling
    d. Discount

11. _____ is the value on a given date of a future payment or series of future payments, discounted to reflect the time value of money and other factors such as investment risk. _____ calculations are widely used in business and economics to provide a means to compare cash flows at different times on a meaningful 'like to like' basis.

    The most commonly applied model of the time value of money is compound interest.

    a. Net present value
    b. Present value of benefits
    c. Negative gearing
    d. Present value

12. In financial accounting, the term _____ is most commonly used to describe any part of shareholders' equity, except for basic share capital. Sometimes, the term is used instead of the term provision; such a use, however, is inconsistent with the terminology suggested by International Accounting Standards Board. For more information about provisions, see provision (accounting.)
    a. Reserve
    b. Closing entries
    c. Treasury stock
    d. FIFO and LIFO accounting

13. In finance, the value of an option consists of two components, its intrinsic value and its _____. Time value is simply the difference between option value and intrinsic value. _____ is also known as theta, extrinsic value, or instrumental value.
    a. Debt buyer
    b. Global Squeeze
    c. Conservatism
    d. Time value

14. Simply put, _____ is the value of money figuring in a given amount of interest for a given amount of time. For example 100 dollars of todays money held for a year at 5 percent interest is worth 105 dollars, therefore 100 dollars paid now or 105 dollars paid exactly one year from now is the same amount of payment of money with that given intersest at that given amount of time. This notion dates at least to Martín de Azpilcueta of the School of Salamanca.

    All of the standard calculations for _____ derive from the most basic algebraic expression for the present value of a future sum, 'discounted' to the present by an amount equal to the _____. For example, a sum of FV to be received in one year is discounted (at the rate of interest r) to give a sum of PV at present: PV = FV -- r·PV = FV/(1+r).

    a. Coefficient of variation
    b. Time value of money
    c. Zero-coupon bond
    d. Current account

15. In the stock market, a _____ is the stock of a company that is regarded as a leader in its given industry. The performance of the stock is said to reflect the performance of the industry in general. These stocks are used as barometers for the rest of the market. General Motors is an example of a _____ stock. As the major auto maker in the US, it sets the tone for the rest of the industry. General Motors also has contracts with companies in other industries so its performance is reflected in other sectors of the market.
    a. Bellwether
    b. 529 plan
    c. 7-Eleven
    d. 4-4-5 Calendar

16. The _____ is a United States government corporation created by the Glass-Steagall Act of 1933. It provides deposit insurance, which guarantees the safety of checking and savings deposits in member banks, currently up to $250,000 per depositor per bank. Insured deposits are backed by the full faith and credit of the United States.
    a. Ford Foundation
    b. FASB
    c. NYSE Group
    d. Federal Deposit Insurance Corporation

17. _____ is a term applied in many countries to a reference interest rate used by banks. The term originally indicated the rate of interest at which banks lent to favored customers, i.e., those with high credibility, though this is no longer always the case. Some variable interest rates may be expressed as a percentage above or below _____.
    a. Time deposit
    b. Credit bureau
    c. Prime rate
    d. Reserve requirement

Chapter 9. Interest Rates

18. In finance, the yield curve is the relation between the interest rate (or cost of borrowing) and the time to maturity of the debt for a given borrower in a given currency. For example, the current U.S. dollar interest rates paid on U.S. Treasury securities for various maturities are closely watched by many traders, and are commonly plotted on a graph such as the one on the right which is informally called 'the yield curve.' More formal mathematical descriptions of this relation are often called the _____.

The yield of a debt instrument is the annualized percentage increase in the value of the investment.

   a. 4-4-5 Calendar
   c. 7-Eleven
   b. Term structure of interest rates
   d. 529 plan

19. In finance, the _____ is the global financial market for short-term borrowing and lending. It provides short-term liquidity funding for the global financial system. The _____ is where short-term obligations such as Treasury bills, commercial paper and bankers' acceptances are bought and sold.
   a. Cramdown
   c. Money market
   b. Debt-for-equity swap
   d. Consumer debt

20. A _____ s a time deposit, a financial product commonly offered to consumers by banks, thrift institutions, and credit unions.

They are similar to savings accounts in that they are insured and thus virtually risk-free; they are 'money in the bank'. They are different from savings accounts in that they have a specific, fixed term (often three months, six months, or one to five years), and, usually, a fixed interest rate.

   a. Time deposit
   c. Certificate of deposit
   b. Reserve requirement
   d. Variable rate mortgage

21. In the global money market, _____ is an unsecured promissory note with a fixed maturity of one to 270 days. _____ is a money-market security issued (sold) by large banks and corporations to get money to meet short term debt obligations (for example, payroll), and is only backed by an issuing bank or corporation's promise to pay the face amount on the maturity date specified on the note. Since it is not backed by collateral, only firms with excellent credit ratings from a recognized rating agency will be able to sell their _____ at a reasonable price.
   a. Book building
   c. Trade-off theory
   b. Financial distress
   d. Commercial paper

22. The institution most often referenced by the word '_____' is a public or publicly traded _____, the shares of which are traded on a public stock exchange (e.g., the New York Stock Exchange or Nasdaq in the United States) where shares of stock of _____s are bought and sold by and to the general public. Most of the largest businesses in the world are publicly traded _____s. However, the majority of _____s are said to be closely held, privately held or close _____s, meaning that no ready market exists for the trading of shares.
   a. Protect
   c. Federal Home Loan Mortgage Corporation
   b. Depository Trust Company
   d. Corporation

23. The _____ is an interest rate a central bank charges depository institutions that borrow reserves from it.

The term _____ has two meanings:

- the same as interest rate; the term 'discount' does not refer to the meaning of the word, but to the purpose of using the quantity, such as computations of present value, e.g. net present value / discounted cash flow

- the annual effective _____, which is the annual interest divided by the capital including that interest; this rate is lower than the interest rate; it corresponds to using the value after a year as the nominal value, and seeing the initial value as the nominal value minus a discount; it is used for Treasury Bills and similar financial instruments

The annual effective _____ is the annual interest divided by the capital including that interest, which is the interest rate divided by 100% plus the interest rate. It is the annual discount factor to be applied to the future cash flow, to find the discount, subtracted from a future value to find the value one year earlier.

For example, suppose there is a government bond that sells for $95 and pays $100 in a year's time.

a. Discount rate
c. Black-Scholes
b. Stochastic volatility
d. Fisher equation

24. In the United States, the _____ is the interest rate at which private depository institutions (mostly banks) lend balances (federal funds) at the Federal Reserve to other depository institutions, usually overnight. Changing the target rate is one form of open market operations that the Chairman of the Federal Reserve uses to regulate the supply of money in the U.S. economy.

U.S. banks and thrift institutions are obligated by law to maintain certain levels of reserves, either as reserves with the Fed or as vault cash.

a. Federal funds rate
c. Regulation T
b. 4-4-5 Calendar
d. Taylor rule

25. In finance, a _____ is collateral that the holder of a position in securities, options, or futures contracts has to deposit to cover the credit risk of his counterparty (most often his broker.) This risk can arise if the holder has done any of the following:

- borrowed cash from the counterparty to buy securities or options,
- sold securities or options short, or
- entered into a futures contract.

The collateral can be in the form of cash or securities, and it is deposited in a _____ account. On U.S. futures exchanges, '_____' was formally called performance bond.

_____ buying is buying securities with cash borrowed from a broker, using other securities as collateral.

a. Share
b. Procter ' Gamble
c. Credit
d. Margin

26. The collateral can be in the form of cash or securities, and it is deposited in a _____. On U.S. futures exchanges, 'margin' was formally called performance bond.

Margin buying is buying securities with cash borrowed from a broker, using other securities as collateral.

a. Margin account
b. Forward contract
c. Dollar roll
d. Risk-neutral measure

27. A _____, reserve bank, or monetary authority is the entity responsible for the monetary policy of a country or of a group of member states. It is a bank that can lend money to other banks in times of need. Its primary responsibility is to maintain the stability of the national currency and money supply, but more active duties include controlling subsidized-loan interest rates, and acting as a lender of last resort to the banking sector during times of financial crisis (private banks often being integral to the national financial system.)

a. Central bank
b. 4-4-5 Calendar
c. 7-Eleven
d. 529 plan

28. _____, in bookkeeping, refers to assets, liabilities, income, and expenses recorded on individual pages of the so called book of final entry or ledger. Changes in _____ value are made by chronologically posting debit (DR) and credit (CR) entries to its page. Examples of _____s are cash, _____s receivable, mortgages, loans, land and buildings, common stock, sales, services provided, wages, and payroll overhead.

a. Alpha
b. Account
c. Option
d. Accretion

29. In financial accounting, a _____ or statement of financial position is a summary of a person's or organization's balances. Assets, liabilities and ownership equity are listed as of a specific date, such as the end of its financial year. A _____ is often described as a snapshot of a company's financial condition.

a. Statement of retained earnings
b. Statement on Auditing Standards No. 70: Service Organizations
c. Financial statements
d. Balance sheet

30. _____s are deposits denominated in United States dollars at banks outside the United States, and thus are not under the jurisdiction of the Federal Reserve. Consequently, such deposits are subject to much less regulation than similar deposits within the United States, allowing for higher margins. There is nothing 'European' about _____ deposits; a US dollar-denominated deposit in Tokyo or Caracas would likewise be deemed _____ deposits.

a. ABN Amro
b. AAB
c. A Random Walk Down Wall Street
d. Eurodollar

31. The _____ (NYSE: FNM), commonly known as Fannie Mae, is a stockholder-owned corporation chartered by Congress in 1968 as a government sponsored enterprise (GSE), but founded in 1938 during the Great Depression. The corporation's purpose is to purchase and securitize mortgages in order to ensure that funds are consistently available to the institutions that lend money to home buyers.

Chapter 9. Interest Rates

On September 7, 2008, James Lockhart, director of the Federal Housing Finance Agency (FHFA), announced that Fannie Mae and Freddie Mac were being placed into conservatorship of the FHFA.

   a. Federal National Mortgage Association
   b. General partnership
   c. SPDR
   d. The Depository Trust ' Clearing Corporation

32. The _____ (NYSE: FRE) is an insolvent government sponsored enterprise (GSE) of the United States federal government.

The _____ was created in 1970 to expand the secondary market for mortgages in the US. Along with other GSEs, Freddie Mac buys mortgages on the secondary market, pools them, and sells them as mortgage-backed securities to investors on the open market.

   a. Federal Home Loan Mortgage Corporation
   b. Governmental Accounting Standards Board
   c. The Depository Trust ' Clearing Corporation
   d. Public company

33. The _____ is a daily reference rate based on the interest rates at which banks borrow unsecured funds from banks in the London wholesale money market (or interbank market.) It is roughly comparable to the U.S. Federal funds rate.

During 1984 it became apparent that an increasing number of banks were trading actively in a variety of relatively new market instruments, notably interest rate swaps, foreign currency options and forward rate agreements.

   a. Risk-free interest rate
   b. Fixed interest
   c. Shanghai Interbank Offered Rate
   d. London Interbank Offered Rate

34. In business and accounting, _____s are everything of value that is owned by a person or company. The balance sheet of a firm records the monetary value of the _____s owned by the firm. The two major _____ classes are tangible _____s and intangible _____s.
   a. EBITDA
   b. Accounts payable
   c. Asset
   d. Income

35. A _____ is a unit that is equal to 1/100th of a percentage point. It is frequently used to express percentage point changes of less than 1%. It avoids the ambiguity between relative and absolute discussions about rates.
   a. 529 plan
   b. 4-4-5 Calendar
   c. Basis point
   d. Bond market

36. _____ is an economic concept with commonplace familiarity. It is the price that a good or service is offered at, or will fetch, in the marketplace. It is of interest mainly in the study of microeconomics.
   a. Delta hedging
   b. Central Securities Depository
   c. Convertible arbitrage
   d. Market price

37. A _____ is a fungible, negotiable instrument representing financial value. They are broadly categorized into debt securities (such as banknotes, bonds and debentures), and equity securities; e.g., common stocks. The company or other entity issuing the _____ is called the issuer.

Chapter 9. Interest Rates

a. Book entry
c. Securities lending
b. Tracking stock
d. Security

38. The _____ for an investment is a calculated annual yield for an investment, which may not pay out yearly. This allows investments which payout with different frequencies to be compared.
   a. Bond equivalent yield
   c. 4-4-5 Calendar
   b. 529 plan
   d. 7-Eleven

39. The terms _____ , nominal _____, and effective _____ describe the interest rate for a whole year (annualized), rather than just a monthly fee/rate, as applied on a loan, mortgage, credit card, etc. Those terms have formal, legal definitions in some countries or legal jurisdictions, but in general:

   • The nominal _____ is the simple-interest rate (for a year.)
   • The effective _____ is the fee+compound interest rate (calculated across a year.)

The nominal _____ is calculated as: the rate, for a payment period, multiplied by the number of payment periods in a year. However, the exact legal definition of 'effective _____' can vary greatly in each jurisdiction, depending on the type of fees included, such as participation fees, loan origination fees, monthly service charges, or late fees. The effective _____ has been called the 'mathematically-true' interest rate for each year. The computation for the effective _____, as the fee+compound interest rate, can also vary depending on whether the up-front fees, such as origination or participation fees, are added to the entire amount, or treated as a short-term loan due in the first payment.

   a. AAB
   c. A Random Walk Down Wall Street
   b. Annual percentage rate
   d. ABN Amro

40. The _____, effective annual interest rate, Annual Equivalent Rate (AER) or simply effective rate is the interest rate on a loan or financial product restated from the nominal interest rate as an interest rate with annual compound interest. It is used to compare the annual interest between loans with different compounding terms (daily, monthly, annually, or other.)

The _____ differs in two important respects from the annual percentage rate (APR):

   1. the _____ generally does not incorporate one-time charges such as front-end fees;
   2. the _____ is (generally) not defined by legal or regulatory authorities (as APR is in many jurisdictions.)

By contrast, the 'effective APR' is used as a legal term, where front-fees and other costs can be included, as defined by local law.

Annual Percentage Yield or effective annual yield is the analogous concept used for savings or investment products, such as a certificate of deposit.

   a. Effective interest rate
   c. AAB
   b. ABN Amro
   d. A Random Walk Down Wall Street

Chapter 9. Interest Rates

41. An _____ is a contract written by a seller that conveys to the buyer the right -- but not the obligation -- to buy (in the case of a call _____) or to sell (in the case of a put _____) a particular asset, such as a piece of property such as, among others, a futures contract. In return for granting the _____, the seller collects a payment (the premium) from the buyer.

For example, buying a call _____ provides the right to buy a specified quantity of a security at a set strike price at some time on or before expiration, while buying a put _____ provides the right to sell.

- a. Amortization
- b. Option
- c. AT'T Mobility LLC
- d. Annuity

42. _____ refers to any type of investment that yields a regular (or fixed) return.

For example, if you lend money to a borrower and the borrower has to pay interest once a month, you have been issued a fixed-income security. When a company does this, it is often called a bond or corporate bank debt (although preferred stock is also sometimes considered to be _____).

- a. Fixed income
- b. Bond market
- c. 529 plan
- d. 4-4-5 Calendar

43. In finance, the _____ is the relation between the interest rate (or cost of borrowing) and the time to maturity of the debt for a given borrower in a given currency. For example, the current U.S. dollar interest rates paid on U.S. Treasury securities for various maturities are closely watched by many traders, and are commonly plotted on a graph such as the one on the right which is informally called 'the _____.' More formal mathematical descriptions of this relation are often called the term structure of interest rates.

The yield of a debt instrument is the annualized percentage increase in the value of the investment.

- a. 529 plan
- b. 4-4-5 Calendar
- c. 7-Eleven
- d. Yield curve

44. The _____ is a financial market where participants buy and sell debt securities, usually in the form of bonds. As of 2006, the size of the international _____ is an estimated $45 trillion, of which the size of the outstanding U.S. _____ debt was $25.2 trillion.

Nearly all of the $923 billion average daily trading volume in the U.S. _____ takes place between broker-dealers and large institutions in a decentralized, over-the-counter market.

- a. 529 plan
- b. Fixed income
- c. Bond market
- d. 4-4-5 Calendar

45. A _____ is a listing of bonds or fixed income instruments and a statistic reflecting the composite value of its components. It is used as a tool to represent the characteristics of its component fixed income instruments. They differ from stock market indices in their complexity.

Chapter 9. Interest Rates

a. 529 plan
c. 7-Eleven
b. 4-4-5 Calendar
d. Bond market index

46. _____ is the provision of resources (such as granting a loan) by one party to another party where that second party does not reimburse the first party immediately, thereby generating a debt, and instead arranges either to repay or return those resources (or material(s) of equal value) at a later date. The first party is called a creditor, also known as a lender, while the second party is called a debtor, also known as a borrower.

Movements of financial capital are normally dependent on either _____ or equity transfers.

a. Warrant
c. Credit
b. Comparable
d. Clearing house

47. The _____ , a component of the Federal Reserve System, is charged under United States law with overseeing the nation's open market operations. It is the Federal Reserve Committee that makes key decisions about interest rates and the growth jam of the United States money supply. It is the principal organ of United States national monetary policy.

a. Federal Open Market Committee
c. Tax incidence
b. Fiscal policy
d. Tax exemption

48. _____ (also trust indenture or deed of trust) is a legal document issued to lenders and describes key terms such as the interest rate, maturity date, convertibility, pledge, promises, representations, covenants, and other terms of the bond offering. When the Offering Memorandum is prepared in advance of marketing a Bond, the indenture will typically be summarised in the 'Description of Notes' section.

a. Court of Audit of Belgium
c. McFadden Act
b. Fair Labor Standards Act
d. Bond indenture

49. A _____ is a bond issued by a corporation. The term is usually applied to longer-term debt instruments, generally with a maturity date falling at least a year after their issue date. (The term 'commercial paper' is sometimes used for instruments with a shorter maturity.)

a. Serial bond
c. Government bond
b. Corporate bond
d. Brady bonds

50. In economics, a _____ is a mechanism that allows people to easily buy and sell (trade) financial securities (such as stocks and bonds), commodities (such as precious metals or agricultural goods), and other fungible items of value at low transaction costs and at prices that reflect the efficient-market hypothesis.

_____s have evolved significantly over several hundred years and are undergoing constant innovation to improve liquidity.

Both general markets (where many commodities are traded) and specialized markets (where only one commodity is traded) exist.

a. Financial Market
c. Secondary market
b. Delta hedging
d. Cost of carry

51. The _____ is a U.S. government-owned corporation within the Department of Housing and Urban Development

Ginnie Mae provides guarantees on mortgage-backed securities backed by federally insured or guaranteed loans, mainly loans issued by the Federal Housing Administration, Department of Veterans Affairs, Rural Housing Service, and Office of Public and Indian Housing. Ginnie Mae securities are the only MBS that are guaranteed by the United States government.

   a. Government National Mortgage Association
   b. Jumbo mortgage
   c. 4-4-5 Calendar
   d. Graduated payment mortgage

52. A _____ is a bond issued by a national government denominated in the country's own currency. Bonds issued by national governments in foreign currencies are normally referred to as sovereign bonds. The first ever _____ was issued by the British government in 1693 to raise money to fund a war against France.

   a. Collateralized debt obligations
   b. Government bond
   c. Municipal bond
   d. Zero-coupon bond

53. In finance, a _____ (non-investment grade bond, speculative grade bond or junk bond) is a bond that is rated below investment grade at the time of purchase. These bonds have a higher risk of default or other adverse credit events, but typically pay higher yields than better quality bonds in order to make them attractive to investors.

   a. Private equity
   b. Sharpe ratio
   c. Volatility
   d. High yield bond

54. In the United States, a _____ is a bond issued by a city or other local government, or their agencies. Potential issuers of these bonds include cities, counties, redevelopment agencies, school districts, publicly owned airports and seaports, and any other governmental entity (or group of governments) below the state level. They may be general obligations of the issuer or secured by specified revenues.

   a. Premium bond
   b. Senior debt
   c. Puttable bond
   d. Municipal bond

55. _____ is a life of security. It may also refer to the final payment date of a loan or other financial instrument, at which point all remaining interest and principal is due to be paid.

1, 3, 6 months _____ band can be calculated by using 30-day per month periods.

   a. Replacement cost
   b. False billing
   c. Primary market
   d. Maturity

56. A _____ is a legal pledge in United States municipal finance, in which an entity pledges its full faith and credit to repay its debt, typically a _____ bond.

   a. General obligation
   b. Financial Institutions Reform Recovery and Enforcement Act
   c. Covenant
   d. Letter of credit

57. In business, _____ is income that a company receives from its normal business activities, usually from the sale of goods and services to customers. Some companies also receive _____ from interest, dividends or royalties paid to them by other companies. _____ may refer to business income in general, or it may refer to the amount, in a monetary unit, received during a period of time, as in 'Last year, Company X had _____ of $32 million.'

Chapter 9. Interest Rates

In many countries, including the UK, _____ is referred to as turnover.

a. Matching principle
c. Revenue

b. Furniture, Fixtures and Equipment
d. Bottom line

58. _____ are bonds issued by governments, authorities, or public benefit corporations that are guaranteed by the revenue flow of the issuing agency.

The Supreme Court decision of Pollock versus Farmer's Loan and Trust Company of 1895 initiated a wave or series of innovations for the financial services community in both tax-treatment and regulation from government. This specific case, according to a leading investment bank's research, resulted in the 'intergovernmental tax immunity doctrine,' ultimately leading to 'tax-free status.' Municipal bonds are generally exempt from federal tax on their interest payments (not capital gains.)

a. Callable bond
c. Gilts

b. Private activity bond
d. Revenue bonds

59. A _____ is a bond bought at a price lower than its face value, with the face value repaid at the time of maturity. It does not make periodic interest payments, or so-called 'coupons,' hence the term zero-coupon bond. Investors earn return from the compounded interest all paid at maturity plus the difference between the discounted price of the bond and its par value.

a. Municipal bond
c. Callable bond

b. Bowie bonds
d. Zero coupon bond

60. The coupon or _____ of a bond is the amount of interest paid per year expressed as a percentage of the face value of the bond.

For example if you hold $10,000 nominal of a bond described as a 4.5% loan stock, you will receive $450 in interest each year (probably in two installments of $225 each.)

Not all bonds have coupons.

a. Zero-coupon bond
c. Puttable bond

b. Revenue bonds
d. Coupon rate

61. _____ measures the nominal future sum of money that a given sum of money is 'worth' at a specified time in the future assuming a certain interest rate rate of return; it is the present value multiplied by the accumulation function.

The value does not include corrections for inflation or other factors that affect the true value of money in the future. This is used in time value of money calculations.

a. Future value
c. Discounted cash flow

b. Present value of costs
d. Future-oriented

62. In economics, the _____ is the proposition by Irving Fisher that the real interest rate is independent of monetary measures, especially the nominal interest rate. The Fisher equation is

$r_r = r_n - \pi^e$.

This means, the real interest rate (r_r) equals the nominal interest rate (r_n) minus expected rate of inflation (π^e.) Here all the rates are continuously compounded.

a. 529 plan
b. 4-4-5 Calendar
c. 7-Eleven
d. Fisher hypothesis

63. In economics, _____ is a rise in the general level of prices of goods and services in an economy over a period of time. The term '_____' once referred to increases in the money supply (monetary _____); however, economic debates about the relationship between money supply and price levels have led to its primary use today in describing price _____. _____ can also be described as a decline in the real value of money--a loss of purchasing power in the medium of exchange which is also the monetary unit of account.

a. A Random Walk Down Wall Street
b. AAB
c. ABN Amro
d. Inflation

64. In finance and economics _____ refers to the rate of interest before adjustment for inflation (in contrast with the real interest rate); or, for interest balls stated' without adjustment for the full effect of compounding (also referred to as the nominal annual rate.) An interest rate is called nominal if the frequency of compounding (e.g. a month) is not identical to the basic time unit (normally a year.)

The real interest rate includes compensation for the lender's lost value due to inflation, whereas the _____ excludes inflation.

a. SIBOR
b. Shanghai Interbank Offered Rate
c. Cash accumulation equation
d. Nominal interest rate

65. The '_____' is approximately the nominal interest rate minus the inflation rate Since the inflation rate over the course of a loan is not known initially, volatility in inflation represents a risk to both the lender and the borrower.

In economics and finance, an individual who lends money for repayment at a later point in time expects to be compensated for the time value of money, or not having the use of that money while it is lent.

a. 529 plan
b. 4-4-5 Calendar
c. 7-Eleven
d. Real interest rate

66. _____ are the inflation-indexed bonds issued by the U.S. Treasury. The principal is adjusted to the Consumer Price Index, the commonly used measure of inflation. The coupon rate is constant, but generates a different amount of interest when multiplied by the inflation-adjusted principal, thus protecting the holder against inflation. _____ are currently offered in 5-year, 10-year and 20-year maturities.

Chapter 9. Interest Rates

a. 4-4-5 Calendar
b. Treasury securities
c. Treasury Inflation Protected Securities
d. Treasury Inflation-Protected Securities

67. The _____ or forward rate is the agreed upon price of an asset in a forward contract. Using the rational pricing assumption, we can express the _____ in terms of the spot price and any dividends etc., so that there is no possibility for arbitrage.

The _____ is given by:

$$F = \left(S_0 - \sum_{i} D_i e^{-r t_i}\right) e^{(r-q)T}$$

where

F is the _____ to be paid at time T
e^x is the exponential function
r is the risk-free interest rate
q is the cost-of-carry
S_0 is the spot price of the asset (i.e. what it would sell for at time 0)
D_i is a dividend which is guaranteed to be paid at time t_i where $0 < t_i < T$.

The two questions here are what price the short position (the seller of the asset) should offer to maximize his gain, and what price the long position (the buyer of the asset) should accept to maximize his gain?

At the very least we know that both do not want to lose any money in the deal.

a. Financial Gerontology
b. Biweekly Mortgage
c. Security interest
d. Forward price

68. _____ in finance is a risk management technique, related to hedging, that mixes a wide variety of investments within a portfolio. Because the fluctuations of a single security have less impact on a diverse portfolio, _____ minimizes the risk from any one investment.

A simple example of _____ is the following: On a particular island the entire economy consists of two companies: one that sells umbrellas and another that sells sunscreen.

a. 4-4-5 Calendar
b. 529 plan
c. 7-Eleven
d. Diversification

69. _____ is the risk (variability in value) borne by an interest-bearing asset, such as a loan or a bond, due to variability of interest rates. In general, as rates rise, the price of a fixed rate bond will fall, and vice versa. _____ is commonly measured by the bond's duration.

a. Interest rate risk
b. International Fisher effect
c. Official bank rate
d. A Random Walk Down Wall Street

Chapter 9. Interest Rates

70.

In finance, the _____ can be the expected rate of return above the risk-free interest rate. When measuring risk, a common sense approach is to compare the risk-free return on T-bills and the very risky return on other investments. The difference between these two returns can be interpreted as a measure of the excess return on the average risky asset. This excess return is known as the _____.

a. Risk adjusted return on capital
c. Risk aversion

b. Risk modeling
d. Risk premium

71. In finance, _____ occurs when a debtor has not met its legal obligations according to the debt contract, e.g. it has not made a scheduled payment, or has violated a loan covenant (condition) of the debt contract. _____ may occur if the debtor is either unwilling or unable to pay their debt. This can occur with all debt obligations including bonds, mortgages, loans, and promissory notes.

a. Debt validation
c. Vendor finance

b. Default
d. Credit crunch

72. _____ is the risk of loss due to a debtor's non-payment of a loan or other line of credit (either the principal or interest (coupon) or both)

Most lenders employ their own models (credit scorecards) to rank potential and existing customers according to risk, and then apply appropriate strategies. With products such as unsecured personal loans or mortgages, lenders charge a higher price for higher risk customers and vice versa. With revolving products such as credit cards and overdrafts, risk is controlled through careful setting of credit limits.

a. Market risk
c. Transaction risk

b. Liquidity risk
d. Credit risk

73. _____ is a measure of the ability of a debtor to pay their debts as and when they fall due. It is usually expressed as a ratio or a percentage of current liabilities.

For a corporation with a published balance sheet there are various ratios used to calculate a measure of liquidity.

a. Operating profit margin
c. Operating leverage

b. Invested capital
d. Accounting liquidity

74. _____ is a term used to explain a difference between two types of financial securities (e.g. stocks), that have all the same qualities except liquidity. For example:

_____ is a segment of a three-part theory that works to explain the behavior of yield curves for interest rates. The upwards-curving component of the interest yield can be explained by the _____.

a. 4-4-5 Calendar
c. 529 plan

b. 7-Eleven
d. Liquidity premium

75. _____ arises from situations in which a party interested in trading an asset cannot do it because nobody in the market wants to trade that asset. _____ becomes particularly important to parties who are about to hold or currently hold an asset, since it affects their ability to trade.

Manifestation of _____ is very different from a drop of price to zero.

   a. Tracking error
   c. Credit risk
   b. Currency risk
   d. Liquidity Risk

Chapter 10. Bond Prices and Yields

1. In finance, a _____ is a debt security, in which the authorized issuer owes the holders a debt and, depending on the terms of the _____, is obliged to pay interest (the coupon) and/or to repay the principal at a later date, termed maturity.

Thus a _____ is a loan: the issuer is the borrower, the _____ holder is the lender, and the coupon is the interest. _____s provide the borrower with external funds to finance long-term investments, or, in the case of government _____s, to finance current expenditure.

a. Bond
c. Convertible bond
b. Catastrophe bonds
d. Puttable bond

2. The coupon or _____ of a bond is the amount of interest paid per year expressed as a percentage of the face value of the bond.

For example if you hold $10,000 nominal of a bond described as a 4.5% loan stock, you will receive $450 in interest each year (probably in two installments of $225 each.)

Not all bonds have coupons.

a. Zero-coupon bond
c. Puttable bond
b. Revenue bonds
d. Coupon rate

3. The _____, interest yield, income yield, flat yield or running yield is a financial term used in reference to bonds and other fixed-interest securities such as gilts. It is the ratio of the annual interest payment and the bond's current price.

The _____ only therefore refers to the yield of the bond at the current moment. It does not reflect the total return over the life of the bond. In particular, it takes no account of reinvestment risk (the uncertainty about the rate at which future cashflows can be reinvested) or the fact that bonds usually mature at par value, which can be an important component of a bond's return.

a. Stochastic volatility
c. Modified Internal Rate of Return
b. Perpetuity
d. Current yield

4. _____ is the coupon rate of a fixed income security, which is a fixed percentage of the par value. Unlike current yield, it does not vary with the market price of the security. .

a. Bond fund
c. Nominal yield
b. Zero-coupon bond
d. Bond valuation

5. In business and accounting, _____s are everything of value that is owned by a person or company. The balance sheet of a firm records the monetary value of the _____s owned by the firm. The two major _____ classes are tangible _____s and intangible _____s.

a. Accounts payable
c. Income
b. EBITDA
d. Asset

6. _____ is a term used to refer to how an investor distributes his or her investments among various classes of investment vehicles (e.g., stocks and bonds).

A large part of financial planning is finding an _____ that is appropriate for a given person in terms of their appetite for and ability to shoulder risk. This can depend on various factors; see investor profile.

- a. Investment performance
- b. Alternative investment
- c. Investing online
- d. Asset allocation

7. A _____ is a unit that is equal to 1/100th of a percentage point. It is frequently used to express percentage point changes of less than 1%. It avoids the ambiguity between relative and absolute discussions about rates.
- a. 529 plan
- b. 4-4-5 Calendar
- c. Bond market
- d. Basis point

8. _____ is a life of security. It may also refer to the final payment date of a loan or other financial instrument, at which point all remaining interest and principal is due to be paid.

1, 3, 6 months _____ band can be calculated by using 30-day per month periods.

- a. Primary market
- b. Maturity
- c. Replacement cost
- d. False billing

9. In finance, the term _____ describes the amount in cash that returns to the owners of a security. Normally it does not include the price variations, at the difference of the total return. _____ applies to various stated rates of return on stocks (common and preferred, and convertible), fixed income instruments (bonds, notes, bills, strips, zero coupon), and some other investment type insurance products (e.g. annuities.)
- a. Yield
- b. Yield to maturity
- c. 4-4-5 Calendar
- d. Macaulay duration

10. The _____ or redemption yield is the yield promised to the bondholder on the assumption that the bond or other fixed-interest security such as gilts will be held to maturity, that all coupon and principal payments will be made and coupon payments are reinvested at the bond's promised yield at the same rate as invested. It is a measure of the return of the bond. This technique in theory allows Investors to calculate the fair value of different financial instruments
- a. Macaulay duration
- b. 4-4-5 Calendar
- c. Yield
- d. Yield to maturity

11. In finance, _____ is the interest that has accumulated since the principal investment, or since the previous interest payment if there has been one already. For a financial instrument such as a bond, interest is calculated and paid in set intervals.

The primary formula for calculating the interest accrued in a given period is:

$$I_A = T \times P \times R$$

where I_A is the _____, T is the fraction of the year, P is the principal, and R is the annualized interest rate.

a. A Random Walk Down Wall Street
b. Accrued interest
c. ABN Amro
d. AAB

12. _____ is a fee paid on borrowed assets. It is the price paid for the use of borrowed money, or, money earned by deposited funds. Assets that are sometimes lent with _____ include money, shares, consumer goods through hire purchase, major assets such as aircraft, and even entire factories in finance lease arrangements.
   a. Interest
   b. AAB
   c. Insolvency
   d. A Random Walk Down Wall Street

13. An _____ is a contract written by a seller that conveys to the buyer the right -- but not the obligation -- to buy (in the case of a call _____) or to sell (in the case of a put _____) a particular asset, such as a piece of property such as, among others, a futures contract. In return for granting the _____, the seller collects a payment (the premium) from the buyer.

For example, buying a call _____ provides the right to buy a specified quantity of a security at a set strike price at some time on or before expiration, while buying a put _____ provides the right to sell.

   a. AT'T Mobility LLC
   b. Option
   c. Amortization
   d. Annuity

14. A '_____' is a 'Charge' that is paid to obtain the right to delay a payment. Essentially, the payer purchases the right to make a given payment in the future instead of in the Present. The '_____', or 'Charge' that must be paid to delay the payment, is simply the difference between what the payment amount would be if it were paid in the present and what the payment amount would be paid if it were paid in the future.
   a. Value at risk
   b. Risk aversion
   c. Risk modeling
   d. Discount

15. A _____ is a bond bought at a price lower than its face value, with the face value repaid at the time of maturity. It does not make periodic interest payments, or so-called 'coupons,' hence the term zero-coupon bond. Investors earn return from the compounded interest all paid at maturity plus the difference between the discounted price of the bond and its par value.
   a. Municipal bond
   b. Callable bond
   c. Bowie bonds
   d. Zero coupon bond

16. A _____ is a generic term for any bond selling for more than 100% of par value, i.e., at a price greater than 100.00, which typically occurs for high coupon bonds in a falling interest rate climate.
   a. Municipal bond
   b. Premium bond
   c. Revenue bonds
   d. Nominal yield

17. In finance, the _____ is the price of a bond excluding any interest that has accrued since issue or the most recent coupon payment. This is to be compared with the dirty price, which is the price of a bond including the accrued interest.

When bond prices are quoted on a Bloomberg Terminal or Reuters they are quoted using the _____.

Chapter 10. Bond Prices and Yields

a. Bond valuation
c. Bowie bonds
b. Gilts
d. Clean price

18. The _____ of a bond represents the value of a bond, exclusive of any commissions or fees. The _____ is also called the 'full price.'

Bonds, as well as a variety of other fixed income securities, provide for coupon payments to be made to bond holders on a fixed schedule. The _____ of a bond will decrease on the days coupons are paid, resulting in a saw-tooth pattern for the bond value.

a. Serial bond
c. Dirty price
b. Premium bond
d. Collateralized debt obligations

19. _____ are government bonds issued by the United States Department of the Treasury through the Bureau of the Public Debt. They are the debt financing instruments of the U.S. Federal government, and they are often referred to simply as Treasuries or Treasurys. There are four types of marketable _____: Treasury bills, Treasury notes, Treasury bonds, and Treasury Inflation Protected Securities (TIPS.)

a. Treasury securities
c. Treasury Inflation Protected Securities
b. 4-4-5 Calendar
d. Treasury Inflation-Protected Securities

20. _____ is a type of bond that allows the issuer of the bond to retain the privilege of redeeming the bond at some point before the bond reaches the date of maturity. In other words, on the call dates, the issuer has the right, but not the obligation, to buy back the bonds from the bond holders at the call price. Technically speaking, the bonds are not really bought and held by the issuer but cancelled immediately.

a. Callable bond
c. Bond fund
b. Gilts
d. Coupon rate

21. The institution most often referenced by the word '_____' is a public or publicly traded _____, the shares of which are traded on a public stock exchange (e.g., the New York Stock Exchange or Nasdaq in the United States) where shares of stock of _____s are bought and sold by and to the general public. Most of the largest businesses in the world are publicly traded _____s. However, the majority of _____s are said to be closely held, privately held or close _____s, meaning that no ready market exists for the trading of shares.

a. Depository Trust Company
c. Corporation
b. Federal Home Loan Mortgage Corporation
d. Protect

22. In financial accounting, _____s are precautions for which the amount or probability of occurrence are not known. Typical examples are _____s for warranty costs and _____ for taxes the term reserve is used instead of term _____; such a use, however, is inconsistent with the terminology suggested by International Accounting Standards Board.

a. Momentum Accounting and Triple-Entry Bookkeeping
c. Money measurement concept
b. Provision
d. Petty cash

23. _____ in finance is a risk management technique, related to hedging, that mixes a wide variety of investments within a portfolio. Because the fluctuations of a single security have less impact on a diverse portfolio, _____ minimizes the risk from any one investment.

A simple example of _____ is the following: On a particular island the entire economy consists of two companies: one that sells umbrellas and another that sells sunscreen.

   a. 4-4-5 Calendar   b. 7-Eleven
   c. Diversification   d. 529 plan

24. An _____ is the price a borrower pays for the use of money they do not own, and the return a lender receives for deferring the use of funds, by lending it to the borrower. _____s are normally expressed as a percentage rate over the period of one year.

_____s targets are also a vital tool of monetary policy and are used to control variables like investment, inflation, and unemployment.

   a. AAB   b. ABN Amro
   c. A Random Walk Down Wall Street   d. Interest rate

25. _____ is the risk (variability in value) borne by an interest-bearing asset, such as a loan or a bond, due to variability of interest rates. In general, as rates rise, the price of a fixed rate bond will fall, and vice versa. _____ is commonly measured by the bond's duration.
   a. A Random Walk Down Wall Street   b. Interest rate risk
   c. International Fisher effect   d. Official bank rate

26. In finance, the _____ of a financial asset measures the sensitivity of the asset's price to interest rate movements, expressed as a number of years. The reason for expressing this sensitivity in years is that the time that will elapse until a cash flow is received allows more interest to accumulate. Therefore the price of an asset with long term cashflows has more interest rate sensitivity than an asset with cashflows in the near future.
   a. Duration   b. Yield to maturity
   c. Macaulay duration   d. 4-4-5 Calendar

27. A _____ is a collective investment scheme that invests in bonds and other debt securities. _____s yield monthly dividends that include interest payments on the fund's underlying securities plus any capital appreciation in the prices of the portfolio's bonds. _____s tend to pay higher dividends than CDs and money market accounts, and they generally pay out dividends more frequently and regularly than individual bonds.
   a. Premium bond   b. Private activity bond
   c. Gilts   d. Bond fund

28. A _____ is a pool of assets forming an independent legal entity that are bought with the contributions to a pension plan for the exclusive purpose of financing pension plan benefits.

_____s are important shareholders of listed and private companies. They are especially important to the stock market where large institutional investors like the Ontario Teachers' Pension Plan dominate.

   a. Leveraged buyout   b. Leverage
   c. Limited liability company   d. Pension fund

Chapter 10. Bond Prices and Yields

29. _____ is the weighted average maturity of a bond where the weights are the relative discounted cash flows in each period.

It will be seen that this is the same formula for the duration as given above.

Macaulay showed that an unweighted average maturity is not useful in predicting interest rate risk.

a. Yield
b. Yield to maturity
c. 4-4-5 Calendar
d. Macaulay duration

30. A _____ is a financial contract between two parties, the buyer and the seller of this type of option. Often it is simply labeled a 'call'. The buyer of the option has the right, but not the obligation to buy an agreed quantity of a particular commodity or financial instrument (the underlying instrument) from the seller of the option at a certain time (the expiration date) for a certain price (the strike price.)

a. Bull spread
b. Bear spread
c. Bear call spread
d. Call option

31. _____, in finance and accounting, means stated value or face value. From this comes the expressions at par (at the _____), over par (over _____) and under par (under _____.)

The term '_____' has several meanings depending on context and geography.

a. FIDC
b. Global Squeeze
c. Sinking fund
d. Par value

32. The _____, in terms of finance and investing, describes how the expected return of a stock or portfolio is correlated to the return of the financial market as a whole.

An asset with a beta of 0 means that its price is not at all correlated with the market; that asset is independent. A positive beta means that the asset generally follows the market.

a. LIBOR market model
b. Beta coefficient
c. Perpetuity
d. Current yield

33. _____ is one of the main genres of financial risk. The term describes the risk that a particular investment might be canceled or stopped somehow, that one may have to find a new place to invest that money with the risk being there might not be a similarly attractive investment available. This primarily occurs if bonds (which are portions of loans to entities) are paid back earlier then expected.

a. Standard of deferred payment
b. Debt cash flow
c. Biweekly Mortgage
d. Reinvestment risk

Chapter 11. Diversification and Risky Asset Allocation

1. _____ in finance is a risk management technique, related to hedging, that mixes a wide variety of investments within a portfolio. Because the fluctuations of a single security have less impact on a diverse portfolio, _____ minimizes the risk from any one investment.

A simple example of _____ is the following: On a particular island the entire economy consists of two companies: one that sells umbrellas and another that sells sunscreen.

   a. 7-Eleven   b. 4-4-5 Calendar
   c. 529 plan   d. Diversification

2. The _____ is the weighted-average most likely outcome in gambling, probability theory, economics or finance.

In gambling and probability theory, there is usually a discrete set of possible outcomes. In this case, _____ is a measure of the relative balance of win or loss weighted by their chances of occurring.

   a. ABN Amro   b. AAB
   c. A Random Walk Down Wall Street   d. Expected return

3. In probability and statistics, the _____ of a collection of numbers is a measure of the dispersion of the numbers from their expected (mean) value. It can apply to a probability distribution, a random variable, a population or a data set. The _____ is usually denoted with the letter σ (lowercase sigma.)

   a. Kurtosis   b. Mean
   c. Sample size   d. Standard deviation

4. In probability theory and statistics, the _____ of a random variable, probability distribution averaging the squared distance of its possible values from the expected value (mean.) Whereas the mean is a way to describe the location of a distribution, the _____ is a way to capture its scale or degree of being spread out. The unit of _____ is the square of the unit of the original variable.

   a. Harmonic mean   b. Semivariance
   c. Variance   d. Monte Carlo methods

5. Depending on the nature of the investment, the type of _____ will vary.

A common concern with any investment is that you may lose the money you invest - your capital. This risk is therefore often referred to as 'capital risk.'

If the assets you invest in are held in another currency there is a risk that currency movements alone may affect the value.

   a. AAB   b. ABN Amro
   c. A Random Walk Down Wall Street   d. Investment risk

6.

Chapter 11. Diversification and Risky Asset Allocation

In finance, the _____ can be the expected rate of return above the risk-free interest rate. When measuring risk, a common sense approach is to compare the risk-free return on T-bills and the very risky return on other investments. The difference between these two returns can be interpreted as a measure of the excess return on the average risky asset. This excess return is known as the _____.

    a. Risk modeling
    b. Risk adjusted return on capital
    c. Risk aversion
    d. Risk premium

7. _____ is the discipline of identifying, monitoring and limiting risks. In some cases the acceptable risk may be near zero. Risks can come from accidents, natural causes and disasters as well as deliberate attacks from an adversary.
    a. Risk management
    b. 4-4-5 Calendar
    c. Penny stock
    d. FIFO

8. Modern portfolio theory (MPT) proposes how rational investors will use diversification to optimize their portfolios, and how a risky asset should be priced. The basic concepts of the theory are Markowitz diversification, the _____, capital asset pricing model, the alpha and beta coefficients, the Capital Market Line and the Securities Market Line.

MPT models an asset's return as a random variable, and models a portfolio as a weighted combination of assets so that the return of a portfolio is the weighted combination of the assets' returns.

    a. ABN Amro
    b. A Random Walk Down Wall Street
    c. Efficient frontier
    d. AAB

9. In business and accounting, _____s are everything of value that is owned by a person or company. The balance sheet of a firm records the monetary value of the _____s owned by the firm. The two major _____ classes are tangible _____s and intangible _____s.
    a. Income
    b. EBITDA
    c. Accounts payable
    d. Asset

10. _____ is a term used to refer to how an investor distributes his or her investments among various classes of investment vehicles (e.g., stocks and bonds.)

A large part of financial planning is finding an _____ that is appropriate for a given person in terms of their appetite for and ability to shoulder risk. This can depend on various factors; see investor profile.

    a. Asset allocation
    b. Investing online
    c. Investment performance
    d. Alternative investment

11. The _____, in terms of finance and investing, describes how the expected return of a stock or portfolio is correlated to the return of the financial market as a whole.

An asset with a beta of 0 means that its price is not at all correlated with the market; that asset is independent. A positive beta means that the asset generally follows the market.

Chapter 11. Diversification and Risky Asset Allocation

a. Beta coefficient
c. LIBOR market model
b. Current yield
d. Perpetuity

12. A _____ is the direction in which a financial market is moving. _____s can be classified as primary trends, secondary trends (short-term), and secular trends (long-term.) This principle incorporates the idea that market cycles occur with regularity and persistence.
   a. 4-4-5 Calendar
   c. 529 plan
   b. 7-Eleven
   d. Market trend

13. The _____ is one of several stock market indices, created by nineteenth-century Wall Street Journal editor and Dow Jones ' Company co-founder Charles Dow. Dow compiled the index to gauge the performance of the industrial sector of the American stock market. It is the second-oldest U.S. market index, after the Dow Jones Transportation Average, which Dow also created.
   a. 7-Eleven
   c. 4-4-5 Calendar
   b. Dow Jones Industrial Average
   d. 529 plan

14. In business and finance, a _____ (also referred to as equity _____) of stock means a _____ of ownership in a corporation (company.) In the plural, stocks is often used as a synonym for _____s especially in the United States, but it is less commonly used that way outside of North America.

In the United Kingdom, South Africa, and Australia, stock can also refer to completely different financial instruments such as government bonds or, less commonly, to all kinds of marketable securities.

   a. Share
   c. Procter ' Gamble
   b. Bucket shop
   d. Margin

15. _____ is the action of bringing a portfolio of investments that has deviated away from one's target asset allocation back into line. Under-weighted securities can be purchased with newly saved money; alternatively, over-weighted securities can be sold to purchase under-weighted securities.

The investments in a portfolio will perform according to the market.

   a. Security market line
   c. Rebalancing
   b. Divestment
   d. Market timing

16. In probability theory and statistics, _____ indicates the strength and direction of a linear relationship between two random variables. That is in contrast with the usage of the term in colloquial speech, which denotes any relationship, not necessarily linear. In general statistical usage, _____ or co-relation refers to the departure of two random variables from independence.
   a. Variance
   c. Geometric mean
   b. Probability distribution
   d. Correlation

17. In economics and finance, _____ is the practice of taking advantage of a price differential between two or more markets: striking a combination of matching deals that capitalize upon the imbalance, the profit being the difference between the market prices. When used by academics, an _____ is a transaction that involves no negative cash flow at any probabilistic or temporal state and a positive cash flow in at least one state; in simple terms, a risk-free profit.

Chapter 11. Diversification and Risky Asset Allocation

a. Initial margin
b. Efficient-market hypothesis
c. Issuer
d. Arbitrage

18. In finance, a _____ is a debt security, in which the authorized issuer owes the holders a debt and, depending on the terms of the _____, is obliged to pay interest (the coupon) and/or to repay the principal at a later date, termed maturity.

Thus a _____ is a loan: the issuer is the borrower, the _____ holder is the lender, and the coupon is the interest. _____s provide the borrower with external funds to finance long-term investments, or, in the case of government _____s, to finance current expenditure.

a. Bond
b. Puttable bond
c. Convertible bond
d. Catastrophe bonds

19. A _____ is a collective investment scheme that invests in bonds and other debt securities. _____s yield monthly dividends that include interest payments on the fund's underlying securities plus any capital appreciation in the prices of the portfolio's bonds. _____s tend to pay higher dividends than CDs and money market accounts, and they generally pay out dividends more frequently and regularly than individual bonds.

a. Premium bond
b. Gilts
c. Private activity bond
d. Bond fund

20. A _____, securities exchange or (in Europe) bourse is a corporation or mutual organization which provides 'trading' facilities for stock brokers and traders, to trade stocks and other securities. _____s also provide facilities for the issue and redemption of securities as well as other financial instruments and capital events including the payment of income and dividends. The securities traded on a _____ include: shares issued by companies, unit trusts and other pooled investment products and bonds.

a. 7-Eleven
b. 529 plan
c. 4-4-5 Calendar
d. Stock exchange

21. A _____ or equity fund is a fund that invests in Equities more commonly known as stocks. Such funds are typically held either in stock or cash, as opposed to Bonds, notes, or other securities. This may be a mutual fund or exchange-traded fund.

a. Money market funds
b. Mutual fund fees and expenses
c. Closed-end fund
d. Stock fund

22. A _____ is a situation that involves losing one quality or aspect of something in return for gaining another quality or aspect. It implies a decision to be made with full comprehension of both the upside and downside of a particular choice.

In economics the term is expressed as opportunity cost, referring the most preferred alternative given up.

a. Trade-off
b. Break-even point
c. Capital outflow
d. Total revenue

23. An _____ or index tracker is a collective investment scheme (usually a mutual fund or exchange-traded fund) that aims to replicate the movements of an index of a specific financial market regardless of market conditions.

Tracking can be achieved by trying to hold all of the securities in the index, in the same proportions as the index. Other methods include statistically sampling the market and holding 'representative' securities.

a. Investment company
b. A Random Walk Down Wall Street
c. Index Fund
d. AAB

24. A _____ is a method of measuring a section of the stock market. Many indices are cited by news or financial services firms and are used to benchmark the performance of portfolios such as mutual funds.
a. Trading curb
b. Program trading
c. Stop order
d. Stock market index

25. A _____ is a fungible, negotiable instrument representing financial value. They are broadly categorized into debt securities (such as banknotes, bonds and debentures), and equity securities; e.g., common stocks. The company or other entity issuing the _____ is called the issuer.
a. Securities lending
b. Security
c. Book entry
d. Tracking stock

26. A _____ is a professionally managed type of collective investment scheme that pools money from many investors and invests it in stocks, bonds, short-term money market instruments, and/or other securities. The _____ will have a fund manager that trades the pooled money on a regular basis. Currently, the worldwide value of all _____ s totals more than $26 trillion.

Since 1940, there have been three basic types of investment companies in the United States: open-end funds, also known in the US as _____ s; unit investment trusts (UITs); and closed-end funds.

a. Net asset value
b. Financial intermediary
c. Trust company
d. Mutual fund

27. An _____ is a document a company presents at an annual general meeting for approval by its shareholders, or a charitable organization presents its trustees. The report is made up of reports, which may include the following:

- Chairman's report
- CEO's report
- Auditor's report on corporate governance
- Mission statement
- Corporate governance statement of compliance
- Statement of directors' responsibilities
- Invitation to the company's AGM

as well as financial statements including:

- Auditor's report on the financial statements
- Balance sheet
- Statement of retained earnings
- Income statement
- Cash flow statement
- Notes to the financial statements
- Accounting policies

Other information deemed relevant to stakeholders may be included, such as a report on operations for manufacturing firms. In the case of larger companies, it is usually a sleek, colorful, high gloss publication.

The details provided in the report are of use to investors to understand the company's financial position and future direction.

a. Accrued liabilities
b. Annual report
c. Outstanding balance
d. Amortization schedule

Chapter 12. Return, Risk, and the Security Market Line

1. Depending on the nature of the investment, the type of _____ will vary.

A common concern with any investment is that you may lose the money you invest - your capital. This risk is therefore often referred to as 'capital risk.'

If the assets you invest in are held in another currency there is a risk that currency movements alone may affect the value.

   a. ABN Amro
   c. AAB
   b. A Random Walk Down Wall Street
   d. Investment risk

2.

In finance, the _____ can be the expected rate of return above the risk-free interest rate. When measuring risk, a common sense approach is to compare the risk-free return on T-bills and the very risky return on other investments. The difference between these two returns can be interpreted as a measure of the excess return on the average risky asset. This excess return is known as the _____.

   a. Risk modeling
   c. Risk adjusted return on capital
   b. Risk premium
   d. Risk aversion

3. A _____ is a fungible, negotiable instrument representing financial value. They are broadly categorized into debt securities (such as banknotes, bonds and debentures), and equity securities; e.g., common stocks. The company or other entity issuing the _____ is called the issuer.
   a. Book entry
   c. Securities lending
   b. Security
   d. Tracking stock

4. In Modern Portfolio Theory, the _____ is the graphical representation of the Capital Asset Pricing Model. It displays the expected rate of return for an overall market as a function of systematic (non-diversifiable) risk (beta.)

The Y-Intercept (beta=0) of the _____ is equal to the risk-free interest rate.

   a. Divestment
   c. Certificate in Investment Performance Measurement
   b. Rebalancing
   d. Security market line

5. _____ is the discipline of identifying, monitoring and limiting risks. In some cases the acceptable risk may be near zero. Risks can come from accidents, natural causes and disasters as well as deliberate attacks from an adversary.
   a. 4-4-5 Calendar
   c. Penny stock
   b. FIFO
   d. Risk management

6. A '_____' is a 'Charge' that is paid to obtain the right to delay a payment. Essentially, the payer purchases the right to make a given payment in the future instead of in the Present. The '_____', or 'Charge' that must be paid to delay the payment, is simply the difference between what the payment amount would be if it were paid in the present and what the payment amount would be paid if it were paid in the future.
   a. Risk aversion
   c. Discount
   b. Value at risk
   d. Risk modeling

Chapter 12. Return, Risk, and the Security Market Line

7. The institution most often referenced by the word '_____' is a public or publicly traded _____, the shares of which are traded on a public stock exchange (e.g., the New York Stock Exchange or Nasdaq in the United States) where shares of stock of _____s are bought and sold by and to the general public. Most of the largest businesses in the world are publicly traded _____s. However, the majority of _____s are said to be closely held, privately held or close _____s, meaning that no ready market exists for the trading of shares.

   a. Federal Home Loan Mortgage Corporation   b. Depository Trust Company
   c. Protect   d. Corporation

8. _____ in finance is a risk management technique, related to hedging, that mixes a wide variety of investments within a portfolio. Because the fluctuations of a single security have less impact on a diverse portfolio, _____ minimizes the risk from any one investment.

A simple example of _____ is the following: On a particular island the entire economy consists of two companies: one that sells umbrellas and another that sells sunscreen.

   a. Diversification   b. 4-4-5 Calendar
   c. 529 plan   d. 7-Eleven

9. In finance, _____ is that risk which is common to an entire market and not to any individual entity or component thereof. It should be distinguished from systemic risk which is the risk that the entire financial system will collapse as a result of some catastrophic event.

Risks can be reduced in four main ways: Avoidance, Reduction, Retention and Transfer.

   a. Conglomerate merger   b. Primary market
   c. Systematic risk   d. Capital surplus

10. _____ is the risk that the value of an investment will decrease due to moves in market factors. The five standard _____ factors are:

- Equity risk, the risk that stock prices will change.
- Interest rate risk, the risk that interest rates will change.
- Currency risk, the risk that foreign exchange rates will change.
- Commodity risk, the risk that commodity prices (e.g. grains, metals) will change.

As with other forms of risk, _____ may be measured in a number of ways. Traditionally, this is done using a Value at Risk methodology. Value at risk is well established as a risk management technique, but it contains a number of limiting assumptions that constrain its accuracy.

   a. Currency risk   b. Market risk
   c. Transaction risk   d. Tracking error

11. The _____ on a portfolio of investments takes into account not only the capital appreciation on the portfolio, but also the income received on the portfolio. The income typically consists of interest, dividends, and securities lending fees. This contrasts with the price return, which takes into account only the capital gain on an investment.

Chapter 12. Return, Risk, and the Security Market Line

a. Total return
c. Capitalization rate
b. Global tactical asset allocation
d. Profitability index

12. Modern portfolio theory (MPT) proposes how rational investors will use diversification to optimize their portfolios, and how a risky asset should be priced. The basic concepts of the theory are Markowitz diversification, the _____, capital asset pricing model, the alpha and beta coefficients, the Capital Market Line and the Securities Market Line.

MPT models an asset's return as a random variable, and models a portfolio as a weighted combination of assets so that the return of a portfolio is the weighted combination of the assets' returns.

a. A Random Walk Down Wall Street
c. Efficient frontier
b. ABN Amro
d. AAB

13. In the portfolio management field, Eugene Fama and Kenneth French developed the highly successful _____ to describe market behavior.

CAPM uses a single factor, beta, to compare the excess returns of a portfolio with the excess returns of the market as a whole. But it oversimplifies the complex market. Fama and French started with the observation that two classes of stocks have tended to do better than the market as a whole: small caps and (ii) stocks with a high book-to-market ratio (BM, customarily called value stocks, and different from growth stocks). They then added two factors to CAPM to reflect a portfolio's exposure to these two classes:

Here r is the portfolio's return rate, R_f is the risk-free return rate, and K_m is the return of the whole stock market. The 'three factor' >β is analogous to the classical >β but not equal to it, since there are now two additional factors to do some of the work. SMB stands for 'small minus big' and HML for 'high (book-to-price ratio) minus low'; they measure the historic excess returns of small caps over big caps and of value stocks over growth stocks.

a. Mitigating Control
c. Reputational risk
b. Guaranteed investment contracts
d. Fama-French three factor model

14. The _____, in terms of finance and investing, describes how the expected return of a stock or portfolio is correlated to the return of the financial market as a whole.

An asset with a beta of 0 means that its price is not at all correlated with the market; that asset is independent. A positive beta means that the asset generally follows the market.

a. Perpetuity
c. Current yield
b. LIBOR market model
d. Beta coefficient

15. In economics and finance, _____ is the practice of taking advantage of a price differential between two or more markets: striking a combination of matching deals that capitalize upon the imbalance, the profit being the difference between the market prices. When used by academics, an _____ is a transaction that involves no negative cash flow at any probabilistic or temporal state and a positive cash flow in at least one state; in simple terms, a risk-free profit.

   a. Initial margin
   b. Arbitrage
   c. Efficient-market hypothesis
   d. Issuer

16. The _____ is the weighted-average most likely outcome in gambling, probability theory, economics or finance.

In gambling and probability theory, there is usually a discrete set of possible outcomes. In this case, _____ is a measure of the relative balance of win or loss weighted by their chances of occurring.

   a. AAB
   b. A Random Walk Down Wall Street
   c. ABN Amro
   d. Expected return

17. A _____ is a payment made by a corporation to its shareholder members. When a corporation earns a profit or surplus, that money can be put to two uses: it can either be re-invested in the business (called retained earnings), or it can be paid to the shareholders as a _____. Many corporations retain a portion of their earnings and pay the remainder as a _____.

   a. Dividend puzzle
   b. Dividend yield
   c. Special dividend
   d. Dividend

18. In finance, _____ is the risk involved in using models to value financial securities. Rebonato considers alternative definitions including:

1) After observing a set of prices for the underlying and hedging instruments, different but identically calibrated models might produce different prices for the same exotic product. 2) Losses will be incurred because of an 'incorrect' hedging strategy suggested by a model.

   a. Takeover
   b. Duty of loyalty
   c. Price-to-book ratio
   d. Model risk

19. In finance, the _____ is used to determine a theoretically appropriate required rate of return of an asset, if that asset is to be added to an already well-diversified portfolio, given that asset's non-diversifiable risk. The model takes into account the asset's sensitivity to non-diversifiable risk (also known as systemic risk or market risk), often represented by the quantity beta (β) in the financial industry, as well as the expected return of the market and the expected return of a theoretical risk-free asset.

The model was introduced by Jack Treynor (1961, 1962), William Sharpe (1964), John Lintner (1965a,b) and Jan Mossin (1966) independently, building on the earlier work of Harry Markowitz on diversification and modern portfolio theory.

   a. Cox-Ingersoll-Ross model
   b. Hull-White model
   c. Capital asset pricing model
   d. Random walk hypothesis

Chapter 12. Return, Risk, and the Security Market Line

20. The term _____ has three unrelated technical definitions, and is also used in a variety of non-technical ways.

- In financial economics, it refers to any asset used to make money, as opposed to assets used for personal enjoyment or consumption. This is an important distinction because two people can disagree sharply about the value of personal assets, one person might think a sports car is more valuable than a pickup truck, another person might have the opposite taste. But if an asset is held for the purpose of making money, taste has nothing to do with it, only differences of opinion about how much money the asset will produce. With the further assumption that people agree on the probability distribution of future cash flows, it is possible to have an objective _____ pricing model. Even without the assumption of agreement, it is possible to set rational limits on _____ value.
- In governmental accounting, it is defined as any asset used in operations with an initial useful life extending beyond one reporting period. Generally, government managers have a 'stewardship' duty to maintain _____s under their control. See International Public Sector Accounting Standards for details.
- In US tax accounting, it is defined as any property other than a list of exceptions. The main exceptions are anything held for sale, and any real estate or depreciable property used in business. Almost everything you own and use for personal purposes, pleasure or investment is a _____. If something is a _____ for tax purposes, gains or losses on sale or disposition are capital gains or capital losses. For individuals, however, capital losses on property held for personal use are generally not deductible. See the IRS publication Tax Facts about Capital Gains and Losses for details.

A well-known financial accounting textbook advises that the term be avoided except in tax accounting because it is used in so many different senses, not all of them well-defined. For example it is often used as a synonym for fixed assets or for investments in securities.

A common non-technical usage occurs when people ask that employees or the environment or something else be treated as a _____.

a. Political risk
c. Solvency
b. Settlement date
d. Capital asset

21. A _____ is a portfolio consisting of a weighted sum of every asset in the market, with weights in the proportions that they exist in the market (with the necessary assumption that these assets are infinitely divisible.)

Neha Tyagi's critique (1977) states that this is only a theoretical concept, as to create a _____ for investment purposes in practice would necessarily include every single possible available asset, including real estate, precious metals, stamp collections, jewelry, and anything with any worth, as the theoretical market being referred to would be the world market. As a result, proxies for the market are used in practice by investors.

a. Market portfolio
c. Central Securities Depository
b. Market price
d. Delta neutral

22. In business and accounting, _____s are everything of value that is owned by a person or company. The balance sheet of a firm records the monetary value of the _____s owned by the firm. The two major _____ classes are tangible _____s and intangible _____s.

a. EBITDA
c. Income
b. Asset
d. Accounts payable

Chapter 12. Return, Risk, and the Security Market Line

23. In finance, _____ is the process of estimating the potential market value of a financial asset or liability. they can be done on assets (for example, investments in marketable securities such as stocks, options, business enterprises, or intangible assets such as patents and trademarks) or on liabilities (e.g., Bonds issued by a company.) _____s are required in many contexts including investment analysis, capital budgeting, merger and acquisition transactions, financial reporting, taxable events to determine the proper tax liability, and in litigation.
   - a. Valuation
   - b. Share
   - c. Margin
   - d. Procter ' Gamble

24. In probability theory and statistics, _____ is a measure of how much two variables change together (variance is a special case of the _____ when the two variables are identical.)

If two variables tend to vary together (that is, when one of them is above its expected value, then the other variable tends to be above its expected value too), then the _____ between the two variables will be positive. On the other hand, when one of them is above its expected value the other variable tends to be below its expected value, then the _____ between the two variables will be negative.

   - a. Probability distribution
   - b. Stratified sampling
   - c. Frequency distribution
   - d. Covariance

25. In business and finance, a _____ (also referred to as equity _____) of stock means a _____ of ownership in a corporation (company.) In the plural, stocks is often used as a synonym for _____s especially in the United States, but it is less commonly used that way outside of North America.

In the United Kingdom, South Africa, and Australia, stock can also refer to completely different financial instruments such as government bonds or, less commonly, to all kinds of marketable securities.

   - a. Procter ' Gamble
   - b. Bucket shop
   - c. Margin
   - d. Share

26. _____ mature in one year or less. Like zero-coupon bonds, they do not pay interest prior to maturity; instead they are sold at a discount of the par value to create a positive yield to maturity. Many regard _____ as the least risky investment available to U.S. investors.
   - a. Treasury securities
   - b. 4-4-5 Calendar
   - c. Treasury Inflation Protected Securities
   - d. Treasury bills

27. _____ is the provision of resources (such as granting a loan) by one party to another party where that second party does not reimburse the first party immediately, thereby generating a debt, and instead arranges either to repay or return those resources (or material(s) of equal value) at a later date. The first party is called a creditor, also known as a lender, while the second party is called a debtor, also known as a borrower.

Movements of financial capital are normally dependent on either _____ or equity transfers.

   - a. Comparable
   - b. Credit
   - c. Warrant
   - d. Clearing house

Chapter 12. Return, Risk, and the Security Market Line

28. A _____ assesses the credit worthiness of an individual, corporation, or even a country. _____s are calculated from financial history and current assets and liabilities. Typically, a _____ tells a lender or investor the probability of the subject being able to pay back a loan.
    a. Credit report monitoring
    b. Debenture
    c. Credit cycle
    d. Credit rating

29. The _____ is a financial ratio used to compare a company's book value to its current market price. Book value is an accounting term denoting the portion of the company held by the shareholders; in other words, the company's total tangible assets less its total liabilities. The calculation can be performed in two ways, but the result should be the same each way. In the first way, the company's market capitalization can be divided by the company's total book value from its balance sheet. The second way, using per-share values, is to divide the company's current share price by the book value per share (i.e. its book value divided by the number of outstanding shares).
    a. Whisper numbers
    b. Stop order
    c. Stock repurchase
    d. Price-to-book ratio

30. _____ is a measurement of corporate or economic size equal to the share price times the number of shares outstanding of a public company. As owning stock represents owning the company, including all its equity, capitalization could represent the public opinion of a company's net worth and is a determining factor in stock valuation. Likewise, the capitalization of stock markets or economic regions may be compared to other economic indicators.
    a. Synthetic CDO
    b. Just-in-time
    c. Proxy fight
    d. Market capitalization

Chapter 13. Performance Evaluation and Risk Management

1. Depending on the nature of the investment, the type of _____ will vary.

A common concern with any investment is that you may lose the money you invest - your capital. This risk is therefore often referred to as 'capital risk.'

If the assets you invest in are held in another currency there is a risk that currency movements alone may affect the value.

   a. Investment risk
   c. ABN Amro
   b. A Random Walk Down Wall Street
   d. AAB

2. _____ is the discipline of identifying, monitoring and limiting risks. In some cases the acceptable risk may be near zero. Risks can come from accidents, natural causes and disasters as well as deliberate attacks from an adversary.
   a. Risk management
   c. Penny stock
   b. 4-4-5 Calendar
   d. FIFO

3. The _____ is a measure of the excess return (or Risk Premium) per unit of risk in an investment asset or a trading strategy it is defined as:

$$S = \frac{R - R_f}{\sigma} = \frac{E[R - R_f]}{\sqrt{\text{var}[R - R_f]}},$$

where R is the asset return, R_f is the return on a benchmark asset, such as the risk free rate of return, $E[R - R_f]$ is the expected value of the excess of the asset return over the benchmark return, and σ is the standard deviation of the asset excess return.

Note, if R_f is a constant risk free return throughout the period,

$$\sqrt{\text{var}[R - R_f]} = \sqrt{\text{var}[R]}.$$

The _____ is used to characterize how well the return of an asset compensates the investor for the risk taken. When comparing two assets each with the expected return E[R] against the same benchmark with return R_f, the asset with the higher _____ gives more return for the same risk.

   a. Current ratio
   c. Receivables turnover ratio
   b. Sharpe ratio
   d. P/E ratio

4. The _____ is a measurement of the returns earned in excess of that which could have been earned on a riskless investment (i.e. Treasury Bill) (per each unit of market risk assumed).

Chapter 13. Performance Evaluation and Risk Management

The _____ relates excess return over the risk-free rate to the additional risk taken; however systematic risk instead of total risk is used. The higher the _____, the better the performance under analysis.

$$T_i = \frac{r_i - r_f}{\beta_i}$$

where

T_i > _____,

r_i > portfolio i's return,

r_f > risk free rate

β_i > portfolio i's beta

a. Revolving credit
c. Channel stuffing
b. Creditor
d. Treynor ratio

5. _____ is a risk-adjusted measure of the so-called active return on an investment. It is the return in excess of the compensation for the risk borne, and thus commonly used to assess active managers' performances. Often, the return of a benchmark is subtracted in order to consider relative performance, which yields Jensen's _____.

a. Option
c. Amortization
b. Annuity
d. Alpha

6. The _____ is the weighted-average most likely outcome in gambling, probability theory, economics or finance.

In gambling and probability theory, there is usually a discrete set of possible outcomes. In this case, _____ is a measure of the relative balance of win or loss weighted by their chances of occurring.

a. A Random Walk Down Wall Street
c. Expected return
b. ABN Amro
d. AAB

7. A _____ is a portfolio consisting of a weighted sum of every asset in the market, with weights in the proportions that they exist in the market (with the necessary assumption that these assets are infinitely divisible.)

Neha Tyagi's critique (1977) states that this is only a theoretical concept, as to create a _____ for investment purposes in practice would necessarily include every single possible available asset, including real estate, precious metals, stamp collections, jewelry, and anything with any worth, as the theoretical market being referred to would be the world market. As a result, proxies for the market are used in practice by investors.

Chapter 13. Performance Evaluation and Risk Management

a. Market portfolio
c. Central Securities Depository
b. Market price
d. Delta neutral

8. In business and finance, a _____ (also referred to as equity _____) of stock means a _____ of ownership in a corporation (company.) In the plural, stocks is often used as a synonym for _____s especially in the United States, but it is less commonly used that way outside of North America.

In the United Kingdom, South Africa, and Australia, stock can also refer to completely different financial instruments such as government bonds or, less commonly, to all kinds of marketable securities.

a. Procter ' Gamble
c. Share
b. Margin
d. Bucket shop

9. _____ proposes how rational investors will use diversification to optimize their portfolios, and how a risky asset should be priced. The basic concepts of the theory are Markowitz diversification, the efficient frontier, capital asset pricing model, the alpha and beta coefficients, the Capital Market Line and the Securities Market Line.

_____ models an asset's return as a random variable, and models a portfolio as a weighted combination of assets so that the return of a portfolio is the weighted combination of the assets' returns.

a. Market value
c. Modern Portfolio Theory
b. Payback period
d. Consumer basket

10. A _____ or equity fund is a fund that invests in Equities more commonly known as stocks. Such funds are typically held either in stock or cash, as opposed to Bonds, notes, or other securities. This may be a mutual fund or exchange-traded fund.

a. Money market funds
c. Mutual fund fees and expenses
b. Closed-end fund
d. Stock Fund

11. Behavioral economics and _____ are closely related fields that have evolved to be a separate branch of economic and financial analysis which applies scientific research on human and social, cognitive and emotional factors to better understand economic decisions by, say, consumers, borrowers, investors, and how they affect market prices, returns and the allocation of resources.

The field is primarily concerned with the bounds of rationality (selfishness, self-control) of economic agents. Behavioral models typically integrate insights from psychology with neo-classical economic theory.

a. Market structure
c. Medium of exchange
b. Behavioral finance
d. Recession

12. A _____ is a professionally managed type of collective investment scheme that pools money from many investors and invests it in stocks, bonds, short-term money market instruments, and/or other securities. The _____ will have a fund manager that trades the pooled money on a regular basis. Currently, the worldwide value of all _____s totals more than $26 trillion.

Since 1940, there have been three basic types of investment companies in the United States: open-end funds, also known in the US as _____s; unit investment trusts (UITs); and closed-end funds.

   a. Mutual fund
   c. Trust company
   b. Net asset value
   d. Financial intermediary

13. In business and accounting, _____s are everything of value that is owned by a person or company. The balance sheet of a firm records the monetary value of the _____s owned by the firm. The two major _____ classes are tangible _____s and intangible _____s.
   a. Accounts payable
   c. Income
   b. EBITDA
   d. Asset

14. _____ is a term used to refer to how an investor distributes his or her investments among various classes of investment vehicles (e.g., stocks and bonds.)

A large part of financial planning is finding an _____ that is appropriate for a given person in terms of their appetite for and ability to shoulder risk. This can depend on various factors; see investor profile.

   a. Investment performance
   c. Alternative investment
   b. Investing online
   d. Asset allocation

15. In finance, a _____ is a debt security, in which the authorized issuer owes the holders a debt and, depending on the terms of the _____, is obliged to pay interest (the coupon) and/or to repay the principal at a later date, termed maturity.

Thus a _____ is a loan: the issuer is the borrower, the _____ holder is the lender, and the coupon is the interest. _____s provide the borrower with external funds to finance long-term investments, or, in the case of government _____s, to finance current expenditure.

   a. Puttable bond
   c. Convertible bond
   b. Bond
   d. Catastrophe bonds

16. A _____ is a collective investment scheme that invests in bonds and other debt securities. _____s yield monthly dividends that include interest payments on the fund's underlying securities plus any capital appreciation in the prices of the portfolio's bonds. _____s tend to pay higher dividends than CDs and money market accounts, and they generally pay out dividends more frequently and regularly than individual bonds.
   a. Private activity bond
   c. Gilts
   b. Premium bond
   d. Bond fund

17. A _____, securities exchange or (in Europe) bourse is a corporation or mutual organization which provides 'trading' facilities for stock brokers and traders, to trade stocks and other securities. _____s also provide facilities for the issue and redemption of securities as well as other financial instruments and capital events including the payment of income and dividends. The securities traded on a _____ include: shares issued by companies, unit trusts and other pooled investment products and bonds.

a. 7-Eleven	b. 529 plan
c. 4-4-5 Calendar	d. Stock exchange

18. In finance, a _____ is a position established in one market in an attempt to offset exposure to the price risk of an equal but opposite obligation or position in another market -- usually, but not always, in the context of one's commercial activity. Hedging is a strategy designed to minimize exposure to such business risks as a sharp contraction in demand for one's inventory, while still allowing the business to profit from producing and maintaining that inventory. A typical hedger might be a farmer with 2000 acres of unharvested wheat in the ground, who would rather tend his crop without the distraction of uncertain prices.

a. 7-Eleven	b. 529 plan
c. Hedge	d. 4-4-5 Calendar

19. A _____ is a private investment fund open to a limited range of investors that is permitted by regulators to undertake a wider range of activities than other investment funds and also pays a performance fee to its investment manager. Each fund will have its own strategy which determines the type of investments and the methods of investment it undertakes. _____s as a class invest in a broad range of investments extending over shares, debt, commodities and beyond.

a. Hedge fund	b. 7-Eleven
c. 4-4-5 Calendar	d. 529 plan

20. In economic models, the _____ time frame assumes no fixed factors of production. Firms can enter or leave the marketplace, and the cost (and availability) of land, labor, raw materials, and capital goods can be assumed to vary. In contrast, in the short-run time frame, certain factors are assumed to be fixed, because there is not sufficient time for them to change.

a. Long-run	b. Short-run
c. 529 plan	d. 4-4-5 Calendar

21. In financial mathematics and financial risk management, _____ is a widely used measure of the risk of loss on a specific portfolio of financial assets. For a given portfolio, probability and time horizon, VaR is defined as a threshold value such that the probability that the mark-to-market loss on the portfolio over the given time horizon exceeds this value (assuming normal markets and no trading) is the given probability level.

For example, if a portfolio of stocks has a one-day 5% VaR of $1 million, there is a 5% probability that the portfolio will fall in value by more than $1 million over a one day period, assuming markets are normal and there is no trading.

a. Discount factor	b. Risk aversion
c. Risk modeling	d. Value at risk

Chapter 13. Performance Evaluation and Risk Management

22. An _____ is a document a company presents at an annual general meeting for approval by its shareholders, or a charitable organization presents its trustees. The report is made up of reports, which may include the following:

- Chairman's report
- CEO's report
- Auditor's report on corporate governance
- Mission statement
- Corporate governance statement of compliance
- Statement of directors' responsibilities
- Invitation to the company's AGM

as well as financial statements including:

- Auditor's report on the financial statements
- Balance sheet
- Statement of retained earnings
- Income statement
- Cash flow statement
- Notes to the financial statements
- Accounting policies

Other information deemed relevant to stakeholders may be included, such as a report on operations for manufacturing firms. In the case of larger companies, it is usually a sleek, colorful, high gloss publication.

The details provided in the report are of use to investors to understand the company's financial position and future direction.

   a. Amortization schedule   b. Annual report
   c. Outstanding balance   d. Accrued liabilities

23. The _____ is an important family of continuous probability distributions, applicable in many fields. Each member of the family may be defined by two parameters, location and scale: the mean and variance respectively. The standard _____ is the _____ with a mean of zero and a variance of one
   a. Probability distribution   b. Correlation
   c. Random variables   d. Normal distribution

24. _____ is a step in a risk management process. _____ is the determination of quantitative or qualitative value of risk related to a concrete situation and a recognized threat (also called hazard.) Quantitative _____ requires calculations of two components of risk: R, the magnitude of the potential loss L, and the probability p that the loss will occur.
   a. 529 plan   b. 7-Eleven
   c. 4-4-5 Calendar   d. Risk assessment

25. In probability theory and statistics, the _____ of a random variable, probability distribution averaging the squared distance of its possible values from the expected value (mean.) Whereas the mean is a way to describe the location of a distribution, the _____ is a way to capture its scale or degree of being spread out. The unit of _____ is the square of the unit of the original variable.

Chapter 13. Performance Evaluation and Risk Management   119

a. Harmonic mean
b. Monte Carlo methods
c. Semivariance
d. Variance

26. In probability and statistics, the _____ of a collection of numbers is a measure of the dispersion of the numbers from their expected (mean) value. It can apply to a probability distribution, a random variable, a population or a data set. The _____ is usually denoted with the letter σ (lowercase sigma.)

a. Kurtosis
b. Mean
c. Sample size
d. Standard deviation

27. _____ is a mathematical science pertaining to the collection, analysis, interpretation or explanation, and presentation of data. It also provides tools for prediction and forecasting based on data. It is applicable to a wide variety of academic disciplines, from the natural and social sciences to the humanities, government and business.

a. Sample size
b. Statistics
c. Mean
d. Covariance

Chapter 14. Futures Contracts

1. In finance, a _____ is a debt security, in which the authorized issuer owes the holders a debt and, depending on the terms of the _____, is obliged to pay interest (the coupon) and/or to repay the principal at a later date, termed maturity.

Thus a _____ is a loan: the issuer is the borrower, the _____ holder is the lender, and the coupon is the interest. _____s provide the borrower with external funds to finance long-term investments, or, in the case of government _____s, to finance current expenditure.

   a. Convertible bond
   c. Puttable bond

   b. Bond
   d. Catastrophe bonds

2. The _____ is an American financial and commodity derivative exchange based in Chicago. The _____ was founded in 1898 as the Chicago Butter and Egg Board. Originally, the exchange was a non-profit organization.
   a. Gamelan Council
   c. Financial Crimes Enforcement Network

   b. Chicago Mercantile Exchange
   d. Public Company Accounting Oversight Board

3. A _____ is something for which there is demand, but which is supplied without qualitative differentiation across a market. It is a product that is the same no matter who produces it, such as petroleum, notebook paper, or milk. In other words, copper is copper.
   a. 529 plan
   c. 4-4-5 Calendar

   b. 7-Eleven
   d. Commodity

4. A _____ is a financial contract whose value is derived from the value of something else (known as the underlying.) The underlying on which a _____ is based can be an asset, weather conditions bonds or other forms of credit.
   a. 7-Eleven
   c. Derivative

   b. 529 plan
   d. 4-4-5 Calendar

5. A _____ is a futures contract on a short term interest rate (STIR.) Contracts vary, but are often defined on an interest rate index such as 3-month sterling or US dollar LIBOR.

They are traded across a wide range of currencies, including the G12 country currencies and many others.

   a. Dual currency deposit
   c. Real estate derivatives

   b. Financial future
   d. Notional amount

6. A _____ is an agreement between two parties to buy or sell an asset at a specified point of time in the future. The price of the underlying instrument, in whatever form, is paid before control of the instrument changes. This is one of the many forms of buy/sell orders where the time of trade is not the time where the securities themselves are exchanged.
   a. Derivatives markets
   c. Loan Credit Default Swap Index

   b. Forward contract
   d. Constant maturity credit default swap

7. In finance, a _____ is a standardized contract, to buy or sell a specified commodity of standardized quality at a certain date in the future, at a market determined price (the futures price.)

The price is determined by the instantaneous equilibrium between the forces of supply and demand among competing buy and sell orders on the exchange at the time of the purchase or sale of the contract.

Chapter 14. Futures Contracts

In many cases, the items may be such non-traditional 'commodities' as foreign currencies, commercial or government paper [e.g., bonds], or 'baskets' of corporate equity ['stock indices'] or other financial instruments.

a. Heston model
c. Financial future
b. Repurchase agreement
d. Futures contract

8. A _____ is a central financial exchange where people can trade standardized futures contracts; that is, a contract to buy specific quantities of a commodity or financial instrument at a specified price with delivery set at a specified time in the future.

Though the origins of futures trading can supposedly be traced to Ancient Greek or Phoenician times, the first modern organized _____ began in 1710 at the Dojima Rice Exchange in Osaka, Japan.

The United States followed in the early 1800s.

a. 529 plan
c. 4-4-5 Calendar
b. 7-Eleven
d. Futures Exchange

9. _____ is a fee paid on borrowed assets. It is the price paid for the use of borrowed money, or, money earned by deposited funds. Assets that are sometimes lent with _____ include money, shares, consumer goods through hire purchase, major assets such as aircraft, and even entire factories in finance lease arrangements.

a. AAB
c. Interest
b. Insolvency
d. A Random Walk Down Wall Street

10. An _____ is the price a borrower pays for the use of money they do not own, and the return a lender receives for deferring the use of funds, by lending it to the borrower. _____s are normally expressed as a percentage rate over the period of one year.

_____s targets are also a vital tool of monetary policy and are used to control variables like investment, inflation, and unemployment.

a. ABN Amro
c. A Random Walk Down Wall Street
b. Interest rate
d. AAB

11. An _____ is a futures contract with an interest-bearing instrument as the underlying asset.

Examples include Treasury-bill futures, Treasury-bond futures and Eurodollar futures.

The global market for exchange-traded _____s is notionally valued by the Bank for International Settlements at $5,794,200 million in 2005.

a. Interest rate derivative
c. Interest rate future
b. Open interest
d. Equity swap

Chapter 14. Futures Contracts

12. The _____ , largely the creation of Leo Melamed, is part of the Chicago Mercantile Exchange (CME), the largest futures exchange in the United States and the second largest in the world after Eurex, for the trading of futures contracts and options on futures. The _____ was started on May 16, 1972. Two of the more prevalent contracts traded are currency futures and interest rate futures.
    a. AAB
    b. ABN Amro
    c. A Random Walk Down Wall Street
    d. International Monetary Market

13. A _____ is a method of measuring a section of the stock market. Many indices are cited by news or financial services firms and are used to benchmark the performance of portfolios such as mutual funds.
    a. Stock market index
    b. Program trading
    c. Stop order
    d. Trading curb

14. A _____ is an exchange of promises between two or more parties to do an act which is enforceable in a court of law. It is where an unqualified offer meets a qualified acceptance and the parties reach Consensus ad Idem. The parties must have the necessary capacity to _____ and the _____ must not be either trifling, indeterminate, impossible or illegal.
    a. 4-4-5 Calendar
    b. 529 plan
    c. 7-Eleven
    d. Contract

15. An _____ is a contract written by a seller that conveys to the buyer the right -- but not the obligation -- to buy (in the case of a call _____) or to sell (in the case of a put _____) a particular asset, such as a piece of property such as, among others, a futures contract. In return for granting the _____, the seller collects a payment (the premium) from the buyer.

For example, buying a call _____ provides the right to buy a specified quantity of a security at a set strike price at some time on or before expiration, while buying a put _____ provides the right to sell.

    a. Annuity
    b. Amortization
    c. Option
    d. AT'T Mobility LLC

16. A _____ is a fungible, negotiable instrument representing financial value. They are broadly categorized into debt securities (such as banknotes, bonds and debentures), and equity securities; e.g., common stocks. The company or other entity issuing the _____ is called the issuer.
    a. Book entry
    b. Securities lending
    c. Security
    d. Tracking stock

17. The _____ was formed in 1881 as a cash market for grains. The exchange launched its first futures contract, hard red spring wheat two years later. Today, it is a nonprofit member organization, trading futures and options on hard red spring wheat, white wheat, durum wheat, cottonseed, and Twin Cities on- and off-peak electricity.
    a. 4-4-5 Calendar
    b. 529 plan
    c. 7-Eleven
    d. Minneapolis Grain Exchange

18. In finance, a _____ in a security, such as a stock or a bond means the holder of the position owns the security and will profit if the price of the security goes up.

Chapter 14. Futures Contracts

Similarly, a _____ in a futures contract or similar derivative, means the holder of the position will profit if the price of the underlying security goes up. Going long is the more conventional practice of investing and is contrasted with going short

- Short (finance)

a. Central Securities Depository
b. Forward market
c. Long position
d. Delta hedging

19. Days to Cover (DTC) is a numerical term that describes the relationship between the amount of shares in a given equity that have been short sold and the number of days of typical trading that it would require to 'cover' all _____ outstanding. For example, if there are ten million shares of XYZ Inc. that are currently short sold and the average daily volume of XYZ shares traded each day is one million, it would require ten days of trading for all _____ to be covered (10 million / 1 million.)

a. Stock or scrip dividends
b. Cash budget
c. Guaranteed investment contracts
d. Short positions

20. In finance, a _____ is a position established in one market in an attempt to offset exposure to the price risk of an equal but opposite obligation or position in another market -- usually, but not always, in the context of one's commercial activity. Hedging is a strategy designed to minimize exposure to such business risks as a sharp contraction in demand for one's inventory, while still allowing the business to profit from producing and maintaining that inventory. A typical hedger might be a farmer with 2000 acres of unharvested wheat in the ground, who would rather tend his crop without the distraction of uncertain prices.

a. 7-Eleven
b. 4-4-5 Calendar
c. 529 plan
d. Hedge

21. _____, in bookkeeping, refers to assets, liabilities, income, and expenses recorded on individual pages of the so called book of final entry or ledger. Changes in _____ value are made by chronologically posting debit (DR) and credit (CR) entries to its page. Examples of _____s are cash, _____s receivable, mortgages, loans, land and buildings, common stock, sales, services provided, wages, and payroll overhead.

a. Account
b. Alpha
c. Accretion
d. Option

22. The _____ requirement is the amount required to be collateralized in order to open a position. Thereafter, the amount required to be kept in collateral until the position is closed is the maintenance requirement. The maintenance requirement is the minimum amount to be collateralized in order to keep an open position.

a. Initial margin
b. Efficient-market hypothesis
c. Arbitrage
d. Issuer

23. The variation margin or _____ is not collateral, but a daily offsetting of profits and losses. Futures are marked-to-market every day, so the current price is compared to the previous day's price. The profit or loss on the day of a position is then paid to or debited from the holder by the futures exchange.

a. Total return swap
b. Delivery month
c. Maintenance margin
d. SPI 200 futures contract

24. In finance, a _____ is collateral that the holder of a position in securities, options, or futures contracts has to deposit to cover the credit risk of his counterparty (most often his broker.) This risk can arise if the holder has done any of the following:

- borrowed cash from the counterparty to buy securities or options,
- sold securities or options short, or
- entered into a futures contract.

The collateral can be in the form of cash or securities, and it is deposited in a _____ account. On U.S. futures exchanges, '_____' was formally called performance bond.

_____ buying is buying securities with cash borrowed from a broker, using other securities as collateral.

a. Credit
b. Procter ' Gamble
c. Share
d. Margin

25. The collateral can be in the form of cash or securities, and it is deposited in a _____. On U.S. futures exchanges, 'margin' was formally called performance bond.

Margin buying is buying securities with cash borrowed from a broker, using other securities as collateral.

a. Dollar roll
b. Forward contract
c. Risk-neutral measure
d. Margin account

26. The _____ is the amount required to be collateralized in order to open a position. Thereafter, the amount required to be kept in collateral until the position is closed is the maintenance requirement. The maintenance requirement is the minimum amount to be collateralized in order to keep an open position.

a. ABN Amro
b. A Random Walk Down Wall Street
c. Initial margin requirement
d. AAB

27. In financial accounting, a _____ or statement of financial position is a summary of a person's or organization's balances. Assets, liabilities and ownership equity are listed as of a specific date, such as the end of its financial year. A _____ is often described as a snapshot of a company's financial condition.

a. Statement of retained earnings
b. Financial statements
c. Statement on Auditing Standards No. 70: Service Organizations
d. Balance sheet

28. The _____ or cash market is a commodities or securities market in which goods are sold for cash and delivered immediately. Contracts bought and sold on these markets are immediately effective. _____s can operate wherever the infrastructure exists to conduct the transaction.

a. Non-deliverable forward
b. Spot market
c. Foreign exchange controls
d. Currency swap

Chapter 14. Futures Contracts

29. The _____ or spot rate of a commodity, a security or a currency is the price that is quoted for immediate (spot) settlement (payment and delivery.) Spot settlement is normally one or two business days from trade date. This is in contrast with the forward price established in a forward contract or futures contract, where contract terms (price) are set now, but delivery and payment will occur at a future date.
   a. Market price
   b. Cost of carry
   c. Spot price
   d. Central Securities Depository

30. In economics and finance, _____ is the practice of taking advantage of a price differential between two or more markets: striking a combination of matching deals that capitalize upon the imbalance, the profit being the difference between the market prices. When used by academics, an _____ is a transaction that involves no negative cash flow at any probabilistic or temporal state and a positive cash flow in at least one state; in simple terms, a risk-free profit.
   a. Arbitrage
   b. Issuer
   c. Efficient-market hypothesis
   d. Initial margin

31. _____ , in finance, is a general theory of asset pricing, that has become influential in the pricing of stocks.

   _____ holds that the expected return of a financial asset can be modeled as a linear function of various macro-economic factors or theoretical market indices, where sensitivity to changes in each factor is represented by a factor-specific beta coefficient. The model-derived rate of return will then be used to price the asset correctly - the asset price should equal the expected end of period price discounted at the rate implied by model.

   a. ABN Amro
   b. Arbitrage pricing theory
   c. AAB
   d. A Random Walk Down Wall Street

32. _____ is a form of corporation equity ownership represented in the securities. It is dangerous in comparison to preferred shares and some other investment options, in that in the event of bankruptcy, _____ investors receive their funds after preferred stockholders, bondholders, creditors, etc. On the other hand, common shares on average perform better than preferred shares or bonds over time.
   a. Stop-limit order
   b. Stock split
   c. Stock market bubble
   d. Common stock

33. _____ are futures contracts with the underlying asset being one particular stock, usually in batches of 100. When purchased, no transmission of share rights or dividends occurs. Being futures contracts they are traded on margin, thus offering leverage, and they are not subject to the short selling limitations that stocks are.
   a. Heston model
   b. Weather derivatives
   c. Single-stock futures
   d. Volatility swap

34. In business and accounting, _____ s are everything of value that is owned by a person or company. The balance sheet of a firm records the monetary value of the _____ s owned by the firm. The two major _____ classes are tangible _____ s and intangible _____ s.
   a. Income
   b. Asset
   c. Accounts payable
   d. EBITDA

35. _____ is a term used to refer to how an investor distributes his or her investments among various classes of investment vehicles (e.g., stocks and bonds.)

Chapter 14. Futures Contracts

A large part of financial planning is finding an _____ that is appropriate for a given person in terms of their appetite for and ability to shoulder risk. This can depend on various factors; see investor profile.

a. Alternative investment
b. Investment performance
c. Investing online
d. Asset allocation

36. In business and finance, a _____ (also referred to as equity _____) of stock means a _____ of ownership in a corporation (company.) In the plural, stocks is often used as a synonym for _____s especially in the United States, but it is less commonly used that way outside of North America.

In the United Kingdom, South Africa, and Australia, stock can also refer to completely different financial instruments such as government bonds or, less commonly, to all kinds of marketable securities.

a. Margin
b. Bucket shop
c. Procter ' Gamble
d. Share

37. A _____ is a payment made by a corporation to its shareholder members. When a corporation earns a profit or surplus, that money can be put to two uses: it can either be re-invested in the business (called retained earnings), or it can be paid to the shareholders as a _____. Many corporations retain a portion of their earnings and pay the remainder as a _____.

a. Special dividend
b. Dividend puzzle
c. Dividend yield
d. Dividend

38. The _____ is an American stock exchange. It is the largest electronic screen-based equity securities trading market in the United States. With approximately 3,200 companies, it has more trading volume per day than any other stock exchange in the world.
a. NASDAQ
b. 4-4-5 Calendar
c. 7-Eleven
d. 529 plan

39. _____ is casually defined as the use of computers in stock markets to engage in arbitrage and portfolio insurance strategies. However, the New York Stock Exchange (NYSE) defines the term as 'a wide range of portfolio trading strategies involving the purchase or sale of 15 or more stocks having a total market value of $1 million or more' without any direct reference to the use of computers. The word 'program' can be interpreted in its earlier, more general meaning of a defined and pre-arranged sequence of steps, rather than specifically a computer program.
a. Wash sale
b. Share price
c. Stop order
d. Program trading

40. _____ in finance is a risk management technique, related to hedging, that mixes a wide variety of investments within a portfolio. Because the fluctuations of a single security have less impact on a diverse portfolio, _____ minimizes the risk from any one investment.

A simple example of _____ is the following: On a particular island the entire economy consists of two companies: one that sells umbrellas and another that sells sunscreen.

Chapter 14. Futures Contracts

a. 7-Eleven
b. 529 plan
c. 4-4-5 Calendar
d. Diversification

41. _____ is the risk that the value of an investment will decrease due to moves in market factors. The five standard _____ factors are:

- Equity risk, the risk that stock prices will change.
- Interest rate risk, the risk that interest rates will change.
- Currency risk, the risk that foreign exchange rates will change.
- Commodity risk, the risk that commodity prices (e.g. grains, metals) will change.

As with other forms of risk, _____ may be measured in a number of ways. Traditionally, this is done using a Value at Risk methodology. Value at risk is well established as a risk management technique, but it contains a number of limiting assumptions that constrain its accuracy.

a. Tracking error
b. Transaction risk
c. Market risk
d. Currency risk

42. _____ is the last hour of the stock market trading session (3:00-4:00 P.M., New York Time) on the third Friday of every March, June, September, and December. Those days are the expiration of three kinds of securities:

- Stock index futures.
- Stock market index options.
- Stock options.

The simultaneous expirations generally increases the trading volume of options, futures and the underlying stocks, and occasionally increases volatility of prices of related securities.

With the introduction of

- Single stock futures expiring on the same days, triple witching has become quadruple witching

The term 'triple witching' is conventionally thought to originate from the three witches in Shakespeare's play Macbeth. While the terms 'double witching' and 'quadruple witching' are sometimes used too, it doesn't carry the same foreboding connotation as triple witching. The phrase is intended to connote the extra volatility leading up to the event resulting from the expiration dates of three financing instruments.

a. Repurchase agreement
b. STIRT
c. Quality spread differential
d. Triple witching hour

43. The _____, in terms of finance and investing, describes how the expected return of a stock or portfolio is correlated to the return of the financial market as a whole.

An asset with a beta of 0 means that its price is not at all correlated with the market; that asset is independent. A positive beta means that the asset generally follows the market.

a. Current yield
b. LIBOR market model
c. Perpetuity
d. Beta coefficient

44. A _____ is a private or public market for the trading of company stock and derivatives of company stock at an agreed price; these are securities listed on a stock exchange as well as those only traded privately.

The size of the world _____ is estimated at about $36.6 trillion US at the beginning of October 2008 . The world derivatives market has been estimated at about $480 trillion face or nominal value, 12 times the size of the entire world economy.

a. Andrew Tobias
b. Adolph Coors
c. Anton Gelonkin
d. Stock market

45. In finance, the _____ of a financial asset measures the sensitivity of the asset's price to interest rate movements, expressed as a number of years. The reason for expressing this sensitivity in years is that the time that will elapse until a cash flow is received allows more interest to accumulate. Therefore the price of an asset with long term cashflows has more interest rate sensitivity than an asset with cashflows in the near future.

a. Macaulay duration
b. Yield to maturity
c. 4-4-5 Calendar
d. Duration

46. _____ is the risk (variability in value) borne by an interest-bearing asset, such as a loan or a bond, due to variability of interest rates. In general, as rates rise, the price of a fixed rate bond will fall, and vice versa. _____ is commonly measured by the bond's duration.

a. Official bank rate
b. International Fisher effect
c. A Random Walk Down Wall Street
d. Interest rate risk

47. In financial accounting, the term _____ is most commonly used to describe any part of shareholders' equity, except for basic share capital. Sometimes, the term is used instead of the term provision; such a use, however, is inconsistent with the terminology suggested by International Accounting Standards Board. For more information about provisions, see provision (accounting.)

a. Treasury stock
b. FIFO and LIFO accounting
c. Closing entries
d. Reserve

48. _____ are government bonds issued by the United States Department of the Treasury through the Bureau of the Public Debt. They are the debt financing instruments of the U.S. Federal government, and they are often referred to simply as Treasuries or Treasurys. There are four types of marketable _____: Treasury bills, Treasury notes, Treasury bonds, and Treasury Inflation Protected Securities (TIPS.)

a. Treasury Inflation Protected Securities
b. Treasury Inflation-Protected Securities
c. 4-4-5 Calendar
d. Treasury securities

Chapter 15. Stock Options

1. An _____ is a contract written by a seller that conveys to the buyer the right -- but not the obligation -- to buy (in the case of a call _____) or to sell (in the case of a put _____) a particular asset, such as a piece of property such as, among others, a futures contract. In return for granting the _____, the seller collects a payment (the premium) from the buyer.

For example, buying a call _____ provides the right to buy a specified quantity of a security at a set strike price at some time on or before expiration, while buying a put _____ provides the right to sell.

   a. Annuity
   b. AT'T Mobility LLC
   c. Amortization
   d. Option

2. A _____ is a financial contract between two parties, the buyer and the seller of this type of option. Often it is simply labeled a 'call'. The buyer of the option has the right, but not the obligation to buy an agreed quantity of a particular commodity or financial instrument (the underlying instrument) from the seller of the option at a certain time (the expiration date) for a certain price (the strike price.)
   a. Bear spread
   b. Call option
   c. Bear call spread
   d. Bull spread

3. In banking and finance, _____ denotes all activities from the time a commitment is made for a transaction until it is settled. _____ is necessary because the speed of trades is much faster than the cycle time for completing the underlying transaction.

In its widest sense _____ involves the management of post-trading, pre-settlement credit exposures, to ensure that trades are settled in accordance with market rules, even if a buyer or seller should become insolvent prior to settlement.

   a. Procter ' Gamble
   b. Clearing
   c. Share
   d. Clearing house

4. The institution most often referenced by the word '_____' is a public or publicly traded _____, the shares of which are traded on a public stock exchange (e.g., the New York Stock Exchange or Nasdaq in the United States) where shares of stock of _____s are bought and sold by and to the general public. Most of the largest businesses in the world are publicly traded _____s, However, the majority of _____s are said to be closely held, privately held or close _____s, meaning that no ready market exists for the trading of shares.
   a. Depository Trust Company
   b. Protect
   c. Federal Home Loan Mortgage Corporation
   d. Corporation

5. A _____ is a financial contract whose value is derived from the value of something else (known as the underlying.) The underlying on which a _____ is based can be an asset, weather conditions bonds or other forms of credit.
   a. 7-Eleven
   b. 4-4-5 Calendar
   c. 529 plan
   d. Derivative

6. In options, the _____ is a key variable in a derivatives contract between two parties. Where the contract requires delivery of the underlying instrument, the trade will be at the _____, regardless of the spot price (market price) of the underlying instrument at that time.

Chapter 15. Stock Options

Definition - The fixed price at which the owner of an option can purchase, in the case of a call in the case of a put, the underlying security or commodity.

a. Moneyness
b. Strike price
c. Swaption
d. Naked put

7. A _____ is a financial contract between two parties, the seller (writer) and the buyer of the option. The put allows its buyer the right but not the obligation to sell a commodity or financial instrument (the underlying instrument) to the writer (seller) of the option at a certain time for a certain price (the strike price.) The writer (seller) has the obligation to purchase the underlying asset at that strike price, if the buyer exercises the option.

a. Debit spread
b. Bear call spread
c. Bear spread
d. Put option

8. A _____ is an exchange of promises between two or more parties to do an act which is enforceable in a court of law. It is where an unqualified offer meets a qualified acceptance and the parties reach Consensus ad Idem. The parties must have the necessary capacity to _____ and the _____ must not be either trifling, indeterminate, impossible or illegal.

a. 7-Eleven
b. 4-4-5 Calendar
c. Contract
d. 529 plan

9. A _____ is a fungible, negotiable instrument representing financial value. They are broadly categorized into debt securities (such as banknotes, bonds and debentures), and equity securities; e.g., common stocks. The company or other entity issuing the _____ is called the issuer.

a. Tracking stock
b. Securities lending
c. Book entry
d. Security

10. In finance, _____ is the process of estimating the potential market value of a financial asset or liability. they can be done on assets (for example, investments in marketable securities such as stocks, options, business enterprises, or intangible assets such as patents and trademarks) or on liabilities (e.g., Bonds issued by a company.) _____s are required in many contexts including investment analysis, capital budgeting, merger and acquisition transactions, financial reporting, taxable events to determine the proper tax liability, and in litigation.

a. Procter ' Gamble
b. Margin
c. Valuation
d. Share

11. The _____ is an American stock exchange. It is the largest electronic screen-based equity securities trading market in the United States. With approximately 3,200 companies, it has more trading volume per day than any other stock exchange in the world.

a. 529 plan
b. 7-Eleven
c. 4-4-5 Calendar
d. NASDAQ

12. A _____, securities exchange or (in Europe) bourse is a corporation or mutual organization which provides 'trading' facilities for stock brokers and traders, to trade stocks and other securities. _____s also provide facilities for the issue and redemption of securities as well as other financial instruments and capital events including the payment of income and dividends. The securities traded on a _____ include: shares issued by companies, unit trusts and other pooled investment products and bonds.

Chapter 15. Stock Options

a. 529 plan
b. 4-4-5 Calendar
c. 7-Eleven
d. Stock Exchange

13. In finance, the term _____ describes the amount in cash that returns to the owners of a security. Normally it does not include the price variations, at the difference of the total return. _____ applies to various stated rates of return on stocks (common and preferred, and convertible), fixed income instruments (bonds, notes, bills, strips, zero coupon), and some other investment type insurance products (e.g. annuities.)

a. Macaulay duration
b. Yield to maturity
c. 4-4-5 Calendar
d. Yield

14. In finance, a _____ is a debt security, in which the authorized issuer owes the holders a debt and, depending on the terms of the _____, is obliged to pay interest (the coupon) and/or to repay the principal at a later date, termed maturity.

Thus a _____ is a loan: the issuer is the borrower, the _____ holder is the lender, and the coupon is the interest. _____s provide the borrower with external funds to finance long-term investments, or, in the case of government _____s, to finance current expenditure.

a. Catastrophe bonds
b. Convertible bond
c. Bond
d. Puttable bond

15. _____ is a form of corporation equity ownership represented in the securities. It is dangerous in comparison to preferred shares and some other investment options, in that in the event of bankruptcy, _____ investors receive their funds after preferred stockholders, bondholders, creditors, etc. On the other hand, common shares on average perform better than preferred shares or bonds over time.

a. Stock split
b. Stock market bubble
c. Stop-limit order
d. Common stock

16. _____, is when a company issues common stock or shares to the public for the first time. They are often issued by smaller, younger companies seeking capital to expand, but can also be done by large privately-owned companies looking to become publicly traded.

In an _____ the issuer may obtain the assistance of an underwriting firm, which helps it determine what type of security to issue (common or preferred), best offering price and time to bring it to market.

a. Initial public offering
b. Insolvency
c. Interest
d. Asian Financial Crisis

17. In business and finance, a _____ (also referred to as equity _____) of stock means a _____ of ownership in a corporation (company.) In the plural, stocks is often used as a synonym for _____s especially in the United States, but it is less commonly used that way outside of North America.

In the United Kingdom, South Africa, and Australia, stock can also refer to completely different financial instruments such as government bonds or, less commonly, to all kinds of marketable securities.

a. Bucket shop
b. Procter ' Gamble
c. Share
d. Margin

18. An _____ option has no intrinsic value. A call option is _____ when the strike price is above the spot price of the underlying security. A put option is _____ when the strike price is below the spot price.
   a. ABN Amro
   b. AAB
   c. A Random Walk Down Wall Street
   d. Out-of-the-money

19. The _____ is the price the buyer of the options contract pays for the right to buy or sell a security at a specified price in the future.
   a. AAB
   b. ABN Amro
   c. A Random Walk Down Wall Street
   d. Option premium

20. _____ is a term used to describe any option trading strategy that involves selling options. An option writer sells options to potentially profit from the decline of extrinsic value on options, sometimes referred to as time value.

   _____ strategies include covered calls, naked calls and naked puts, bear call spreads, bull put spreads, ratio credit spreads, short strangles and short straddles.

   a. AAB
   b. ABN Amro
   c. Options writing
   d. A Random Walk Down Wall Street

21. _____ is the difference between price and the costs of bringing to market whatever it is that is accounted as an enterprise (whether by harvest, extraction, manufacture, or purchase) in terms of the component costs of delivered goods and/or services and any operating or other expenses.

   A key difficulty in measuring profit is in defining costs. Pure economic monetary profits can be zero or negative even in competitive equilibrium when accounted monetized costs exceed monetized price.

   a. Accounting profit
   b. A Random Walk Down Wall Street
   c. AAB
   d. Economic profit

22. A _____ is a transaction in which the seller of call options already owns the corresponding amount of the underlying instrument, such as shares of a stock or other securities. These owned shares provide the 'cover' as they can be handed over to the buyer of the options when he decides to exercise them, instead of having to buy the optioned shares at unfavorable market prices in the case of 'uncovered' or short call. Thus, the _____ limits the (potentially unlimited) loss that results from a short call when the price of the underlying stock moves above the strike price of the option.
   a. 4-4-5 Calendar
   b. 529 plan
   c. 7-Eleven
   d. Covered call

23. In finance, a _____ is an investment strategy involving the purchase or sale of particular option derivatives that allows the holder to profit based on how much the price of the underlying security moves, regardless of the direction of price movement. The purchase of particular option derivatives is known as a long _____, while the sale of the option derivatives is known as a short _____.

An option payoff diagram for a long _____ position

Chapter 15. Stock Options

A long _____ involves going long, i.e., purchasing, both a call option and a put option on some stock, interest rate, index or other underlying.

 a. Moneyness
 b. Bear call spread
 c. Put option
 d. Straddle

24. In economics and finance, _____ is the practice of taking advantage of a price differential between two or more markets: striking a combination of matching deals that capitalize upon the imbalance, the profit being the difference between the market prices. When used by academics, an _____ is a transaction that involves no negative cash flow at any probabilistic or temporal state and a positive cash flow in at least one state; in simple terms, a risk-free profit.
 a. Issuer
 b. Efficient-market hypothesis
 c. Initial margin
 d. Arbitrage

25. In finance, _____ refers to the value of a security which is intrinsic to or contained in the security itself. It is also frequently called fundamental value. It is ordinarily calculated by summing the future income generated by the asset, and discounting it to the present value.
 a. Intrinsic value
 b. Accretion
 c. Amortization
 d. Alpha

26. An _____ is a call option on the common stock of a company, issued as a form of non-cash compensation. Restrictions on the option (such as vesting and limited transferability) attempt to align the holder's interest with those of the business' shareholders. If the company's stock rises, holders of options experience a direct financial benefit.
 a. Employee stock option
 b. Operating ratio
 c. Underwriting contract
 d. Internal financing

27. In financial mathematics, _____ defines a relationship between the price of a call option and a put option--both with the identical strike price and expiry. To derive the _____ relationship, the assumption is that the options are not exercised before expiration day, which necessarily applies to European options. _____ can be derived in a manner that is largely model independent.
 a. Hull-White model
 b. Rendleman-Bartter model
 c. Cox-Ingersoll-Ross model
 d. Put-call parity

28. The _____ is one of several stock market indices, created by nineteenth-century Wall Street Journal editor and Dow Jones' Company co-founder Charles Dow. Dow compiled the index to gauge the performance of the industrial sector of the American stock market. It is the second-oldest U.S. market index, after the Dow Jones Transportation Average, which Dow also created.
 a. 529 plan
 b. 7-Eleven
 c. 4-4-5 Calendar
 d. Dow Jones Industrial Average

29. _____ is a heterodox theory on stock price movements that is used as the basis for technical analysis. The theory was derived from 255 Wall Street Journal editorials written by Charles H. Dow (1851-1902), journalist, founder and first editor of the Wall Street Journal and co-founder of Dow Jones and Company. Following Dow's death, William P. Hamilton, Robert Rhea and E. George Schaefer organized and collectively represented '_____,' based on Dow's editorials.

a. Money flow
b. Dow theory
c. Technical analysis
d. Point and figure

30. A _____ is a method of measuring a section of the stock market. Many indices are cited by news or financial services firms and are used to benchmark the performance of portfolios such as mutual funds.
   a. Program trading
   b. Stock market index
   c. Stop order
   d. Trading curb

31. In financial mathematics, the _____ of an option contract is the volatility implied by the market price of the option based on an option pricing model. In other words, it is the volatility that, given a particular pricing model, yields a theoretical value for the option equal to the current market price. Non-option financial instruments that have embedded optionality, such as an interest rate cap, can also have an _____.
   a. Interest rate future
   b. Equity derivative
   c. Implied volatility
   d. Interest rate derivative

32. _____ most frequently refers to the standard deviation of the continuously compounded returns of a financial instrument with a specific time horizon. It is often used to quantify the risk of the instrument over that time period. _____ is typically expressed in annualized terms, and it may either be an absolute number ($5) or a fraction of the mean (5%).
   a. Portfolio insurance
   b. Seasoned equity offering
   c. Currency swap
   d. Volatility

Chapter 16. Option Valuation

1. _____ mature in one year or less. Like zero-coupon bonds, they do not pay interest prior to maturity; instead they are sold at a discount of the par value to create a positive yield to maturity. Many regard _____ as the least risky investment available to U.S. investors.
   a. Treasury securities
   b. Treasury Inflation Protected Securities
   c. 4-4-5 Calendar
   d. Treasury bills

2. _____ are government bonds issued by the United States Department of the Treasury through the Bureau of the Public Debt. They are the debt financing instruments of the U.S. Federal government, and they are often referred to simply as Treasuries or Treasurys. There are four types of marketable _____: Treasury bills, Treasury notes, Treasury bonds, and Treasury Inflation Protected Securities (TIPS.)
   a. 4-4-5 Calendar
   b. Treasury securities
   c. Treasury Inflation Protected Securities
   d. Treasury Inflation-Protected Securities

3. A _____ is a government debt issued by the United States Department of the Treasury through the Bureau of the Public Debt. They are the debt financing instruments of the United States Federal government, and they are often referred to simply as Treasuries. There are four types of marketable treasury securities: Treasury bills, Treasury notes, Treasury bonds, and Treasury Inflation Protected Securities (TIPS.)
   a. International trade
   b. OTC Bulletin Board
   c. Insolvency
   d. United States Treasury security

4. In finance, a _____ is a debt security, in which the authorized issuer owes the holders a debt and, depending on the terms of the _____, is obliged to pay interest (the coupon) and/or to repay the principal at a later date, termed maturity.

Thus a _____ is a loan: the issuer is the borrower, the _____ holder is the lender, and the coupon is the interest. _____s provide the borrower with external funds to finance long-term investments, or, in the case of government _____s, to finance current expenditure.

   a. Puttable bond
   b. Convertible bond
   c. Catastrophe bonds
   d. Bond

5. An _____ is a contract written by a seller that conveys to the buyer the right -- but not the obligation -- to buy (in the case of a call _____) or to sell (in the case of a put _____) a particular asset, such as a piece of property such as, among others, a futures contract. In return for granting the _____, the seller collects a payment (the premium) from the buyer.

For example, buying a call _____ provides the right to buy a specified quantity of a security at a set strike price at some time on or before expiration, while buying a put _____ provides the right to sell.

   a. Option
   b. Annuity
   c. AT'T Mobility LLC
   d. Amortization

6. A _____ is a fungible, negotiable instrument representing financial value. They are broadly categorized into debt securities (such as banknotes, bonds and debentures), and equity securities; e.g., common stocks. The company or other entity issuing the _____ is called the issuer.

a. Securities lending b. Security
c. Book entry d. Tracking stock

7. A _____, securities exchange or (in Europe) bourse is a corporation or mutual organization which provides 'trading' facilities for stock brokers and traders, to trade stocks and other securities. _____s also provide facilities for the issue and redemption of securities as well as other financial instruments and capital events including the payment of income and dividends. The securities traded on a _____ include: shares issued by companies, unit trusts and other pooled investment products and bonds.
   a. Stock Exchange b. 7-Eleven
   c. 529 plan d. 4-4-5 Calendar

8. The _____ is the weighted-average most likely outcome in gambling, probability theory, economics or finance.

In gambling and probability theory, there is usually a discrete set of possible outcomes. In this case, _____ is a measure of the relative balance of win or loss weighted by their chances of occurring.

   a. ABN Amro b. A Random Walk Down Wall Street
   c. Expected return d. AAB

9. An _____ is a call option on the common stock of a company, issued as a form of non-cash compensation. Restrictions on the option (such as vesting and limited transferability) attempt to align the holder's interest with those of the business' shareholders. If the company's stock rises, holders of options experience a direct financial benefit.
   a. Employee stock option b. Underwriting contract
   c. Operating ratio d. Internal financing

10. In finance, _____ is the process of estimating the potential market value of a financial asset or liability. they can be done on assets (for example, investments in marketable securities such as stocks, options, business enterprises, or intangible assets such as patents and trademarks) or on liabilities (e.g., Bonds issued by a company.) _____s are required in many contexts including investment analysis, capital budgeting, merger and acquisition transactions, financial reporting, taxable events to determine the proper tax liability, and in litigation.
    a. Procter ' Gamble b. Margin
    c. Share d. Valuation

11. The role of the _____ is to issue accounting standards in the United Kingdom. It is recognised for that purpose under the Companies Act 1985. It took over the task of setting accounting standards from the Accounting Standards Committee (ASC) in 1990.
    a. AAB b. Accounting Standards Board
    c. ABN Amro d. A Random Walk Down Wall Street

12. _____ is the field of accountancy concerned with the preparation of financial statements for decision makers, such as stockholders, suppliers, banks, employees, government agencies, owners, and other stakeholders. The fundamental need for _____ is to reduce principal-agent problem by measuring and monitoring agents' performance and reporting the results to interested users.

_____ is used to prepare accounting information for people outside the organization or not involved in the day to day running of the company.

Chapter 16. Option Valuation

a. 529 plan
b. 4-4-5 Calendar
c. 7-Eleven
d. Financial Accounting

13. The _____ is a private, not-for-profit organization whose primary purpose is to develop generally accepted accounting principles (GAAP) within the United States in the public's interest. The Securities and Exchange Commission (SEC) designated the _____ as the organization responsible for setting accounting standards for public companies in the U.S. It was created in 1973, replacing the Accounting Principles Board and the Committee on Accounting Procedure of the American Institute of Certified Public Accountants. The _____'s mission is 'to establish and improve standards of financial accounting and reporting for the guidance and education of the public, including issuers, auditors, and users of financial information.'

The _____ is not a governmental body.

a. Financial Accounting Standards Board
b. KPMG
c. Federal Deposit Insurance Corporation
d. World Congress of Accountants

14. A _____ is the price of a single share of a no. of saleable stocks of the company. Once the stock is purchased, the owner becomes a shareholder of the company that issued the share.
a. Stock split
b. Share price
c. Whisper numbers
d. Trading curb

15. In options, the _____ is a key variable in a derivatives contract between two parties. Where the contract requires delivery of the underlying instrument, the trade will be at the _____, regardless of the spot price (market price) of the underlying instrument at that time.

Definition - The fixed price at which the owner of an option can purchase, in the case of a call in the case of a put, the underlying security or commodity.

a. Moneyness
b. Swaption
c. Strike price
d. Naked put

16. _____ most frequently refers to the standard deviation of the continuously compounded returns of a financial instrument with a specific time horizon. It is often used to quantify the risk of the instrument over that time period. _____ is typically expressed in annualized terms, and it may either be an absolute number ($5) or a fraction of the mean (5%).
a. Currency swap
b. Seasoned equity offering
c. Volatility
d. Portfolio insurance

17. _____ is a fee paid on borrowed assets. It is the price paid for the use of borrowed money , or, money earned by deposited funds . Assets that are sometimes lent with _____ include money, shares, consumer goods through hire purchase, major assets such as aircraft, and even entire factories in finance lease arrangements.
a. A Random Walk Down Wall Street
b. AAB
c. Insolvency
d. Interest

18. An _____ is the price a borrower pays for the use of money they do not own, and the return a lender receives for deferring the use of funds, by lending it to the borrower. _____s are normally expressed as a percentage rate over the period of one year.

_____s targets are also a vital tool of monetary policy and are used to control variables like investment, inflation, and unemployment.

a. A Random Walk Down Wall Street
b. AAB
c. Interest rate
d. ABN Amro

19. A _____ is a financial contract between two parties, the buyer and the seller of this type of option. Often it is simply labeled a 'call'. The buyer of the option has the right, but not the obligation to buy an agreed quantity of a particular commodity or financial instrument (the underlying instrument) from the seller of the option at a certain time (the expiration date) for a certain price (the strike price.)

a. Call option
b. Bull spread
c. Bear spread
d. Bear call spread

20. A _____ is a payment made by a corporation to its shareholder members. When a corporation earns a profit or surplus, that money can be put to two uses: it can either be re-invested in the business (called retained earnings), or it can be paid to the shareholders as a _____. Many corporations retain a portion of their earnings and pay the remainder as a _____.

a. Special dividend
b. Dividend
c. Dividend puzzle
d. Dividend yield

21. The _____ on a company stock is the company's annual dividend payments divided by its market cap, or the dividend per share divided by the price per share. It is often expressed as a percentage.

Dividend payments on preferred shares are stipulated by the prospectus.

a. Dividend yield
b. Dividend reinvestment plan
c. Special dividend
d. Dividend imputation

22. A _____ is a financial contract between two parties, the seller (writer) and the buyer of the option. The put allows its buyer the right but not the obligation to sell a commodity or financial instrument (the underlying instrument) to the writer (seller) of the option at a certain time for a certain price (the strike price.) The writer (seller) has the obligation to purchase the underlying asset at that strike price, if the buyer exercises the option.

a. Put option
b. Bear spread
c. Bear call spread
d. Debit spread

23. In finance, the term _____ describes the amount in cash that returns to the owners of a security. Normally it does not include the price variations, at the difference of the total return. _____ applies to various stated rates of return on stocks (common and preferred, and convertible), fixed income instruments (bonds, notes, bills, strips, zero coupon), and some other investment type insurance products (e.g. annuities).

a. 4-4-5 Calendar
b. Yield to maturity
c. Macaulay duration
d. Yield

Chapter 16. Option Valuation

24. In financial mathematics, the _____ of an option contract is the volatility implied by the market price of the option based on an option pricing model. In other words, it is the volatility that, given a particular pricing model, yields a theoretical value for the option equal to the current market price. Non-option financial instruments that have embedded optionality, such as an interest rate cap, can also have an _____.
    - a. Equity derivative
    - b. Interest rate future
    - c. Interest rate derivative
    - d. Implied volatility

25. In probability and statistics, the _____ of a collection of numbers is a measure of the dispersion of the numbers from their expected (mean) value. It can apply to a probability distribution, a random variable, a population or a data set. The _____ is usually denoted with the letter σ (lowercase sigma.)
    - a. Mean
    - b. Kurtosis
    - c. Sample size
    - d. Standard deviation

26. A _____ is a private or public market for the trading of company stock and derivatives of company stock at an agreed price; these are securities listed on a stock exchange as well as those only traded privately.

    The size of the world _____ is estimated at about $36.6 trillion US at the beginning of October 2008 . The world derivatives market has been estimated at about $480 trillion face or nominal value, 12 times the size of the entire world economy.
    - a. Anton Gelonkin
    - b. Adolph Coors
    - c. Stock market
    - d. Andrew Tobias

27. A _____ is a method of measuring a section of the stock market. Many indices are cited by news or financial services firms and are used to benchmark the performance of portfolios such as mutual funds.
    - a. Trading curb
    - b. Stop order
    - c. Program trading
    - d. Stock market index

28. _____ is a form of corporation equity ownership represented in the securities. It is dangerous in comparison to preferred shares and some other investment options, in that in the event of bankruptcy, _____ investors receive their funds after preferred stockholders, bondholders, creditors, etc. On the other hand, common shares on average perform better than preferred shares or bonds over time.
    - a. Stop-limit order
    - b. Stock market bubble
    - c. Stock split
    - d. Common stock

29. In business and accounting, _____s are everything of value that is owned by a person or company. The balance sheet of a firm records the monetary value of the _____s owned by the firm. The two major _____ classes are tangible _____s and intangible _____s.
    - a. Accounts payable
    - b. Asset
    - c. EBITDA
    - d. Income

30. _____ is a term used to refer to how an investor distributes his or her investments among various classes of investment vehicles (e.g., stocks and bonds.)

    A large part of financial planning is finding an _____ that is appropriate for a given person in terms of their appetite for and ability to shoulder risk. This can depend on various factors; see investor profile.

a. Investing online
b. Investment performance
c. Asset allocation
d. Alternative investment

31. In business and finance, a _____ (also referred to as equity _____) of stock means a _____ of ownership in a corporation (company.) In the plural, stocks is often used as a synonym for _____s especially in the United States, but it is less commonly used that way outside of North America.

In the United Kingdom, South Africa, and Australia, stock can also refer to completely different financial instruments such as government bonds or, less commonly, to all kinds of marketable securities.

a. Procter ' Gamble
b. Bucket shop
c. Margin
d. Share

32. The _____, in terms of finance and investing, describes how the expected return of a stock or portfolio is correlated to the return of the financial market as a whole.

An asset with a beta of 0 means that its price is not at all correlated with the market; that asset is independent. A positive beta means that the asset generally follows the market.

a. LIBOR market model
b. Beta coefficient
c. Current yield
d. Perpetuity

33. An _____ or index tracker is a collective investment scheme (usually a mutual fund or exchange-traded fund) that aims to replicate the movements of an index of a specific financial market regardless of market conditions.

Tracking can be achieved by trying to hold all of the securities in the index, in the same proportions as the index. Other methods include statistically sampling the market and holding 'representative' securities.

a. Investment company
b. A Random Walk Down Wall Street
c. AAB
d. Index fund

Chapter 17. Projecting Cash Flow and Earnings

1. An _____ is a document a company presents at an annual general meeting for approval by its shareholders, or a charitable organization presents its trustees. The report is made up of reports, which may include the following:

- Chairman's report
- CEO's report
- Auditor's report on corporate governance
- Mission statement
- Corporate governance statement of compliance
- Statement of directors' responsibilities
- Invitation to the company's AGM

as well as financial statements including:

- Auditor's report on the financial statements
- Balance sheet
- Statement of retained earnings
- Income statement
- Cash flow statement
- Notes to the financial statements
- Accounting policies

Other information deemed relevant to stakeholders may be included, such as a report on operations for manufacturing firms. In the case of larger companies, it is usually a sleek, colorful, high gloss publication.

The details provided in the report are of use to investors to understand the company's financial position and future direction.

a. Amortization schedule
c. Annual report
b. Accrued liabilities
d. Outstanding balance

2. _____ are formal records of a business' financial activities.

_____ provide an overview of a business' financial condition in both short and long term. There are four basic _____:

1. **Balance sheet**: also referred to as statement of financial position or condition, reports on a company's assets, liabilities, and net equity as of a given point in time.
2. **Income statement**: also referred to as Profit and Loss statement (or a 'P'L'), reports on a company's income, expenses, and profits over a period of time.
3. **Statement of retained earnings**: explains the changes in a company's retained earnings over the reporting period.
4. **Statement of cash flows**: reports on a company's cash flow activities, particularly its operating, investing and financing activities.

a. Financial statements

b. Notes to the Financial Statements

c. Statement of retained earnings

d. Statement on Auditing Standards No. 70: Service Organizations

3. The U.S. Securities and Exchange Commission's (SEC's) Regulation Fair Disclosure, also commonly referred to as _____ was an SEC ruling implemented in October 2000 (.) It mandated that all publicly traded companies must disclose material information to all investors at the same time.

The regulation sought to stamp out selective disclosure, in which some investors (often large institutional investors) received market moving information before others (often smaller, individual investors.)

a. Revenue recognition

b. Commodity Pool Operator

c. Regulation FD

d. Regulation Fair Disclosure

4. In financial accounting, a _____ or statement of financial position is a summary of a person's or organization's balances. Assets, liabilities and ownership equity are listed as of a specific date, such as the end of its financial year. A _____ is often described as a snapshot of a company's financial condition.

a. Statement on Auditing Standards No. 70: Service Organizations

b. Statement of retained earnings

c. Balance sheet

d. Financial statements

5. A _____ is a fungible, negotiable instrument representing financial value. They are broadly categorized into debt securities (such as banknotes, bonds and debentures), and equity securities; e.g., common stocks. The company or other entity issuing the _____ is called the issuer.

a. Securities lending

b. Book entry

c. Security

d. Tracking stock

6. In business and accounting, _____s are everything of value that is owned by a person or company. The balance sheet of a firm records the monetary value of the _____s owned by the firm. The two major _____ classes are tangible _____s and intangible _____s.

a. EBITDA

b. Accounts payable

c. Income

d. Asset

7. _____ is the balance of the amounts of cash being received and paid by a business during a defined period of time, sometimes tied to a specific project. Measurement of _____ can be used

- to evaluate the state or performance of a business or project.
- to determine problems with liquidity. Being profitable does not necessarily mean being liquid. A company can fail because of a shortage of cash, even while profitable.
- to generate project rate of returns. The time of _____s into and out of projects are used as inputs to financial models such as internal rate of return, and net present value.
- to examine income or growth of a business when it is believed that accrual accounting concepts do not represent economic realities. Alternately, _____ can be used to 'validate' the net income generated by accrual accounting.

Chapter 17. Projecting Cash Flow and Earnings 143

_____ as a generic term may be used differently depending on context, and certain _____ definitions may be adapted by analysts and users for their own uses. Common terms include operating _____ and free _____.

_____s can be classified into:

1. Operational _____s: Cash received or expended as a result of the company's core business activities.
2. Investment _____s: Cash received or expended through capital expenditure, investments or acquisitions.
3. Financing _____s: Cash received or expended as a result of financial activities, such as interests and dividends.

All three together - the net _____ - are necessary to reconcile the beginning cash balance to the ending cash balance. Loan draw downs or equity injections, that is just shifting of capital but no expenditure as such, are not considered in the net _____.

a. Real option
b. Corporate finance
c. Shareholder value
d. Cash flow

8. In financial accounting, a _____ or statement of cash flows is a financial statement that shows a company's flow of cash. The money coming into the business is called cash inflow, and money going out from the business is called cash outflow. The statement shows how changes in balance sheet and income accounts affect cash and cash equivalents, and breaks the analysis down to operating, investing, and financing activities.

a. 529 plan
b. 7-Eleven
c. 4-4-5 Calendar
d. Cash flow statement

9. In accounting, a _____ is an asset on the balance sheet which is expected to be sold or otherwise used up in the near future, usually within one year, or one business cycle - whichever is longer. Typical _____s include cash, cash equivalents, accounts receivable, inventory, the portion of prepaid accounts which will be used within a year, and short-term investments.

On the balance sheet, assets will typically be classified into _____s and long-term assets.

a. Historical cost
b. Current asset
c. Write-off
d. Long-term liabilities

10. _____ plant, and equipment, is a term used in accountancy for assets and property which cannot easily be converted into cash. This can be compared with current assets such as cash or bank accounts, which are described as liquid assets. In most cases, only tangible assets are referred to as fixed.

a. Petty cash
b. Remittance advice
c. Percentage of Completion
d. Fixed asset

11. _____ is an accounting term used to reflect the portion of the book value of a business entity not directly attributable to its assets and liabilities; it normally arises only in case of an acquisition. It reflects the ability of the entity to make a higher profit than would be derived from selling the tangible assets. _____ is also known as an intangible asset.

    a. Net profit
    b. Consolidation
    c. Goodwill
    d. Cost of goods sold

12. _____, refers to consumption opportunity gained by an entity within a specified time frame, which is generally expressed in monetary terms. However, for households and individuals, '_____ is the sum of all the wages, salaries, profits, interests payments, rents and other forms of earnings received... in a given period of time.' For firms, _____ generally refers to net-profit: what remains of revenue after expenses have been subtracted.

    a. Income
    b. Accrual
    c. OIBDA
    d. Annual report

13. An _____ is a financial statement for companies that indicates how Revenue is transformed into net income The purpose of the _____ is to show managers and investors whether the company made or lost money during the period being reported.

The important thing to remember about an _____ is that it represents a period of time.

    a. ABN Amro
    b. AAB
    c. A Random Walk Down Wall Street
    d. Income statement

14. In accounting, _____ are considered liabilities of the business that are to be settled in cash within the fiscal year or the operating cycle, whichever period is longer.

For example accounts payable for goods, services or supplies that were purchased for use in the operation of the business and payable within a normal period of time would be _____.

Bonds, mortgages and loans that are payable over a term exceeding one year would be fixed liabilities.

    a. Current liabilities
    b. Gross sales
    c. Net income
    d. Closing entries

15. _____ are defined as identifiable non-monetary assets that cannot be seen, touched or physically measured, which are created through time and/or effort and that are identifiable as a separate asset. There are two primary forms of intangibles - legal intangibles (such as trade secrets (e.g., customer lists), copyrights, patents, trademarks, and goodwill) and competitive intangibles (such as knowledge activities (know-how, knowledge), collaboration activities, leverage activities, and structural activities.) Legal intangibles generate legal property rights defensible in a court of law.

    a. ABN Amro
    b. AAB
    c. A Random Walk Down Wall Street
    d. Intangible assets

16. In economic models, the _____ time frame assumes no fixed factors of production. Firms can enter or leave the marketplace, and the cost (and availability) of land, labor, raw materials, and capital goods can be assumed to vary. In contrast, in the short-run time frame, certain factors are assumed to be fixed, because there is not sufficient time for them to change.

Chapter 17. Projecting Cash Flow and Earnings

a. 4-4-5 Calendar
b. 529 plan
c. Long-run
d. Short-run

17. _____ is that which is owed; usually referencing assets owed, but the term can cover other obligations. In the case of assets, _____ is a means of using future purchasing power in the present before a summation has been earned. Some companies and corporations use _____ as a part of their overall corporate finance strategy.

a. Debt
b. Credit cycle
c. Partial Payment
d. Cross-collateralization

18. _____, _____ includes the direct costs attributable to the production of the goods sold by a company. This amount includes the materials cost used in creating the goods along with the direct labor costs used to produce the good. It excludes indirect expenses such as distribution costs and sales force costs.

a. Goodwill
b. Cost of goods sold
c. Net profit
d. Deferred financing costs

19. In economics, business, and accounting, a _____ is the value of money that has been used up to produce something, and hence is not available for use anymore. In business, the _____ may be one of acquisition, in which case the amount of money expended to acquire it is counted as _____. In this case, money is the input that is gone in order to acquire the thing.

a. Fixed costs
b. Cost
c. Marginal cost
d. Sliding scale fees

20. _____ is a term used in accounting, economics and finance to spread the cost of an asset over the span of several years.

In simple words we can say that _____ is the reduction in the value of an asset due to usage, passage of time, wear and tear, technological outdating or obsolescence, depletion or other such factors.

In accounting, _____ is a term used to describe any method of attributing the historical or purchase cost of an asset across its useful life, roughly corresponding to normal wear and tear.

a. Depreciation
b. Dottom line
c. Deferred financing costs
d. Matching principle

21. In accounting, _____ or sales profit is the difference between revenue and the cost of making a product or providing a service, before deducting overhead, payroll, taxation, and interest payments. Note that this is different than operating profit.

Net sales are calculated:

Net sales = Sales - Sales returns and allowances

_____ is found by deducting the cost of goods sold:

_____ = Net sales - Cost of goods sold

Chapter 17. Projecting Cash Flow and Earnings

_____ should not be confused with net income:

Net income = _____ - Total operating expenses

Cost of goods sold is calculated differently for merchandising business than for a manufacturer.

a. Cash flow
c. Gross income
b. Real option
d. Gross profit

22. In bookkeeping, accounting, and finance, _____ are operating revenues earned by a company when it sells its products. Revenue _____ are reported directly on the income statement as Sales or _____.

In financial ratios that use income statement sales values, 'sales' refers to _____, not gross sales.

a. Closing entries
c. Journal entry
b. Depletion
d. Net sales

23. An _____, operating expenditure, operational expense, operational expenditure or OPEX is an on-going cost for running a product, business, or system. Its counterpart, a capital expenditure (CAPEX), is the cost of developing or providing non-consumable parts for the product or system. For example, the purchase of a photocopier is the CAPEX, and the annual paper and toner cost is the OPEX.

a. ABN Amro
c. AAB
b. A Random Walk Down Wall Street
d. Operating expense

24. _____ is the difference between operating revenues and operating expenses, but it is also sometimes used as a synonym for EBIT and operating profit. This is true if the firm has no non-_____.

A professional investor contemplating a change to the capital structure of a firm (e.g., through a leveraged buyout) first evaluates a firm's fundamental earnings potential (reflected by Earnings Before Interest, Taxes, Depreciation and Amortization EBITDA and EBIT), and then determines the optimal use of debt vs. equity.

a. ABN Amro
c. AAB
b. A Random Walk Down Wall Street
d. Operating income

25. In accounting, _____ refers to the portion of net income which is retained by the corporation rather than distributed to its owners as dividends. Similarly, if the corporation makes a loss, then that loss is retained and called variously retained losses, accumulated losses or accumulated deficit. _____ and losses are cumulative from year to year with losses offsetting earnings.

a. Matching principle
c. Historical cost
b. Retained earnings
d. Generally Accepted Accounting Principles

26. _____ is the difference between price and the costs of bringing to market whatever it is that is accounted as an enterprise (whether by harvest, extraction, manufacture, or purchase) in terms of the component costs of delivered goods and/or services and any operating or other expenses.

Chapter 17. Projecting Cash Flow and Earnings

A key difficulty in measuring profit is in defining costs. Pure economic monetary profits can be zero or negative even in competitive equilibrium when accounted monetized costs exceed monetized price.

a. Economic profit
b. Accounting profit
c. AAB
d. A Random Walk Down Wall Street

27. A _____ is a payment made by a corporation to its shareholder members. When a corporation earns a profit or surplus, that money can be put to two uses: it can either be re-invested in the business (called retained earnings), or it can be paid to the shareholders as a _____. Many corporations retain a portion of their earnings and pay the remainder as a _____.

a. Dividend puzzle
b. Special dividend
c. Dividend yield
d. Dividend

28. _____ or financing is to provide capital (funds), which means money for a project, a person, a business or any other private or public institutions.

Those funds can be allocated for either short term or long term purposes. The health fund is a new way of _____ private healthcare centers.

a. Proxy fight
b. Product life cycle
c. Synthetic CDO
d. Funding

29. An _____ is a tax levied on the financial income of people, corporations, or other legal entities. Various _____ systems exist, with varying degrees of tax incidence. Income taxation can be progressive, proportional, or regressive.

a. ABN Amro
b. AAB
c. A Random Walk Down Wall Street
d. Income tax

30. _____ is a fee paid on borrowed assets. It is the price paid for the use of borrowed money , or, money earned by deposited funds . Assets that are sometimes lent with _____ include money, shares, consumer goods through hire purchase, major assets such as aircraft, and even entire factories in finance lease arrangements.

a. A Random Walk Down Wall Street
b. AAB
c. Insolvency
d. Interest

31. _____ relates to the cost of borrowing money. It is the price that a lender charges a borrower for the use of the lender's money. _____ is different from OPEX and CAPEX, for it relates to the capital structure of a company.

a. ABN Amro
b. A Random Walk Down Wall Street
c. Interest expense
d. AAB

32. _____ is equal to the income that a firm has after subtracting costs and expenses from the total revenue. _____ can be distributed among holders of common stock as a dividend or held by the firm as retained earnings. _____ is an accounting term; in some countries (such as the UK) profit is the usual term.

a. Historical cost
b. Furniture, Fixtures and Equipment
c. Net income
d. Write-off

33. In financial accounting, _____ , cash flow provided by operations or cash flow from operating activities, refers to the amount of cash a company generates from the revenues it brings in, excluding costs associated with long-term investment on capital items or investment in securities.

_____ = Cash generated from operations less taxation and interest paid, investment income received and less dividends paid gives rise to _____s per International Financial Reporting Standards.

To calculate cash generated from operations, one must calculate cash generated from customers and cash paid to suppliers.

a. Other Comprehensive Basis of Accounting
b. A Random Walk Down Wall Street
c. Appreciation
d. Operating cash flow

34. _____ is a form of corporation equity ownership represented in the securities. It is dangerous in comparison to preferred shares and some other investment options, in that in the event of bankruptcy, _____ investors receive their funds after preferred stockholders, bondholders, creditors, etc. On the other hand, common shares on average perform better than preferred shares or bonds over time.

a. Stock market bubble
b. Stock split
c. Stop-limit order
d. Common stock

35. In accounting, _____ or *Carrying value* is the value of an asset according to its balance sheet account balance. For assets, the value is based on the original cost of the asset less any depreciation, amortization or impairment costs made against the asset. A company's _____ is its total assets minus intangible assets and liabilities.

a. Retained earnings
b. Pro forma
c. Current liabilities
d. Book value

36. The term _____ has three unrelated technical definitions, and is also used in a variety of non-technical ways.

- In financial economics, it refers to any asset used to make money, as opposed to assets used for personal enjoyment or consumption. This is an important distinction because two people can disagree sharply about the value of personal assets, one person might think a sports car is more valuable than a pickup truck, another person might have the opposite taste. But if an asset is held for the purpose of making money, taste has nothing to do with it, only differences of opinion about how much money the asset will produce. With the further assumption that people agree on the probability distribution of future cash flows, it is possible to have an objective _____ pricing model. Even without the assumption of agreement, it is possible to set rational limits on _____ value.
- In governmental accounting, it is defined as any asset used in operations with an initial useful life extending beyond one reporting period. Generally, government managers have a 'stewardship' duty to maintain _____s under their control. See International Public Sector Accounting Standards for details.
- In US tax accounting, it is defined as any property other than a list of exceptions. The main exceptions are anything held for sale, and any real estate or depreciable property used in business. Almost everything you own and use for personal purposes, pleasure or investment is a _____. If something is a _____ for tax purposes, gains or losses on sale or disposition are capital gains or capital losses. For individuals, however, capital losses on property held for personal use are generally not deductible. See the IRS publication Tax Facts about Capital Gains and Losses for details.

Chapter 17. Projecting Cash Flow and Earnings

A well-known financial accounting textbook advises that the term be avoided except in tax accounting because it is used in so many different senses, not all of them well-defined. For example it is often used as a synonym for fixed assets or for investments in securities.

A common non-technical usage occurs when people ask that employees or the environment or something else be treated as a _____.

- a. Political risk
- b. Settlement date
- c. Solvency
- d. Capital asset

37. In finance, the _____ is used to determine a theoretically appropriate required rate of return of an asset, if that asset is to be added to an already well-diversified portfolio, given that asset's non-diversifiable risk. The model takes into account the asset's sensitivity to non-diversifiable risk (also known as systemic risk or market risk), often represented by the quantity beta (β) in the financial industry, as well as the expected return of the market and the expected return of a theoretical risk-free asset.

The model was introduced by Jack Treynor (1961, 1962), William Sharpe (1964), John Lintner (1965a,b) and Jan Mossin (1966) independently, building on the earlier work of Harry Markowitz on diversification and modern portfolio theory.

- a. Cox-Ingersoll-Ross model
- b. Random walk hypothesis
- c. Capital asset pricing model
- d. Hull-White model

38. _____ are the earnings returned on the initial investment amount.

In the US, the Financial Accounting Standards Board (FASB) requires companies' income statements to report _____ for each of the major categories of the income statement: continuing operations, discontinued operations, extraordinary items, and net income.

The _____ formula does not include preferred dividends for categories outside of continued operations and net income.

- a. Inventory turnover
- b. Assets turnover
- c. Average accounting return
- d. Earnings per share

39. _____, Gross profit margin or Gross Profit Rate can be defined as the amount of contribution to the business enterprise, after paying for direct-fixed and direct-variable unit costs, required to cover overheads (fixed commitments) and provide a buffer for unknown items. It expresses the relationship between gross profit and sales revenue.

It can be expressed in absolute terms:

Gross Profit = Revenue >− Cost of Goods Sold

or as the ratio of gross profit to sales revenue, usually in the form of a percentage:

Chapter 17. Projecting Cash Flow and Earnings

_____ Percentage = (Revenue-Cost of Goods Sold)/Revenue

Cost of goods sold includes variable costs and fixed costs directly linked to the product, such as material and labor. It does not include indirect fixed costs like office expenses, rent, administrative costs, etc.

- a. Net profit margin
- b. Profit margin
- c. 4-4-5 Calendar
- d. Gross margin

40. The _____ of a stock is a measure of the price paid for a share relative to the annual income or profit earned by the firm per share. It is a financial ratio used for valuation: a higher _____ means that investors are paying more for each unit of income, so the stock is more expensive compared to one with lower _____.

The _____ has units of years, which can be interpreted as 'number of years of earnings to pay back purchase price'.

- a. Sustainable growth rate
- b. Quick ratio
- c. Return of capital
- d. P/E ratio

41. _____ measures the rate of return on the ownership interest (shareholders' equity) of the common stock owners. _____ is viewed as one of the most important financial ratios. It measures a firm's efficiency at generating profits from every dollar of shareholders' equity (also known as net assets or assets minus liabilities.)
- a. Diluted Earnings Per Share
- b. Return of capital
- c. Return on sales
- d. Return on equity

42. The _____ percentage shows how profitable a company's assets are in generating revenue.

_____ can be computed as:

$$ROA = \frac{\text{Net Income}}{\text{Total Assets}}$$

This number tells you 'what the company can do with what it's got', i.e. how many dollars of earnings they derive from each dollar of assets they control. It's a useful number for comparing competing companies in the same industry.

- a. Receivables turnover ratio
- b. P/E ratio
- c. Return on assets
- d. Return on sales

43. In finance, _____ is the process of estimating the potential market value of a financial asset or liability. they can be done on assets (for example, investments in marketable securities such as stocks, options, business enterprises, or intangible assets such as patents and trademarks) or on liabilities (e.g., Bonds issued by a company.) _____s are required in many contexts including investment analysis, capital budgeting, merger and acquisition transactions, financial reporting, taxable events to determine the proper tax liability, and in litigation.

Chapter 17. Projecting Cash Flow and Earnings

a. Procter ' Gamble
b. Valuation
c. Share
d. Margin

44. In finance, a _____ is collateral that the holder of a position in securities, options, or futures contracts has to deposit to cover the credit risk of his counterparty (most often his broker.) This risk can arise if the holder has done any of the following:

- borrowed cash from the counterparty to buy securities or options,
- sold securities or options short, or
- entered into a futures contract.

The collateral can be in the form of cash or securities, and it is deposited in a _____ account. On U.S. futures exchanges, '_____' was formally called performance bond.

_____ buying is buying securities with cash borrowed from a broker, using other securities as collateral.

a. Credit
b. Share
c. Procter ' Gamble
d. Margin

45. In business and finance, a _____ (also referred to as equity _____) of stock means a _____ of ownership in a corporation (company.) In the plural, stocks is often used as a synonym for _____s especially in the United States, but it is less commonly used that way outside of North America.

In the United Kingdom, South Africa, and Australia, stock can also refer to completely different financial instruments such as government bonds or, less commonly, to all kinds of marketable securities.

a. Share
b. Margin
c. Procter ' Gamble
d. Bucket shop

46. The institution most often referenced by the word '_____' is a public or publicly traded _____, the shares of which are traded on a public stock exchange (e.g., the New York Stock Exchange or Nasdaq in the United States) where shares of stock of _____s are bought and sold by and to the general public. Most of the largest businesses in the world are publicly traded _____s, However, the majority of _____s are said to be closely held, privately held or close _____s, meaning that no ready market exists for the trading of shares.

a. Federal Home Loan Mortgage Corporation
b. Protect
c. Depository Trust Company
d. Corporation

47. The term _____ is a term applied to practices that are perfunctory, or seek to satisfy the minimum requirements or to conform to a convention or doctrine. It has different meanings in different fields.

In accounting, _____ earnings are those earnings of companies in addition to actual earnings calculated under the Generally Accepted Accounting Principles (GAAP) in their quarterly and yearly financial reports.

a. Long-term liabilities
b. Deferred income
c. Deferred financing costs
d. Pro forma

Chapter 17. Projecting Cash Flow and Earnings

48. _____ is the term in economics for the amount of fixed or real capital present in relation to other factors of production, especially labor. At the level of either a production process or the aggregate economy, it may be estimated by the capital/labor ratio, such as from the points along a capital/labor isoquant.

Since the use of tools and machinery makes labor more effective, rising _____ pushes up the productivity of labor, so a society that is more capital intensive tends to have a higher standard of living over the long run than one with low _____.

a. Weighted average cost of capital
c. Cost of capital

b. 4-4-5 Calendar
d. Capital intensity

49. _____ indicates the percentage of a company's earnings that are not paid out in dividends but credited to retained earnings. It is the opposite of the dividend payout ratio, so that also called the retention rate.

_____ = 1 - Dividend Payout Ratio

a. Bankassurer
c. Dow Jones Indexes

b. Fair market value
d. Retention ratio

50. In the theory of capital structure, _____ is the phrase used to describe funds that firms obtain from outside of the firm. It is contrasted to internal financing which consists mainly of profits retained by the firm for investment. There are many kinds of _____.

a. Ownership equity
c. External financing

b. Adjustment
d. Asset-backed commercial paper

51. An _____ is a call option on the common stock of a company, issued as a form of non-cash compensation. Restrictions on the option (such as vesting and limited transferability) attempt to align the holder's interest with those of the business' shareholders. If the company's stock rises, holders of options experience a direct financial benefit.

a. Underwriting contract
c. Employee stock option

b. Operating ratio
d. Internal financing

52. An _____ is a contract written by a seller that conveys to the buyer the right -- but not the obligation -- to buy (in the case of a call _____) or to sell (in the case of a put _____) a particular asset, such as a piece of property such as, among others, a futures contract. In return for granting the _____, the seller collects a payment (the premium) from the buyer.

For example, buying a call _____ provides the right to buy a specified quantity of a security at a set strike price at some time on or before expiration, while buying a put _____ provides the right to sell.

a. Option
c. AT'T Mobility LLC

b. Amortization
d. Annuity

53. In finance, _____ are stocks that appreciate in value and yield a high return on equity (ROE.) Analysts compute ROE by taking the company's net income and dividing it by the company's equity. To be classified as a growth stock, analysts expect to see at least 15 percent return on equity.

Chapter 17. Projecting Cash Flow and Earnings

a. 4-4-5 Calendar
b. Growth stocks
c. Stock valuation
d. Security Analysis

54. _____ is a rent received on a regular basis, with little effort required to maintain it. It is advocated by some authors, especially by Robert Kiyosaki.

Some examples of _____ are:

- Repeated regular income, earned by a sales person, generated from the payment of a product or service that must be renewed on a regular basis, in order to continue receiving its benefits - also called residual income.
- Rental from property;
- Royalties from publishing a book or from licensing a patent or other form of intellectual property;
- Earnings from internet advertisement on your websites;
- Earnings from a business that does not require direct involvement from the owner or merchant;
- Dividend and interest income from owning securities, such as stocks and bonds, are usually referred to as portfolio income, which can be considered a form of _____;
- Pensions.

_____ is usually taxable. The American Internal Revenue Service defines _____ as 'any activity...

a. Fixed exchange rate system
b. 4-4-5 Calendar
c. Horizontal merger
d. Passive income

55. A _____ rocket is a rocket that uses two or more stages, each of which contains its own engines and propellant. A tandem or serial stage is mounted on top of another stage; a parallel stage is attached alongside another stage. The result is effectively two or more rockets stacked on top of or attached next to each other.

a. 529 plan
b. 4-4-5 Calendar
c. Multistage
d. 7-Eleven

Chapter 18. Corporate Bonds

1. In finance, a _____ is a debt security, in which the authorized issuer owes the holders a debt and, depending on the terms of the _____, is obliged to pay interest (the coupon) and/or to repay the principal at a later date, termed maturity.

Thus a _____ is a loan: the issuer is the borrower, the _____ holder is the lender, and the coupon is the interest. _____s provide the borrower with external funds to finance long-term investments, or, in the case of government _____s, to finance current expenditure.

- a. Bond
- b. Catastrophe bonds
- c. Puttable bond
- d. Convertible bond

2. _____ (also trust indenture or deed of trust) is a legal document issued to lenders and describes key terms such as the interest rate, maturity date, convertibility, pledge, promises, representations, covenants, and other terms of the bond offering. When the Offering Memorandum is prepared in advance of marketing a Bond, the indenture will typically be summarised in the 'Description of Notes' section.

- a. Bond indenture
- b. McFadden Act
- c. Fair Labor Standards Act
- d. Court of Audit of Belgium

3. A _____ is a bond issued by a corporation. The term is usually applied to longer-term debt instruments, generally with a maturity date falling at least a year after their issue date. (The term 'commercial paper' is sometimes used for instruments with a shorter maturity.)

- a. Brady bonds
- b. Serial bond
- c. Government bond
- d. Corporate bond

4. _____ is the balance of the amounts of cash being received and paid by a business during a defined period of time, sometimes tied to a specific project. Measurement of _____ can be used

- to evaluate the state or performance of a business or project.
- to determine problems with liquidity. Being profitable does not necessarily mean being liquid. A company can fail because of a shortage of cash, even while profitable.
- to generate project rate of returns. The time of _____s into and out of projects are used as inputs to financial models such as internal rate of return, and net present value.
- to examine income or growth of a business when it is believed that accrual accounting concepts do not represent economic realities. Alternately, _____ can be used to 'validate' the net income generated by accrual accounting.

_____ as a generic term may be used differently depending on context, and certain _____ definitions may be adapted by analysts and users for their own uses. Common terms include operating _____ and free _____.

_____s can be classified into:

1. Operational _____s: Cash received or expended as a result of the company's core business activities.
2. Investment _____s: Cash received or expended through capital expenditure, investments or acquisitions.
3. Financing _____s: Cash received or expended as a result of financial activities, such as interests and dividends.

Chapter 18. Corporate Bonds

All three together - the net _____ - are necessary to reconcile the beginning cash balance to the ending cash balance. Loan draw downs or equity injections, that is just shifting of capital but no expenditure as such, are not considered in the net _____.

    a. Corporate finance
    b. Shareholder value
    c. Cash flow
    d. Real option

5. _____ is a form of corporation equity ownership represented in the securities. It is dangerous in comparison to preferred shares and some other investment options, in that in the event of bankruptcy, _____ investors receive their funds after preferred stockholders, bondholders, creditors, etc. On the other hand, common shares on average perform better than preferred shares or bonds over time.
    a. Stop-limit order
    b. Stock market bubble
    c. Stock split
    d. Common stock

6. The coupon or _____ of a bond is the amount of interest paid per year expressed as a percentage of the face value of the bond.

For example if you hold $10,000 nominal of a bond described as a 4.5% loan stock, you will receive $450 in interest each year (probably in two installments of $225 each.)

Not all bonds have coupons.

    a. Revenue bonds
    b. Zero-coupon bond
    c. Puttable bond
    d. Coupon rate

7. A _____ is a bond issued by a national government denominated in the country's own currency. Bonds issued by national governments in foreign currencies are normally referred to as sovereign bonds. The first ever _____ was issued by the British government in 1693 to raise money to fund a war against France.
    a. Collateralized debt obligations
    b. Zero-coupon bond
    c. Municipal bond
    d. Government bond

8. In the United States, a _____ is a bond issued by a city or other local government, or their agencies. Potential issuers of these bonds include cities, counties, redevelopment agencies, school districts, publicly owned airports and seaports, and any other governmental entity (or group of governments) below the state level. They may be general obligations of the issuer or secured by specified revenues.
    a. Premium bond
    b. Puttable bond
    c. Senior debt
    d. Municipal bond

9. In business and accounting, _____s are everything of value that is owned by a person or company. The balance sheet of a firm records the monetary value of the _____s owned by the firm. The two major _____ classes are tangible _____s and intangible _____s.
    a. EBITDA
    b. Income
    c. Accounts payable
    d. Asset

Chapter 18. Corporate Bonds

10. _____ is a term used to refer to how an investor distributes his or her investments among various classes of investment vehicles (e.g., stocks and bonds.)

A large part of financial planning is finding an _____ that is appropriate for a given person in terms of their appetite for and ability to shoulder risk. This can depend on various factors; see investor profile.

- a. Asset allocation
- b. Investing online
- c. Alternative investment
- d. Investment performance

11. A _____ is a unit that is equal to 1/100th of a percentage point. It is frequently used to express percentage point changes of less than 1%. It avoids the ambiguity between relative and absolute discussions about rates.
- a. 4-4-5 Calendar
- b. 529 plan
- c. Basis point
- d. Bond market

12. _____ is a life of security. It may also refer to the final payment date of a loan or other financial instrument, at which point all remaining interest and principal is due to be paid.

1, 3, 6 months _____ band can be calculated by using 30-day per month periods.

- a. Primary market
- b. Replacement cost
- c. False billing
- d. Maturity

13. In business and finance, a _____ (also referred to as equity _____) of stock means a _____ of ownership in a corporation (company.) In the plural, stocks is often used as a synonym for _____s especially in the United States, but it is less commonly used that way outside of North America.

In the United Kingdom, South Africa, and Australia, stock can also refer to completely different financial instruments such as government bonds or, less commonly, to all kinds of marketable securities.

- a. Margin
- b. Bucket shop
- c. Procter ' Gamble
- d. Share

14. The institution most often referenced by the word '_____' is a public or publicly traded _____, the shares of which are traded on a public stock exchange (e.g., the New York Stock Exchange or Nasdaq in the United States) where shares of stock of _____s are bought and sold by and to the general public. Most of the largest businesses in the world are publicly traded _____s. However, the majority of _____s are said to be closely held, privately held or close _____s, meaning that no ready market exists for the trading of shares.
- a. Corporation
- b. Depository Trust Company
- c. Protect
- d. Federal Home Loan Mortgage Corporation

15. A _____ is defined as a certificate of agreement of loans which is given under the company's stamp and carries an undertaking that the _____ holder will get a fixed return (fixed on the basis of interest rates) and the principal amount whenever the _____ matures.

Chapter 18. Corporate Bonds

In finance, a _____ is a long-term debt instrument used by governments and large companies to obtain funds. It is defined as 'a debt secured only by the debtor's earning power, not by a lien on any specific asset.' It is similar to a bond except the securitization conditions are different.

- a. Collection agency
- b. Debenture
- c. Partial Payment
- d. Collateral Management

16. In finance, a _____ (non-investment grade bond, speculative grade bond or junk bond) is a bond that is rated below investment grade at the time of purchase. These bonds have a higher risk of default or other adverse credit events, but typically pay higher yields than better quality bonds in order to make them attractive to investors.
- a. Volatility
- b. Sharpe ratio
- c. Private equity
- d. High yield bond

17. In finance, _____ refers to any type of debt or general obligation that is not collateralized by a lien on specific assets of the borrower in the case of a bankruptcy or liquidation.

In the event of the bankruptcy of the borrower, the unsecured creditors will have a general claim on the assets of the borrower after the specific pledged assets have been assigned to the secured creditors, although the unsecured creditors will usually realize a smaller proportion of their claims than the secured creditors.

In some legal systems, unsecured creditors who are also indebted to the insolvent debtor are able (and in some jurisdictions, required) to set-off the debts, which actually puts the unsecured creditor with a matured liability to the debtor in a pre-preferential position.

- a. ABN Amro
- b. AAB
- c. A Random Walk Down Wall Street
- d. Unsecured debt

18. An _____ is a mortgage loan where the interest rate on the note is periodically adjusted based on a variety of indices. Among the most common indices are the rates on 1-year constant-maturity Treasury (CMT) securities, the Cost of Funds Index (COFI), and the London Interbank Offered Rate (LIBOR.) A few lenders use their own cost of funds as an index, rather than using other indices.
- a. ABN Amro
- b. A Random Walk Down Wall Street
- c. AAB
- d. Adjustable rate mortgage

19. _____ is the provision of resources (such as granting a loan) by one party to another party where that second party does not reimburse the first party immediately, thereby generating a debt, and instead arranges either to repay or return those resources (or material(s) of equal value) at a later date. The first party is called a creditor, also known as a lender, while the second party is called a debtor, also known as a borrower.

Movements of financial capital are normally dependent on either _____ or equity transfers.

- a. Comparable
- b. Clearing house
- c. Warrant
- d. Credit

20. A _____ assesses the credit worthiness of an individual, corporation, or even a country. _____s are calculated from financial history and current assets and liabilities. Typically, a _____ tells a lender or investor the probability of the subject being able to pay back a loan.
   a. Credit report monitoring
   b. Debenture
   c. Credit cycle
   d. Credit rating

21. _____ is that which is owed; usually referencing assets owed, but the term can cover other obligations. In the case of assets, _____ is a means of using future purchasing power in the present before a summation has been earned. Some companies and corporations use _____ as a part of their overall corporate finance strategy.
   a. Debt
   b. Cross-collateralization
   c. Credit cycle
   d. Partial Payment

22. In lending agreements, _____ is a borrower's pledge of specific property to a lender, to secure repayment of a loan. The _____ serves as protection for a lender against a borrower's risk of default - that is, a borrower failing to pay the principal and interest under the terms of a loan obligation. If a borrower does default on a loan (due to insolvency or other event), that borrower forfeits (gives up) the property pledged as _____ *ollateral* - and the lender then becomes the owner of the _____.
   a. Future-oriented
   b. Nominal value
   c. Collateral
   d. Refinancing risk

23. A _____ is a payment made by a corporation to its shareholder members. When a corporation earns a profit or surplus, that money can be put to two uses: it can either be re-invested in the business (called retained earnings), or it can be paid to the shareholders as a _____. Many corporations retain a portion of their earnings and pay the remainder as a _____.
   a. Dividend puzzle
   b. Special dividend
   c. Dividend yield
   d. Dividend

24. An _____ is a financial security used in aircraft finance, most commonly to take advantage of tax benefits in North America.

In a typical _____ transaction, a 'trust certificate' is sold to investors in order to finance the purchase of an aircraft by a trust managed on the investors' behalf. The trust then leases the aircraft to an airline, and the trustee routes payments through the trust to the investors.

   a. ABN Amro
   b. A Random Walk Down Wall Street
   c. AAB
   d. Equipment trust certificate

25. _____ occurs when an entity that has issued callable bonds calls those debt securities from the debt holders with the express purpose of reissuing new debt at a lower coupon rate. In essence, the issue of new, lower-interest debt allows the company to prematurely refund the older, higher-interest debt.

On the contrary, NonRefundable Bonds may be callable but they cannot be re-issued with a lower coupon rate.

   a. Market neutral
   b. No-arbitrage bounds
   c. Systematic risk
   d. Refunding

Chapter 18. Corporate Bonds

26. _____ is a type of bond that allows the issuer of the bond to retain the privilege of redeeming the bond at some point before the bond reaches the date of maturity. In other words, on the call dates, the issuer has the right, but not the obligation, to buy back the bonds from the bond holders at the call price. Technically speaking, the bonds are not really bought and held by the issuer but cancelled immediately.
   a. Coupon rate
   b. Gilts
   c. Bond fund
   d. Callable bond

27. A _____ is a fungible, negotiable instrument representing financial value. They are broadly categorized into debt securities (such as banknotes, bonds and debentures), and equity securities; e.g., common stocks. The company or other entity issuing the _____ is called the issuer.
   a. Tracking stock
   b. Book entry
   c. Securities lending
   d. Security

28. The U.S. _____ is an independent agency of the United States government which holds primary responsibility for enforcing the federal securities laws and regulating the securities industry, the nation's stock and options exchanges, and other electronic securities markets. The SEC was created by section 4 of the SEC of 1934 (now codified as 15 U.S.C. § 78d and commonly referred to as the 1934 Act.)
   a. Securities and Exchange Commission
   b. 529 plan
   c. 4-4-5 Calendar
   d. 7-Eleven

29. In financial accounting, _____s are precautions for which the amount or probability of occurrence are not known. Typical examples are _____s for warranty costs and _____ for taxes the term reserve is used instead of term _____; such a use, however, is inconsistent with the terminology suggested by International Accounting Standards Board.
   a. Momentum Accounting and Triple-Entry Bookkeeping
   b. Provision
   c. Petty cash
   d. Money measurement concept

30. _____, in accrual accounting, is any account where the asset or liability is not realized until a future date, e.g. annuities, charges, taxes, income, etc. The _____ item may be carried, dependent on type of deferral, as either an asset or liability.See also: accrual

_____ is also used in the university admissions process. It is the action by which a school rejects a student for early admission but still opts to review that student in the general admissions pool.

   a. Net profit
   b. Current asset
   c. Revenue
   d. Deferred

31. _____ is a combination of straight bond and embedded put option. The holder of the _____ has the right, but not the obligation, to demand early repayment of the principal. The put option is usually exercisable on specified dates.
   a. Callable bond
   b. Convertible bond
   c. Brady bonds
   d. Puttable bond

32. In finance, a _____ is a type of bond that can be converted into shares of stock in the issuing company, usually at some pre-announced ratio. It is a hybrid security with debt- and equity-like features. Although it typically has a low coupon rate, the holder is compensated with the ability to convert the bond to common stock, usually at a substantial discount to the stock's market value.
   a. Corporate bond
   b. Bond fund
   c. Convertible bond
   d. Gilts

33. _____ is the value of a property to a particular investor. In the U.S., it is equal to market value for the investor who has the capacity to put the property to good use -- its highest-and-best-use, its most valuable use. For other investors with limited capacity or vision, _____ is lower because they cannot put the property to use in a way that is maximally productive.
   a. Investment value
   b. AAB
   c. ABN Amro
   d. A Random Walk Down Wall Street

34. An _____ option has no intrinsic value. A call option is _____ when the strike price is above the spot price of the underlying security. A put option is _____ when the strike price is below the spot price.
   a. AAB
   b. A Random Walk Down Wall Street
   c. ABN Amro
   d. Out-of-the-money

35. In finance, the term _____ describes the amount in cash that returns to the owners of a security. Normally it does not include the price variations, at the difference of the total return. _____ applies to various stated rates of return on stocks (common and preferred, and convertible), fixed income instruments (bonds, notes, bills, strips, zero coupon), and some other investment type insurance products (e.g. annuities.)
   a. 4-4-5 Calendar
   b. Yield to maturity
   c. Yield
   d. Macaulay duration

36. The _____ or redemption yield is the yield promised to the bondholder on the assumption that the bond or other fixed-interest security such as gilts will be held to maturity, that all coupon and principal payments will be made and coupon payments are reinvested at the bond's promised yield at the same rate as invested. It is a measure of the return of the bond. This technique in theory allows investors to calculate the fair value of different financial instruments.
   a. 4-4-5 Calendar
   b. Yield
   c. Macaulay duration
   d. Yield to maturity

37. In finance, _____ is the interest that has accumulated since the principal investment, or since the previous interest payment if there has been one already. For a financial instrument such as a bond, interest is calculated and paid in set intervals.

The primary formula for calculating the interest accrued in a given period is:

$$I_A = T \times P \times R$$

where I_A is the _____, T is the fraction of the year, P is the principal, and R is the annualized interest rate.

   a. ABN Amro
   b. A Random Walk Down Wall Street
   c. Accrued interest
   d. AAB

Chapter 18. Corporate Bonds

38. _____ is a fee paid on borrowed assets. It is the price paid for the use of borrowed money, or, money earned by deposited funds. Assets that are sometimes lent with _____ include money, shares, consumer goods through hire purchase, major assets such as aircraft, and even entire factories in finance lease arrangements.
    a. A Random Walk Down Wall Street
    b. AAB
    c. Insolvency
    d. Interest

39. In finance, an _____ is a straight bond with an embedded option to exchange the bond for the stock of a company other than the issuer (usually a subsidiary or company in which the issuer owns a stake) at some future date and under prescribed conditions. An _____ is different from a convertible bond. A convertible bond gives the holder the option to convert bond into shares of the issuer.
    a. ABN Amro
    b. AAB
    c. A Random Walk Down Wall Street
    d. Exchangeable bond

40. _____s are financial bonds that mature in installments over a period of time. In effect, a $100,000, 5-year _____ would mature in a $20,000 annuity over a 5-year interval. Bond issues consisting of a series of blocks of securities maturing in sequence, the coupon rate can be different.
    a. Serial bond
    b. Callable bond
    c. Brady bonds
    d. Bond fund

41. A _____ is a fund established by a government agency or business for the purpose of reducing debt.

The _____ was first used in Great Britain in the 18th century to reduce national debt. While used by Robert Walpole in 1716 and effectively in the 1720s and early 1730s, it originated in the commercial tax syndicates of the Italian peninsula of the 14th century to retire redeemable public debt of those cities.

   a. Sinking fund
   b. Debtor
   c. Security interest
   d. Modern portfolio theory

42. _____ are risk-linked securities that transfer a specified set of risks from a sponsor to investors. They are often structured as floating rate corporate bonds whose principal is forgiven if specified trigger conditions are met. They are typically used by insurers as an alternative to traditional catastrophe reinsurance.
    a. Catastrophe bonds
    b. Callable bond
    c. Brady bonds
    d. Clean price

43. _____ refer to services provided by the finance industry.

The finance industry encompasses a broad range of organizations that deal with the management of money. Among these organizations are banks, credit card companies, insurance companies, consumer finance companies, stock brokerages, investment funds and some government sponsored enterprises.

   a. Financial instruments
   b. Delta hedging
   c. Cost of carry
   d. Financial Services

44. A _____, in its most general sense, is a solemn promise to engage in or refrain from a specified action.

Chapter 18. Corporate Bonds

More specifically, a _____, in contrast to a contract, is a one-way agreement whereby the _____er is the only party bound by the promise. A _____ may have conditions and prerequisites that qualify the undertaking, including the actions of second or third parties, but there is no inherent agreement by such other parties to fulfill those requirements.

a. Federal Trade Commission Act
b. Covenant
c. Clayton Antitrust Act
d. Partnership

45. _____ in finance is a risk management technique, related to hedging, that mixes a wide variety of investments within a portfolio. Because the fluctuations of a single security have less impact on a diverse portfolio, _____ minimizes the risk from any one investment.

A simple example of _____ is the following: On a particular island the entire economy consists of two companies: one that sells umbrellas and another that sells sunscreen.

a. 4-4-5 Calendar
b. 7-Eleven
c. 529 plan
d. Diversification

46. In the United States, a _____ is an offering of securities that are not registered with the Securities and Exchange Commission (SEC.) Such offerings exploit an exemption offered by the Securities Act of 1933 that comes with several restrictions, including a prohibition against general solicitation. This exemption allows companies to avoid quarterly reporting requirements and many of the legal liabilities associated with the Sarbanes-Oxley Act.

a. 529 plan
b. Private placement
c. 4-4-5 Calendar
d. 7-Eleven

47. An _____ is an investment vehicle traded on stock exchanges, much like stocks. An ETF holds assets such as stocks or bonds and trades at approximately the same price as the net asset value of its underlying assets over the course of the trading day. Most ETFs track an index, such as the Dow Jones Industrial Average or the S'P 500.

a. ABN Amro
b. AAB
c. Exchange-traded fund
d. A Random Walk Down Wall Street

48. _____ is typically a higher ranking stock than voting shares, and its terms are negotiated between the corporation and the investor.

_____ usually carry no voting rights, but may carry superior priority over common stock in the payment of dividends and upon liquidation. _____ may carry a dividend that is paid out prior to any dividends to common stock holders.

a. Trade-off theory
b. Preferred stock
c. Follow-on offering
d. Second lien loan

49. An _____ or index tracker is a collective investment scheme (usually a mutual fund or exchange-traded fund) that aims to replicate the movements of an index of a specific financial market regardless of market conditions.

Chapter 18. Corporate Bonds

Tracking can be achieved by trying to hold all of the securities in the index, in the same proportions as the index. Other methods include statistically sampling the market and holding 'representative' securities.

a. Index fund
b. Investment company
c. A Random Walk Down Wall Street
d. AAB

50. _____ are those dividends paid out in form of additional stock shares of the issuing corporation or other corporation They are usually issued in proportion to shares owned (for example for every 100 shares of stock owned, 5% stock dividend will yield 5 extra shares). If this payment involves the issue of new shares, this is very similar to a stock split in that it increases the total number of shares while lowering the price of each share and does not change the market capitalization or the total value of the shares held

a. The Hong Kong Securities Institute
b. Time-based currency
c. Database auditing
d. Stock or scrip dividends

51. _____ are bonds that have a variable coupon, equal to a money market reference rate, like LIBOR or federal funds rate, plus a spread. The spread is a rate that remains constant. Almost all _____ have quarterly coupons, i.e. they pay out interest every three months, though counter examples do exist.

a. Floating rate notes
b. Gordon growth model
c. Loan participation
d. CVECAs

52. A _____ refers to any type debt instrument, such as a loan, bond, mortgage that does not have a fixed rate of interest over the life of the instrument. Such debt typically uses an index or other base rate for establishing the interest rate for each relevant period. One of the most common rates to use as the basis for applying interest rates is the London Inter-bank Offered Rate, or LIBOR

a. Floating interest rate
b. Foreign exchange hedge
c. Cost of living
d. Disposal tax effect

53. The value of speculative bonds is affected to a higher degree than investment grade bonds by the possibility of default. For example, in a recession interest rates may drop, and the drop in interest rates tends to increase the value of investment grade bonds; however, a recession tends to increase the possibility of default in speculative-grade bonds.

The original speculative grade bonds were bonds that once had been investment grade at time of issue, but where the credit rating of the issuer had slipped and the possibility of default increased significantly. These bonds are called '_____'.

a. Return on capital employed
b. Sharpe ratio
c. Seed round
d. Fallen angels

54. _____ are government bonds issued by the United States Department of the Treasury through the Bureau of the Public Debt. They are the debt financing instruments of the U.S. Federal government, and they are often referred to simply as Treasuries or Treasurys. There are four types of marketable _____: Treasury bills, Treasury notes, Treasury bonds, and Treasury Inflation Protected Securities (TIPS.)

a. Treasury Inflation-Protected Securities
b. 4-4-5 Calendar
c. Treasury Inflation Protected Securities
d. Treasury securities

Chapter 18. Corporate Bonds

55. In finance, the _____ is the difference between the quoted rates of return on two different investments, usually of different credit quality.

It is a compound of yield and spread.

The '_____ of X over Y' is simply the percentage return on investment (ROI) from financial instrument X minus the percentage return on investment from financial instrument Y (per annum.)

a. Portfolio insurance
b. Yield spread
c. Debtor-in-possession financing
d. Duty of loyalty

56. Behavioral economics and _____ are closely related fields that have evolved to be a separate branch of economic and financial analysis which applies scientific research on human and social, cognitive and emotional factors to better understand economic decisions by, say, consumers, borrowers, investors, and how they affect market prices, returns and the allocation of resources.

The field is primarily concerned with the bounds of rationality (selfishness, self-control) of economic agents. Behavioral models typically integrate insights from psychology with neo-classical economic theory.

a. Recession
b. Market structure
c. Behavioral finance
d. Medium of exchange

57. An _____ is a contract written by a seller that conveys to the buyer the right -- but not the obligation -- to buy (in the case of a call _____) or to sell (in the case of a put _____) a particular asset, such as a piece of property such as, among others, a futures contract. In return for granting the _____, the seller collects a payment (the premium) from the buyer.

For example, buying a call _____ provides the right to buy a specified quantity of a security at a set strike price at some time on or before expiration, while buying a put _____ provides the right to sell.

a. Annuity
b. Option
c. AT'T Mobility LLC
d. Amortization

58. A _____ is a collective investment scheme that invests in bonds and other debt securities. _____s yield monthly dividends that include interest payments on the fund's underlying securities plus any capital appreciation in the prices of the portfolio's bonds. _____s tend to pay higher dividends than CDs and money market accounts, and they generally pay out dividends more frequently and regularly than individual bonds.

a. Gilts
b. Premium bond
c. Private activity bond
d. Bond Fund

59. _____, refers to consumption opportunity gained by an entity within a specified time frame, which is generally expressed in monetary terms. However, for households and individuals, '_____ is the sum of all the wages, salaries, profits, interests payments, rents and other forms of earnings received... in a given period of time.' For firms, _____ generally refers to net-profit: what remains of revenue after expenses have been subtracted.

Chapter 18. Corporate Bonds

a. Annual report
b. Accrual
c. OIBDA
d. Income

60. In financial accounting, the term _____ is most commonly used to describe any part of shareholders' equity, except for basic share capital. Sometimes, the term is used instead of the term provision; such a use, however, is inconsistent with the terminology suggested by International Accounting Standards Board. For more information about provisions, see provision (accounting.)
   a. FIFO and LIFO accounting
   b. Closing entries
   c. Treasury stock
   d. Reserve

61. In finance, _____ refers to Monday, October 19, 1987, when stock markets around the world crashed, shedding a huge value in a very short time. The crash began in Hong Kong, spread west through international time zones to Europe, hitting the United States after other markets had already declined by a significant margin. The Dow Jones Industrial Average (DJIA) dropped by 508 points to 1738.74 (22.61%).
   a. Black Monday
   b. 7-Eleven
   c. 4-4-5 Calendar
   d. 529 plan

62. The _____ is an American stock exchange. It is the largest electronic screen-based equity securities trading market in the United States. With approximately 3,200 companies, it has more trading volume per day than any other stock exchange in the world.
   a. 4-4-5 Calendar
   b. 529 plan
   c. NASDAQ
   d. 7-Eleven

63. A _____, securities exchange or (in Europe) bourse is a corporation or mutual organization which provides 'trading' facilities for stock brokers and traders, to trade stocks and other securities. _____s also provide facilities for the issue and redemption of securities as well as other financial instruments and capital events including the payment of income and dividends. The securities traded on a _____ include: shares issued by companies, unit trusts and other pooled investment products and bonds.
   a. 4-4-5 Calendar
   b. Stock Exchange
   c. 7-Eleven
   d. 529 plan

Chapter 19. Government Bonds

1. A _____ is a bond issued by a national government denominated in the country's own currency. Bonds issued by national governments in foreign currencies are normally referred to as sovereign bonds. The first ever _____ was issued by the British government in 1693 to raise money to fund a war against France.
    a. Government bond
    b. Zero-coupon bond
    c. Municipal bond
    d. Collateralized debt obligations

2. In the United States, a _____ is a bond issued by a city or other local government, or their agencies. Potential issuers of these bonds include cities, counties, redevelopment agencies, school districts, publicly owned airports and seaports, and any other governmental entity (or group of governments) below the state level. They may be general obligations of the issuer or secured by specified revenues.
    a. Senior debt
    b. Municipal bond
    c. Puttable bond
    d. Premium bond

3. In finance, a _____ is a debt security, in which the authorized issuer owes the holders a debt and, depending on the terms of the _____, is obliged to pay interest (the coupon) and/or to repay the principal at a later date, termed maturity.

    Thus a _____ is a loan: the issuer is the borrower, the _____ holder is the lender, and the coupon is the interest. _____s provide the borrower with external funds to finance long-term investments, or, in the case of government _____s, to finance current expenditure.

    a. Catastrophe bonds
    b. Puttable bond
    c. Bond
    d. Convertible bond

4. A _____ is a fungible, negotiable instrument representing financial value. They are broadly categorized into debt securities (such as banknotes, bonds and debentures), and equity securities; e.g., common stocks. The company or other entity issuing the _____ is called the issuer.
    a. Securities lending
    b. Tracking stock
    c. Book entry
    d. Security

5. A '_____' is a 'Charge' that is paid to obtain the right to delay a payment. Essentially, the payer purchases the right to make a given payment in the future instead of in the Present. The '_____', or 'Charge' that must be paid to delay the payment, is simply the difference between what the payment amount would be if it were paid in the present and what the payment amount would be paid if it were paid in the future.
    a. Value at risk
    b. Risk modeling
    c. Risk aversion
    d. Discount

6. _____ is a fee paid on borrowed assets. It is the price paid for the use of borrowed money , or, money earned by deposited funds . Assets that are sometimes lent with _____ include money, shares, consumer goods through hire purchase, major assets such as aircraft, and even entire factories in finance lease arrangements.
    a. Insolvency
    b. AAB
    c. A Random Walk Down Wall Street
    d. Interest

7. _____ is the price at which the issuing company may choose to repurchase a security before its maturity date.

A bond is purchased at a discount if its _____ exceeds its purchase price. It is purchased at a premium if its purchase price exceeds its _____.

Chapter 19. Government Bonds

a. Redemption value
b. Commercial finance
c. Consolidated financial statements
d. Flight-to-quality

8. _____ mature in one year or less. Like zero-coupon bonds, they do not pay interest prior to maturity; instead they are sold at a discount of the par value to create a positive yield to maturity. Many regard _____ as the least risky investment available to U.S. investors.

a. Treasury securities
b. Treasury bills
c. 4-4-5 Calendar
d. Treasury Inflation Protected Securities

9. _____ are government bonds issued by the United States Department of the Treasury through the Bureau of the Public Debt. They are the debt financing instruments of the U.S. Federal government, and they are often referred to simply as Treasuries or Treasurys. There are four types of marketable _____: Treasury bills, Treasury notes, Treasury bonds, and Treasury Inflation Protected Securities (TIPS.)

a. Treasury Inflation Protected Securities
b. 4-4-5 Calendar
c. Treasury Inflation-Protected Securities
d. Treasury securities

10. The coupon or _____ of a bond is the amount of interest paid per year expressed as a percentage of the face value of the bond.

For example if you hold $10,000 nominal of a bond described as a 4.5% loan stock, you will receive $450 in interest each year (probably in two installments of $225 each.)

Not all bonds have coupons.

a. Revenue bonds
b. Puttable bond
c. Zero-coupon bond
d. Coupon rate

11. A _____ is a bond bought at a price lower than its face value, with the face value repaid at the time of maturity. It does not make periodic interest payments, or so-called 'coupons,' hence the term zero-coupon bond. Investors earn return from the compounded interest all paid at maturity plus the difference between the discounted price of the bond and its par value.

a. Callable bond
b. Bowie bonds
c. Municipal bond
d. Zero coupon bond

12. In finance, _____ is the interest that has accumulated since the principal investment, or since the previous interest payment if there has been one already. For a financial instrument such as a bond, interest is calculated and paid in set intervals.

The primary formula for calculating the interest accrued in a given period is:

$$I_A = T \times P \times R$$

where I_A is the _____, T is the fraction of the year, P is the principal, and R is the annualized interest rate.

Chapter 19. Government Bonds

a. ABN Amro
c. Accrued interest
b. A Random Walk Down Wall Street
d. AAB

13. A _____ is a unit that is equal to 1/100th of a percentage point. It is frequently used to express percentage point changes of less than 1%. It avoids the ambiguity between relative and absolute discussions about rates.
  a. Bond market
  c. 529 plan
  b. 4-4-5 Calendar
  d. Basis point

14. In finance, the term _____ describes the amount in cash that returns to the owners of a security. Normally it does not include the price variations, at the difference of the total return. _____ applies to various stated rates of return on stocks (common and preferred, and convertible), fixed income instruments (bonds, notes, bills, strips, zero coupon), and some other investment type insurance products (e.g. annuities.)
  a. Yield to maturity
  c. Yield
  b. 4-4-5 Calendar
  d. Macaulay duration

15. The _____ or redemption yield is the yield promised to the bondholder on the assumption that the bond or other fixed-interest security such as gilts will be held to maturity, that all coupon and principal payments will be made and coupon payments are reinvested at the bond's promised yield at the same rate as invested. It is a measure of the return of the bond. This technique in theory allows investors to calculate the fair value of different financial instruments.
  a. 4-4-5 Calendar
  c. Yield
  b. Yield to maturity
  d. Macaulay duration

16. _____ is a life of security. It may also refer to the final payment date of a loan or other financial instrument, at which point all remaining interest and principal is due to be paid.

1, 3, 6 months _____ band can be calculated by using 30-day per month periods.

  a. Primary market
  c. Maturity
  b. False billing
  d. Replacement cost

17. _____ is that which is owed; usually referencing assets owed, but the term can cover other obligations. In the case of assets, _____ is a means of using future purchasing power in the present before a summation has been earned. Some companies and corporations use _____ as a part of their overall corporate finance strategy.
  a. Partial Payment
  c. Credit cycle
  b. Cross-collateralization
  d. Debt

18. In financial accounting, _____s are precautions for which the amount or probability of occurrence are not known. Typical examples are _____s for warranty costs and _____ for taxes the term reserve is used instead of term _____; such a use, however, is inconsistent with the terminology suggested by International Accounting Standards Board.
  a. Momentum Accounting and Triple-Entry Bookkeeping
  c. Petty cash
  b. Money measurement concept
  d. Provision

19. A _____ or market-based mechanism is any of a wide variety of ways to match up buyers and sellers.

Chapter 19. Government Bonds

An example of a _____ uses announced bid and ask prices. Generally speaking, when two parties wish to engage in a trade, the purchaser will announce a price he is willing to pay (the bid price) and seller will announce a price he is willing to accept (the ask price).

   a. Price mechanism   b. 7-Eleven
   c. 4-4-5 Calendar   d. 529 plan

20. The _____ for securities is the difference between the price quoted by a market maker for an immediate sale and an immediate purchase The size of the bid-offer spread in a given commodity is a measure of the liquidity of the market.

The trader initiating the transaction is said to demand liquidity, and the other party to the transaction supplies liquidity.

   a. Trade-off   b. Capital outflow
   c. Defined contribution plan   d. Bid/offer spread

21. _____ are the inflation-indexed bonds issued by the U.S. Treasury. The principal is adjusted to the Consumer Price Index, the commonly used measure of inflation. The coupon rate is constant, but generates a different amount of interest when multiplied by the inflation-adjusted principal, thus protecting the holder against inflation. _____ are currently offered in 5-year, 10-year and 20-year maturities.

   a. 4-4-5 Calendar   b. Treasury securities
   c. Treasury Inflation Protected Securities   d. Treasury Inflation-Protected Securities

22. A _____ is the highest price that a buyer (i.e., bidder) is willing to pay for a good. It is usually referred to simply as the 'bid.'

In bid and ask, the _____ stands in contrast to the ask price or 'offer', and the difference between the two is called the bid/ask spread.

An unsolicited bid or offer is when a person or company receives a bid even though they are not looking to sell.

   a. Settlement date   b. Mid price
   c. Political risk   d. Bid price

23. In financial accounting, the term _____ is most commonly used to describe any part of shareholders' equity, except for basic share capital. Sometimes, the term is used instead of the term provision; such a use, however, is inconsistent with the terminology suggested by International Accounting Standards Board. For more information about provisions, see provision (accounting.)

   a. FIFO and LIFO accounting   b. Treasury stock
   c. Reserve   d. Closing entries

Chapter 19. Government Bonds

24. A _____, reserve bank, or monetary authority is the entity responsible for the monetary policy of a country or of a group of member states. It is a bank that can lend money to other banks in times of need. Its primary responsibility is to maintain the stability of the national currency and money supply, but more active duties include controlling subsidized-loan interest rates, and acting as a lender of last resort to the banking sector during times of financial crisis (private banks often being integral to the national financial system.)

   a. 7-Eleven
   b. Central bank
   c. 4-4-5 Calendar
   d. 529 plan

25. In economics, _____ is a rise in the general level of prices of goods and services in an economy over a period of time. The term '_____' once referred to increases in the money supply (monetary _____); however, economic debates about the relationship between money supply and price levels have led to its primary use today in describing price _____. _____ can also be described as a decline in the real value of money--a loss of purchasing power in the medium of exchange which is also the monetary unit of account.

   a. AAB
   b. ABN Amro
   c. A Random Walk Down Wall Street
   d. Inflation

26. The institution most often referenced by the word '_____' is a public or publicly traded _____, the shares of which are traded on a public stock exchange (e.g., the New York Stock Exchange or Nasdaq in the United States) where shares of stock of _____s are bought and sold by and to the general public. Most of the largest businesses in the world are publicly traded _____s. However, the majority of _____s are said to be closely held, privately held or close _____s, meaning that no ready market exists for the trading of shares.

   a. Protect
   b. Federal Home Loan Mortgage Corporation
   c. Depository Trust Company
   d. Corporation

27. _____ or financing is to provide capital (funds), which means money for a project, a person, a business or any other private or public institutions.

   Those funds can be allocated for either short term or long term purposes. The health fund is a new way of _____ private healthcare centers.

   a. Proxy fight
   b. Synthetic CDO
   c. Funding
   d. Product life cycle

28. The _____ is a bank that provides financial and technical assistance to developing countries for development programs (e.g. bridges, roads, schools, etc.) with the stated goal of reducing poverty.

   The _____ differs from the _____ Group, in that the _____ comprises only two institutions:

   - International Bank for Reconstruction and Development (IBRD)
   - International Development Association (IDA)

Chapter 19. Government Bonds

Whereas the latter incorporates these two in addition to three more:

- International Finance Corporation (IFC)
- Multilateral Investment Guarantee Agency (MIGA)
- International Centre for Settlement of Investment Disputes (ICSID)

John Maynard Keynes (right) represented the UK at the conference, and Harry Dexter White represented the US.

The _____ was created following the ratification of the United Nations Monetary and Financial Conference | Bretton Woods agreement. The concept was originally conceived in July 1944 at the United Nations Monetary and Financial Conference.

a. 4-4-5 Calendar
c. 7-Eleven
b. World Bank
d. 529 plan

29. An _____ is an investment vehicle traded on stock exchanges, much like stocks. An ETF holds assets such as stocks or bonds and trades at approximately the same price as the net asset value of its underlying assets over the course of the trading day. Most ETFs track an index, such as the Dow Jones Industrial Average or the S'P 500.

a. A Random Walk Down Wall Street
c. ABN Amro
b. Exchange-traded fund
d. AAB

30. An _____ or index tracker is a collective investment scheme (usually a mutual fund or exchange-traded fund) that aims to replicate the movements of an index of a specific financial market regardless of market conditions.

Tracking can be achieved by trying to hold all of the securities in the index, in the same proportions as the index. Other methods include statistically sampling the market and holding 'representative' securities.

a. A Random Walk Down Wall Street
c. Investment company
b. AAB
d. Index fund

31. The _____ is a financial market where participants buy and sell debt securities, usually in the form of bonds. As of 2006, the size of the international _____ is an estimated $45 trillion, of which the size of the outstanding U.S. _____ debt was $25.2 trillion.

Nearly all of the $923 billion average daily trading volume in the U.S. _____ takes place between broker-dealers and large institutions in a decentralized, over-the-counter market.

a. Fixed income
c. 529 plan
b. Bond Market
d. 4-4-5 Calendar

32. A _____ is a collective investment scheme that invests in bonds and other debt securities. _____s yield monthly dividends that include interest payments on the fund's underlying securities plus any capital appreciation in the prices of the portfolio's bonds. _____s tend to pay higher dividends than CDs and money market accounts, and they generally pay out dividends more frequently and regularly than individual bonds.
   a. Gilts
   b. Premium bond
   c. Bond fund
   d. Private activity bond

33. In finance, _____ occurs when a debtor has not met its legal obligations according to the debt contract, e.g. it has not made a scheduled payment, or has violated a loan covenant (condition) of the debt contract. _____ may occur if the debtor is either unwilling or unable to pay their debt. This can occur with all debt obligations including bonds, mortgages, loans, and promissory notes.
   a. Debt validation
   b. Credit crunch
   c. Default
   d. Vendor finance

34. _____ is the risk of loss due to a debtor's non-payment of a loan or other line of credit (either the principal or interest (coupon) or both)

Most lenders employ their own models (credit scorecards) to rank potential and existing customers according to risk, and then apply appropriate strategies. With products such as unsecured personal loans or mortgages, lenders charge a higher price for higher risk customers and vice versa. With revolving products such as credit cards and overdrafts, risk is controlled through careful setting of credit limits.

   a. Liquidity risk
   b. Transaction risk
   c. Market risk
   d. Credit risk

35. _____ in finance is a risk management technique, related to hedging, that mixes a wide variety of investments within a portfolio. Because the fluctuations of a single security have less impact on a diverse portfolio, _____ minimizes the risk from any one investment.

A simple example of _____ is the following: On a particular island the entire economy consists of two companies: one that sells umbrellas and another that sells sunscreen.

   a. Diversification
   b. 7-Eleven
   c. 4-4-5 Calendar
   d. 529 plan

36. A _____ is a bond issued by a corporation. The term is usually applied to longer-term debt instruments, generally with a maturity date falling at least a year after their issue date. (The term 'commercial paper' is sometimes used for instruments with a shorter maturity.)
   a. Brady bonds
   b. Corporate bond
   c. Government bond
   d. Serial bond

37. A _____ is a legal pledge in United States municipal finance, in which an entity pledges its full faith and credit to repay its debt, typically a _____ bond.

Chapter 19. Government Bonds

a. Letter of credit
b. General obligation
c. Financial Institutions Reform Recovery and Enforcement Act
d. Covenant

38. A _____ is a fund established by a government agency or business for the purpose of reducing debt.

The _____ was first used in Great Britain in the 18th century to reduce national debt. While used by Robert Walpole in 1716 and effectively in the 1720s and early 1730s, it originated in the commercial tax syndicates of the Italian peninsula of the 14th century to retire redeemable public debt of those cities.

a. Security interest
b. Debtor
c. Modern portfolio theory
d. Sinking fund

39. _____s are financial bonds that mature in installments over a period of time. In effect, a $100,000, 5-year _____ would mature in a $20,000 annuity over a 5-year interval. Bond issues consisting of a series of blocks of securities maturing in sequence, the coupon rate can be different.

a. Serial bond
b. Callable bond
c. Brady bonds
d. Bond fund

40. _____ is a combination of straight bond and embedded put option. The holder of the _____ has the right, but not the obligation, to demand early repayment of the principal. The put option is usually exercisable on specified dates.

a. Callable bond
b. Brady bonds
c. Convertible bond
d. Puttable bond

41. _____ is a corporate finance term denoting a type of takeover bid. The _____ is a public, open offer or invitation (usually announced in a newspaper advertisement) by a prospective acquirer to all stockholders of a publicly traded corporation (the target corporation) to tender their stock for sale at a specified price during a specified time, subject to the tendering of a minimum and maximum number of shares. In a _____, the bidder contacts shareholders directly; the directors of the company may or may not have endorsed the _____ proposal.

a. Shareholder value
b. Cash is king
c. Follow-on offering
d. Tender offer

42. _____ are bonds that have a variable coupon, equal to a money market reference rate, like LIBOR or federal funds rate, plus a spread. The spread is a rate that remains constant. Almost all _____ have quarterly coupons, i.e. they pay out interest every three months, though counter examples do exist.

a. CVECAs
b. Loan participation
c. Gordon growth model
d. Floating rate notes

43. In business, _____ is income that a company receives from its normal business activities, usually from the sale of goods and services to customers. Some companies also receive _____ from interest, dividends or royalties paid to them by other companies. _____ may refer to business income in general, or it may refer to the amount, in a monetary unit, received during a period of time, as in 'Last year, Company X had _____ of $32 million.'

In many countries, including the UK, _____ is referred to as turnover.

a. Furniture, Fixtures and Equipment
b. Bottom line
c. Matching principle
d. Revenue

44. _____ are bonds issued by governments, authorities, or public benefit corporations that are guaranteed by the revenue flow of the issuing agency.

The Supreme Court decision of Pollock versus Farmer's Loan and Trust Company of 1895 initiated a wave or series of innovations for the financial services community in both tax-treatment and regulation from government. This specific case, according to a leading investment bank's research, resulted in the 'intergovernmental tax immunity doctrine,' ultimately leading to 'tax-free status.' Municipal bonds are generally exempt from federal tax on their interest payments (not capital gains.)

a. Gilts
b. Callable bond
c. Private activity bond
d. Revenue bonds

45. _____ is the provision of resources (such as granting a loan) by one party to another party where that second party does not reimburse the first party immediately, thereby generating a debt, and instead arranges either to repay or return those resources (or material(s) of equal value) at a later date. The first party is called a creditor, also known as a lender, while the second party is called a debtor, also known as a borrower.

Movements of financial capital are normally dependent on either _____ or equity transfers.

a. Clearing house
b. Comparable
c. Warrant
d. Credit

46. A _____ is a document that indicates that the bearer of the document has title to property, such as shares or bonds. They differ from normal registered instruments, in that no records are kept of who owns the underlying property, or of the transactions involving transfer of ownership. Whoever physically holds the bearer bond papers owns the property.
a. Book entry
b. Marketable
c. Bearer instrument
d. Securities lending

47. A _____ is different from normal stock in that it is unregistered - no records are kept of the owner, or the transactions involving ownership. Whoever physically holds the _____ papers owns the stock or corporation. This is useful for investors and corporate officers who wish to retain anonymity.
a. Revenue bonds
b. Clean price
c. Bearer bond
d. Gilts

48. A _____ assesses the credit worthiness of an individual, corporation, or even a country. _____s are calculated from financial history and current assets and liabilities. Typically, a _____ tells a lender or investor the probability of the subject being able to pay back a loan.
a. Credit rating
b. Credit report monitoring
c. Debenture
d. Credit cycle

49. _____ (also trust indenture or deed of trust) is a legal document issued to lenders and describes key terms such as the interest rate, maturity date, convertibility, pledge, promises, representations, covenants, and other terms of the bond offering. When the Offering Memorandum is prepared in advance of marketing a Bond, the indenture will typically be summarised in the 'Description of Notes' section.

   a. McFadden Act

   b. Fair Labor Standards Act

   c. Bond indenture

   d. Court of Audit of Belgium

50. In general, a _____ is a bond issued by or on behalf of local or state government for the purpose of financing the project of a private user.

Section 141(a) of the Internal Revenue Code provides that the term _____ means any bond issued as part of an issue which meets:

> (1) the private business use test of section 141(b)(1) and the private security or payment test of section 141(b)(2), or

> (2) the private loan financing test of § 141(c.)

Under Treasury Regulation section 1.141-2, an interest on a _____ is not excludable from gross income under section 103 (a) of the Internal Revenue Code unless the bond is a qualified bond.

   a. Premium bond

   b. Puttable bond

   c. Private activity bond

   d. Gilts

Chapter 20. Mortgage-Backed Securities

1. A _____ is a financial debt vehicle that was first created in June 1983 by investment banks Salomon Brothers and First Boston for Freddie Mac. (The First Boston team was led by Dexter Senft.) Legally, a _____ is a special purpose entity that is wholly separate from the institution(s) that create it.

   a. 4-4-5 Calendar
   b. Tranche
   c. Yield curve spread
   d. Collateralized mortgage obligation

2. The _____ is a U.S. government-owned corporation within the Department of Housing and Urban Development

Ginnie Mae provides guarantees on mortgage-backed securities backed by federally insured or guaranteed loans, mainly loans issued by the Federal Housing Administration, Department of Veterans Affairs, Rural Housing Service, and Office of Public and Indian Housing. Ginnie Mae securities are the only MBS that are guaranteed by the United States government.

   a. Graduated payment mortgage
   b. 4-4-5 Calendar
   c. Government National Mortgage Association
   d. Jumbo mortgage

3. A _____ is an asset-backed security whose cash flows are backed by the principal and interest payments of a set of mortgage loans. Payments are typically made monthly over the lifetime of the underlying loans.

   a. Conforming loan
   b. Shared appreciation mortgage
   c. Home equity line of credit
   d. Mortgage-backed security

4. _____ is the process of decreasing an amount over a period of time. The word comes from Middle English amortisen to kill, alienate in mortmain, from Anglo-French amorteser, alteration of amortir, from Vulgar Latin admortire to kill, from Latin ad- + mort-, mors death. Particular instances of the term include:

   - _____ (business), the allocation of a lump sum amount to different time periods, particularly for loans and other forms of finance, including related interest or other finance charges.
     - _____ schedule, a table detailing each periodic payment on a loan (typically a mortgage), as generated by an _____ calculator.
     - Negative _____, an _____ schedule where the loan amount actually increases through not paying the full interest
   - Amortized analysis, analyzing the execution cost of algorithms over a sequence of operations.
   - _____ of capital expenditures of certain assets under accounting rules, particularly intangible assets, in a manner analogous to depreciation.
   - _____ (tax law)

_____ is also used in the context of zoning regulations and describes the time in which a property owner has to relocate when the property's use constitutes a preexisting nonconforming use under zoning regulations.

   - Depreciation

   a. Option
   b. AT'T Inc.
   c. Intrinsic value
   d. Amortization

Chapter 20. Mortgage-Backed Securities

5. _____ is the balance of the amounts of cash being received and paid by a business during a defined period of time, sometimes tied to a specific project. Measurement of _____ can be used

- to evaluate the state or performance of a business or project.
- to determine problems with liquidity. Being profitable does not necessarily mean being liquid. A company can fail because of a shortage of cash, even while profitable.
- to generate project rate of returns. The time of _____s into and out of projects are used as inputs to financial models such as internal rate of return, and net present value.
- to examine income or growth of a business when it is believed that accrual accounting concepts do not represent economic realities. Alternately, _____ can be used to 'validate' the net income generated by accrual accounting.

_____ as a generic term may be used differently depending on context, and certain _____ definitions may be adapted by analysts and users for their own uses. Common terms include operating _____ and free _____.

_____s can be classified into:

1. Operational _____s: Cash received or expended as a result of the company's core business activities.
2. Investment _____s: Cash received or expended through capital expenditure, investments or acquisitions.
3. Financing _____s: Cash received or expended as a result of financial activities, such as interests and dividends.

All three together - the net _____ - are necessary to reconcile the beginning cash balance to the ending cash balance. Loan draw downs or equity injections, that is just shifting of capital but no expenditure as such, are not considered in the net _____.

a. Cash flow
b. Real option
c. Corporate finance
d. Shareholder value

6. A _____ is a fungible, negotiable instrument representing financial value. They are broadly categorized into debt securities (such as banknotes, bonds and debentures), and equity securities; e.g., common stocks. The company or other entity issuing the _____ is called the issuer.
a. Tracking stock
b. Book entry
c. Securities lending
d. Security

7. _____ is a structured finance process that involves pooling and repackaging of cash-flow-producing financial assets into securities, which are then sold to investors. The term '_____' is derived from the fact that the form of financial instruments used to obtain funds from the investors are securities. As a portfolio risk backed by amortizing cash flows - and unlike general corporate debt - the credit quality of securitized debt is non-stationary due to changes in volatility that are time- and structure-dependent.
a. Special journals
b. The Glass-Steagall Act of 1933
c. Reputational risk
d. Securitization

8. _____ is the weighted average maturity of a bond where the weights are the relative discounted cash flows in each period.

It will be seen that this is the same formula for the duration as given above.

Macaulay showed that an unweighted average maturity is not useful in predicting interest rate risk.

a. Yield
b. Yield to maturity
c. 4-4-5 Calendar
d. Macaulay duration

9. In finance, the _____ of a financial asset measures the sensitivity of the asset's price to interest rate movements, expressed as a number of years. The reason for expressing this sensitivity in years is that the time that will elapse until a cash flow is received allows more interest to accumulate. Therefore the price of an asset with long term cashflows has more interest rate sensitivity than an asset with cashflows in the near future.

a. Yield to maturity
b. Duration
c. 4-4-5 Calendar
d. Macaulay duration

10. _____ is early repayment of a loan by a borrower.

In the case of a mortgage-backed security (MBS), _____ is perceived as a risk, because mortgage debts are often paid off early in order to incur lower total interest payments through cheaper refinancing. The new financing may be cheaper because the borrower's credit rating has improved or because interest rates are lower, but in either case, the payments that would have been made to the MBS investor would be above market rates.

a. Disposal tax effect
b. Retention ratio
c. Bankruptcy remote
d. Prepayment

11. _____ refers to the replacement of an existing debt obligation with a debt obligation bearing different terms. The most common consumer _____ is for a home mortgage.

_____ may be undertaken to reduce interest rate/interest costs (by _____ at a lower rate), to extend the repayment time, to pay off other debt(s), to reduce one's periodic payment obligations (sometimes by taking a longer-term loan), to reduce or alter risk (such as by _____ from a variable-rate to a fixed-rate loan), and/or to raise cash for investment, consumption, or the payment of a dividend.

a. Refinancing
b. 4-4-5 Calendar
c. 7-Eleven
d. 529 plan

12. An _____ is a table detailing each periodic payment on a amortizing loan (typically a mortgage), as generated by an amortization calculator.

Chapter 20. Mortgage-Backed Securities

While a portion of every payment is applied towards both the interest and the principal balance of the loan, the exact amount applied to principal each time varies (with the remainder going to interest.) An _____ reveals the specific monetary amount put towards interest, as well as the specific put towards the Principal balance, with each payment.

- a. Annual report
- b. Amortization schedule
- c. Adjusted basis
- d. Adjusting entries

13. _____ in finance is a risk management technique, related to hedging, that mixes a wide variety of investments within a portfolio. Because the fluctuations of a single security have less impact on a diverse portfolio, _____ minimizes the risk from any one investment.

A simple example of _____ is the following: On a particular island the entire economy consists of two companies: one that sells umbrellas and another that sells sunscreen.

- a. 4-4-5 Calendar
- b. 7-Eleven
- c. 529 plan
- d. Diversification

14. The _____ is a U.S. government-owned corporation within the Department of Housing and Urban Development

Ginnie Mae provides guarantees on mortgage-backed securities backed by federally insured or guaranteed loans, mainly loans issued by the Federal Housing Administration, Department of Veterans Affairs, Rural Housing Service, and Office of Public and Indian Housing. Ginnie Mae securities are the only MBS that are guaranteed by the United States government.

- a. GNMA
- b. Certified Emission Reductions
- c. Case-Shiller Home Price Indices
- d. Cash budget

15. In finance, _____ occurs when a debtor has not met its legal obligations according to the debt contract, e.g. it has not made a scheduled payment, or has violated a loan covenant (condition) of the debt contract. _____ may occur if the debtor is either unwilling or unable to pay their debt. This can occur with all debt obligations including bonds, mortgages, loans, and promissory notes.
- a. Vendor finance
- b. Default
- c. Credit crunch
- d. Debt validation

16. The institution most often referenced by the word '_____' is a public or publicly traded _____, the shares of which are traded on a public stock exchange (e.g., the New York Stock Exchange or Nasdaq in the United States) where shares of stock of _____s are bought and sold by and to the general public. Most of the largest businesses in the world are publicly traded _____s. However, the majority of _____s are said to be closely held, privately held or close _____s, meaning that no ready market exists for the trading of shares.
- a. Depository Trust Company
- b. Corporation
- c. Federal Home Loan Mortgage Corporation
- d. Protect

Chapter 20. Mortgage-Backed Securities

17. The _____ (NYSE: FNM), commonly known as Fannie Mae, is a stockholder-owned corporation chartered by Congress in 1968 as a government sponsored enterprise (GSE), but founded in 1938 during the Great Depression. The corporation's purpose is to purchase and securitize mortgages in order to ensure that funds are consistently available to the institutions that lend money to home buyers.

On September 7, 2008, James Lockhart, director of the Federal Housing Finance Agency (FHFA), announced that Fannie Mae and Freddie Mac were being placed into conservatorship of the FHFA.

   a. The Depository Trust ' Clearing Corporation   b. SPDR
   c. General partnership   d. Federal National Mortgage Association

18. The _____ (NYSE: FRE) is an insolvent government sponsored enterprise (GSE) of the United States federal government.

The _____ was created in 1970 to expand the secondary market for mortgages in the US. Along with other GSEs, Freddie Mac buys mortgages on the secondary market, pools them, and sells them as mortgage-backed securities to investors on the open market.

   a. Governmental Accounting Standards Board   b. The Depository Trust ' Clearing Corporation
   c. Public company   d. Federal Home Loan Mortgage Corporation

19. In finance, a _____ is a debt security, in which the authorized issuer owes the holders a debt and, depending on the terms of the _____, is obliged to pay interest (the coupon) and/or to repay the principal at a later date, termed maturity.

Thus a _____ is a loan: the issuer is the borrower, the _____ holder is the lender, and the coupon is the interest. _____s provide the borrower with external funds to finance long-term investments, or, in the case of government _____s, to finance current expenditure.

   a. Catastrophe bonds   b. Bond
   c. Convertible bond   d. Puttable bond

20. _____ is a measure of the rate of payments from a bond that pays principal payments in excess of scheduled payments (so-called prepayments.) Such bonds include mortgage-backed securities, CMOs, and ABS, which prepay at some rate usually dependent on the level of interest rates.

_____ is defined as the annualized rate of principal payments beyond the regularly scheduled payments, and is stated as a percentage of outstanding amount of the security or loan minus the scheduled payments.

   a. Profitability index   b. Cash management
   c. Conditional prepayment rate   d. Total return

21. In Modern Portfolio Theory, the _____ is the graphical representation of the Capital Asset Pricing Model. It displays the expected rate of return for an overall market as a function of systematic (non-diversifiable) risk (beta.)

Chapter 20. Mortgage-Backed Securities

The Y-Intercept (beta=0) of the _____ is equal to the risk-free interest rate.

a. Divestment
b. Certificate in Investment Performance Measurement
c. Rebalancing
d. Security market line

22. _____ is a fee paid on borrowed assets. It is the price paid for the use of borrowed money, or, money earned by deposited funds. Assets that are sometimes lent with _____ include money, shares, consumer goods through hire purchase, major assets such as aircraft, and even entire factories in finance lease arrangements.

a. Interest
b. AAB
c. A Random Walk Down Wall Street
d. Insolvency

23. In structured finance, a _____ is one of a number of related securities offered as part of the same transaction. The word _____ is French for slice, section, series, or portion. In the financial sense of the word, each bond is a different slice of the deal's risk.

a. 4-4-5 Calendar
b. Yield curve spread
c. Credit enhancement
d. Tranche

24. In finance, the term _____ describes the amount in cash that returns to the owners of a security. Normally it does not include the price variations, at the difference of the total return. _____ applies to various stated rates of return on stocks (common and preferred, and convertible), fixed income instruments (bonds, notes, bills, strips, zero coupon), and some other investment type insurance products (e.g. annuities.)

a. Macaulay duration
b. Yield to maturity
c. 4-4-5 Calendar
d. Yield

25. An _____ is a contract written by a seller that conveys to the buyer the right -- but not the obligation -- to buy (in the case of a call _____) or to sell (in the case of a put _____) a particular asset, such as a piece of property such as, among others, a futures contract. In return for granting the _____, the seller collects a payment (the premium) from the buyer.

For example, buying a call _____ provides the right to buy a specified quantity of a security at a set strike price at some time on or before expiration, while buying a put _____ provides the right to sell.

a. AT'T Mobility LLC
b. Annuity
c. Amortization
d. Option

26. A _____ is the price of a single share of a no. of saleable stocks of the company. Once the stock is purchased, the owner becomes a shareholder of the company that issued the share.

a. Trading curb
b. Stock split
c. Whisper numbers
d. Share price

27. _____ is the term in economics for the amount of fixed or real capital present in relation to other factors of production, especially labor. At the level of either a production process or the aggregate economy, it may be estimated by the capital/labor ratio, such as from the points along a capital/labor isoquant.

Since the use of tools and machinery makes labor more effective, rising _____ pushes up the productivity of labor, so a society that is more capital intensive tends to have a higher standard of living over the long run than one with low _____.

- a. Cost of capital
- b. 4-4-5 Calendar
- c. Weighted average cost of capital
- d. Capital intensity

28. The _____ is the weighted-average most likely outcome in gambling, probability theory, economics or finance.

In gambling and probability theory, there is usually a discrete set of possible outcomes. In this case, _____ is a measure of the relative balance of win or loss weighted by their chances of occurring.

- a. AAB
- b. A Random Walk Down Wall Street
- c. ABN Amro
- d. Expected return

29. In the United States, the Financial Industry Regulatory Authority (FINRA) is a self-regulatory organization (SRO) under the Securities Exchange Act of 1934, successor to the _____, Inc.

FINRA is responsible for regulatory oversight of all securities firms that do business with the public; professional training, testing and licensing of registered persons; arbitration and mediation; market regulation by contract for The NASDAQ Stock Market, Inc., the American Stock Exchange LLC, and the International Securities Exchange, LLC; and industry utilities, such as Trade Reporting Facilities and other over-the-counter operations.

- a. 529 plan
- b. 7-Eleven
- c. 4-4-5 Calendar
- d. National Association of Securities Dealers

30. In finance, _____ is that risk which is common to an entire market and not to any individual entity or component thereof. It should be distinguished from systemic risk which is the risk that the entire financial system will collapse as a result of some catastrophic event.

Risks can be reduced in four main ways: Avoidance, Reduction, Retention and Transfer.

- a. Systematic risk
- b. Primary market
- c. Conglomerate merger
- d. Capital surplus

31. _____ refer to services provided by the finance industry.

The finance industry encompasses a broad range of organizations that deal with the management of money. Among these organizations are banks, credit card companies, insurance companies, consumer finance companies, stock brokerages, investment funds and some government sponsored enterprises.

- a. Financial instruments
- b. Cost of carry
- c. Delta hedging
- d. Financial Services

ANSWER KEY

Chapter 1

1. b	2. d	3. b	4. d	5. b	6. c	7. d	8. c	9. d	10. d
11. d	12. c	13. a	14. d	15. a	16. d	17. d	18. d	19. d	20. c
21. c	22. a	23. d	24. d	25. d	26. a	27. d	28. b	29. b	30. d
31. b	32. b	33. a	34. d	35. a	36. d	37. d	38. d	39. a	40. a
41. a	42. d	43. a	44. d	45. d					

Chapter 2

1. d	2. d	3. a	4. d	5. d	6. d	7. d	8. b	9. d	10. b
11. b	12. d	13. b	14. b	15. b	16. d	17. c	18. b	19. d	20. d
21. d	22. d	23. d	24. d	25. d	26. c	27. d	28. d	29. b	30. d
31. b	32. d	33. c	34. d	35. d	36. a	37. d	38. d	39. a	40. d
41. c	42. d	43. d	44. a	45. c	46. d	47. b	48. d	49. a	50. d
51. c	52. d	53. a	54. d	55. c	56. c	57. d	58. a	59. d	60. d
61. d									

Chapter 3

1. a	2. c	3. b	4. d	5. c	6. a	7. d	8. c	9. c	10. d
11. d	12. a	13. a	14. d	15. d	16. d	17. d	18. c	19. d	20. d
21. b	22. d	23. a	24. b	25. b	26. b	27. d	28. a	29. d	30. b
31. c	32. b	33. d	34. c	35. d	36. c	37. d	38. d	39. c	40. d
41. b	42. a	43. d	44. b	45. d	46. c	47. d	48. a	49. a	50. b
51. d	52. b	53. a	54. d	55. d	56. d	57. d			

Chapter 4

1. d	2. d	3. c	4. d	5. d	6. d	7. d	8. d	9. d	10. d
11. c	12. c	13. d	14. d	15. c	16. d	17. b	18. d	19. b	20. d
21. d	22. d	23. d	24. b	25. c	26. d	27. d	28. c	29. a	30. d
31. d	32. d	33. a	34. d	35. b	36. b	37. d	38. b	39. d	40. d
41. c	42. a	43. d	44. d	45. d	46. c	47. d	48. d	49. a	50. c
51. d	52. b	53. c							

Chapter 5

1. a	2. d	3. d	4. d	5. a	6. c	7. d	8. d	9. c	10. d
11. b	12. b	13. d	14. d	15. d	16. a	17. d	18. a	19. c	20. c
21. a	22. a	23. a	24. b	25. b	26. b	27. c	28. d	29. b	30. d
31. b	32. d	33. b	34. d	35. a	36. b	37. d	38. b	39. a	40. d
41. d	42. d	43. d	44. d	45. a					

Chapter 6

1. b	2. c	3. c	4. d	5. d	6. d	7. c	8. d	9. d	10. d
11. b	12. a	13. b	14. a	15. d	16. d	17. c	18. d	19. d	20. a
21. a	22. a	23. d	24. c	25. a	26. d	27. d	28. a	29. b	30. b
31. a	32. b	33. c	34. d	35. d	36. b	37. d	38. d	39. a	40. b
41. b	42. a	43. d	44. b	45. d	46. c	47. c	48. d		

Chapter 7

1. d	2. b	3. a	4. a	5. a	6. d	7. d	8. a	9. b	10. d
11. d	12. a	13. c	14. d	15. d	16. d	17. d	18. d	19. c	20. d
21. d	22. a	23. d	24. d	25. b	26. d	27. d	28. b	29. d	30. c
31. d	32. d	33. c	34. d						

Chapter 8

1. c	2. d	3. b	4. d	5. d	6. b	7. d	8. d	9. b	10. a
11. b	12. d	13. d	14. b	15. b	16. c	17. c	18. b	19. a	20. d
21. d	22. b	23. d	24. d	25. b	26. d	27. d	28. c	29. a	30. d
31. d	32. a	33. d	34. d	35. c	36. d				

Chapter 9

1. d	2. d	3. d	4. a	5. d	6. d	7. a	8. a	9. d	10. d
11. d	12. a	13. d	14. b	15. a	16. d	17. c	18. b	19. c	20. c
21. d	22. d	23. a	24. a	25. d	26. a	27. a	28. b	29. d	30. d
31. a	32. a	33. d	34. c	35. c	36. d	37. d	38. a	39. b	40. a
41. b	42. a	43. d	44. c	45. d	46. c	47. a	48. d	49. b	50. a
51. a	52. b	53. d	54. d	55. d	56. a	57. c	58. d	59. d	60. d
61. a	62. d	63. d	64. d	65. d	66. d	67. d	68. d	69. a	70. d
71. b	72. d	73. d	74. d	75. d					

Chapter 10

1. a	2. d	3. d	4. c	5. d	6. d	7. d	8. b	9. a	10. d
11. b	12. a	13. b	14. d	15. d	16. b	17. d	18. c	19. a	20. a
21. c	22. b	23. c	24. d	25. b	26. a	27. d	28. d	29. d	30. d
31. d	32. b	33. d							

Chapter 11

1. d	2. d	3. d	4. c	5. d	6. d	7. a	8. c	9. d	10. a
11. a	12. d	13. b	14. a	15. c	16. d	17. d	18. a	19. d	20. d
21. d	22. a	23. c	24. d	25. b	26. d	27. b			

Chapter 12

1. d	2. b	3. b	4. d	5. d	6. c	7. d	8. a	9. c	10. b
11. a	12. c	13. d	14. d	15. b	16. d	17. d	18. d	19. c	20. d
21. a	22. b	23. a	24. d	25. d	26. d	27. b	28. d	29. d	30. d

Chapter 13

1. a	2. a	3. b	4. d	5. d	6. c	7. a	8. c	9. c	10. d
11. b	12. a	13. d	14. d	15. b	16. d	17. d	18. c	19. a	20. a
21. d	22. b	23. d	24. d	25. d	26. d	27. b			

ANSWER KEY

Chapter 14
1. b	2. b	3. d	4. c	5. b	6. b	7. d	8. d	9. c	10. b
11. c	12. d	13. a	14. d	15. c	16. c	17. d	18. c	19. d	20. d
21. a	22. a	23. c	24. d	25. d	26. c	27. d	28. b	29. c	30. a
31. b	32. d	33. c	34. b	35. d	36. d	37. d	38. a	39. d	40. d
41. c	42. d	43. d	44. d	45. d	46. d	47. d	48. d		

Chapter 15
1. d	2. b	3. b	4. d	5. d	6. b	7. d	8. c	9. d	10. c
11. d	12. d	13. d	14. c	15. d	16. a	17. c	18. d	19. d	20. c
21. a	22. d	23. d	24. d	25. a	26. a	27. d	28. d	29. b	30. b
31. c	32. d								

Chapter 16
1. d	2. b	3. d	4. d	5. a	6. b	7. a	8. c	9. a	10. d
11. b	12. d	13. a	14. b	15. c	16. c	17. d	18. c	19. a	20. b
21. a	22. a	23. d	24. d	25. d	26. c	27. d	28. d	29. b	30. c
31. d	32. b	33. d							

Chapter 17
1. c	2. a	3. c	4. c	5. c	6. d	7. d	8. d	9. b	10. d
11. c	12. a	13. d	14. a	15. d	16. c	17. a	18. b	19. b	20. a
21. d	22. d	23. d	24. d	25. b	26. b	27. d	28. d	29. d	30. d
31. c	32. c	33. d	34. d	35. d	36. d	37. c	38. d	39. d	40. d
41. d	42. c	43. b	44. d	45. a	46. d	47. d	48. d	49. d	50. c
51. c	52. a	53. b	54. d	55. c					

Chapter 18
1. a	2. a	3. d	4. c	5. d	6. d	7. d	8. d	9. d	10. a
11. c	12. d	13. d	14. a	15. b	16. d	17. d	18. d	19. d	20. d
21. a	22. c	23. d	24. d	25. d	26. d	27. d	28. a	29. b	30. d
31. d	32. c	33. a	34. d	35. c	36. d	37. c	38. d	39. d	40. a
41. a	42. a	43. d	44. b	45. d	46. b	47. c	48. b	49. a	50. d
51. a	52. a	53. d	54. d	55. b	56. c	57. b	58. d	59. d	60. d
61. a	62. c	63. b							

Chapter 19
1. a	2. b	3. c	4. d	5. d	6. d	7. a	8. b	9. d	10. d
11. d	12. c	13. d	14. c	15. b	16. c	17. d	18. d	19. a	20. d
21. d	22. d	23. c	24. b	25. d	26. d	27. c	28. b	29. b	30. d
31. b	32. c	33. c	34. d	35. a	36. b	37. b	38. d	39. a	40. d
41. d	42. d	43. d	44. d	45. d	46. c	47. c	48. a	49. c	50. c

Chapter 20

1. d	2. c	3. d	4. d	5. a	6. d	7. d	8. d	9. b	10. d
11. a	12. b	13. d	14. a	15. b	16. b	17. d	18. d	19. b	20. c
21. d	22. a	23. d	24. d	25. d	26. d	27. d	28. d	29. d	30. a
31. d									